Eng'd by Augustus Robin N.Y.

Life of A. P. Dostie;

OR,

The Conflict in New Orleans.

BY

EMILY HAZEN REED.

Snatch from the ashes of your sires
The emblems of their former fires,
And he who in the strife expires,
Will add to theirs a name of fear
That tyranny will quake to hear. — *Byron.*

New York:
WM. P. TOMLINSON, 39 NASSAU STREET.
1868.

TO THE

MEMORY OF THE PATRIOTS

SACRIFICED

UPON THE ALTAR OF FREEDOM,

THIS BOOK

IS AFFECTIONATELY DEDICATED

BY

THE AUTHOR.

"Give me the death of those
Who for their country die,
And oh ! be mine like their repose,
When cold and low they lie !
There loveliest mother earth
Enshrines the fallen brave,
In her sweet lap who gave them birth
They find the tranquil grave."
[*Montgomery.*

PREFACE.

"Will the cause of Liberty suffer through me, because my enemies misinterpret my acts and sayings?" said the dying Dostie.

That the Cause for which thousands have fallen may be promoted, some of those noble "acts and sayings," have been recorded in the following pages, to be preserved as sacred mementoes by the friends of Republican Liberty, who will cherish the patriotic acts and liberal sentiments of one of their standard-bearers in the cause of Universal Freedom.

That the weapons of truth may pierce the hard hearts of traitors and conspirators—who were "all forgiven" by their dying victim—some of the events connected with the life of a patriot and martyr have been narrated.

That the prominent events relating to "The Conflict in New

Orleans" between Slavery and Freedom—between Despotism and Republicanism, may find a place in the history of the Great Rebellion, those events have been recorded in the work before the reader.

New York, April 24, 1868.

CONTENTS.

LIFE OF A. P. DOSTIE;

OR,

The Conflict of New Orleans.

CHAPTER I.

EARLY LIFE OF DOSTIE.

Anthony Paul Dostie was born at Saratoga, New York, on the 20th of June, 1821. His father was of French descent; his mother was of German. His an cestry did not descend like that of the Marquis de Lafayette from the French nobility, nor from the German aristocracy, like that of the Baron de Kalb; but the same enthusiastic love of liberty, which animated those heroes of the first American Revolution, burned in the soul of Dostie during the conflict between republican liberty and slavery, which ended in the triumph of Freedom in the Second American Revolution.

The father of Dostie was a barber by trade. He was an honest, industrious man, of vigorous, but uncultivated intellect. He was a marked character where he lived, noted for his independent bearing, and fearlessness upon all occasions, and respected for his native good sense.

His mother is remembered for her goodness of heart, and industrious habits. These qualities she impressed upon her numerous family, who are all useful American citizens and loyal to republican principles.

The childhood of Dostie was not remarkable for striking events. His education was limited to the advantages of a common public school. Said he, in speaking of those school days, "I was then a lover of the cause of liberty, and often stole away from my companions, to study the lives of those who were devoted to the cause of Freedom.

Generosity of soul, love of liberty, and hatred of oppression characterized the early history of one who was subsequently destined to be a conspicuous victim to the power of oppression.

The intellectual germs implanted in the progressive mind of Dostie were retarded in their development by the influences of his surroundings. Like many of our self-made men, which American history delights to recognize as the upholders of her republican institutions, Dostie, àt a period in his life, when his proud spirit longed to be free from every engagement but that of intellectual culture, was restrained by poverty, and compelled to work for his daily bread, in a barber's shop.

America proudly boasts that, upon her historical record, the names of her noblest heroes and martyrs have not always been taken from the ranks of high-born aristocracy, nor from that chivalric band, whose boast has ever been "That power and wealth must be the passport to honor."

Pure republicanism exalts her patriots, cherishes them for their principles, independent of the accidents of birth, forgetful of their nationality or origin in contemplation of their humanity.

In his nineteenth year, Dostie was married to a lady from Cazenovia, New-York, (Miss Eunice Hull), of uncommon beauty and high intellectual attainments. She was the idol of his heart. Said he, "From the moment my Love possessed my affections, it became my study to become the worthy companion of my beautiful and intellectual wife. I often studied until two o'clock in the morning, and recited the lessons I had learned to the one who sympathized with me in every hope and sorrow. Six years this sacred relation continued, and then my domestic happiness ended. She died, and with her were buried my affections; since then my heart has been buried beneath the tomb."

About the period of his marriage he went to Amsterdam, New York, where he gave his attention to dentistry. He studied his profession in the office of Dr. J. C. Duell, who thus speaks of him:—"During the residence of Dr. Dostie in Amsterdam, he spent all his leisure time in study, and improved his qualities of mind and heart to an almost unprecedented degree, becoming one of the leading men of the town."

In the society of Odd Fellows, of which he was a member, he passed the "Chief Executive Chair" at an early day. Ever faithful in attendance upon the sick, as assistance was required, he will be remembered by all who knew him, as one foremost in every good work. In the profession he had chosen, he became a proficient, and migrated to Chicago to pursue his calling in a broader field. From thence he went to Marshall, Michigan, where he spent a few years, usefully to himself and to society. He visited Amsterdam occasionally, and was always greeted warmly by hosts of friends. His last visit was during the dark days of the rebellion. Upon being called upon to address a meeting convened for the purpose of raising volunteers, he was enthusiastically greeted, and proved of great assistance in revealing the true state of affairs in the South.

He was a man of extensive reading; was possessed of a remarkable memory, and carefully criticised everything of importance in his reading. His nature was genial. He was facinating in conversation, and made friends and admirers wherever he went.

The life of Dr. Dostie in Chicago and Marshall was quiet and uneventful. His time was principally divided between his profession and his studies. Active and industrious in all his undertakings, he was marked by the thoughtful among his friends, as one preparing for a career of usefulness.

CHAPTER II.

DOSTIE'S REMOVAL TO NEW ORLEANS.

In 1852, Dr. Dostie removed to New Orleans, where he was known for years as a popular dentist, and a gentleman of refinement. He was beloved for his upright and benevolent character; admired for his energy and ability, and respected for his love of justice and high sense of honor.

At this period of his life he was a man of commanding figure, and nobly marked features. His habitual expression was sad and thoughtful, and indicative of strong will, noble impulses and benevolent action. In manners, he was gentlemanly and winning. His frankness and gentleness combined, endeared him to a large circle of friends in New Orleans, who dreamed not that the storms of Rebellion would transform their gentle friend into "the turbulent agitator."

As the time approached when the friends of liberty became known as antagonists to the mass of the Southern people, who were wedded to Slavery and its offspring—the Rebellion, a few in New Orleans, dared to express their hatred to treason and oppression. Conspicuous among that number was Dr. Dostie, who stood above a volcano of wrath, and defied the rebellious element that threatened the lives and happiness of those who cherished republican principles. Said Dr. Dostie, at a time in the history of the rebellion when in New Orleans such words were considered worthy of death by the popular verdict, "I hate no human being, but rebellion to republican principles I will never cease to denounce in bitter terms. Principles rise superior to men in this conflict between freedom and slavery, and I would rather see every human being wiped out from the Southern States, than to behold the triumph of treason." Such firmness of principles, strength of virtue, and force of mind, exhibited in the face of rebel vengeance at an early period in the Rebellion marked Dostie a victim to be selected from the revolutionary arena of Louisiana.

The patriotism and loyalty of Dr. Dostie changed his numerous friends to enemies. His popularity was sacrificed before his honesty of soul, and devotion to his Government. Said a rebel (once a friend of the Dr.'s) "Dostie has elements in his character, that might make him the most popular of men, but he has not the most remote idea of policy." Said a friend of Dr. Dostie's, "During the war I was one day walking with him, when one of the lady principals of a Seminary in New Orleans passed us. She cast upon us a look of contempt, so marked that I said to the Dr., "Is that an enemy of yours?" He replied, "She is a lady of intellect and refinement, of whom I was once proud to say, 'she is my friend,' but with a host of old friends, she follows treason, and, judging from her manner, I must say 'she numbers herself among my enemies.' "

Ex-Mayor Monroe says of him, "Dr. Dostie was my friend. He was master of the Masonic Lodge for years to which I belonged. He was an honest Union man, a faithful, candid, conscientious friend." He should have added, and for those virtues I used my power to murder him. "My friend," said Monroe, when the stern, just eye of Shellabarger and an Elliot were fastened upon him, in December, 1866. But in 1860–61. and July 30th, 1866, "My victim."

It is in the tempest of revolution that the inexorable will, boldness and courage of men like Dostie appear to excite traitors to villainous deeds of murder. His daring spirit, patriotic fire, and undying love for the Union made him a conspicuous mark for the venomous darts of those who bid defiance to his cherished principles.

"Dostie shall be hanged, or bow his proud head to treason's yoke," were the words of the conspirators, who acknowledged Jefferson Davis their leader, and his murderous policy, their rule of action.

CHAPTER III.

DOSTIE'S DEPARTURE FOR THE NORTH.

On the 21st of August, 1861, refusing to take the oath of allegiance to the Southern Confederacy, Dostie left New Orleans and went to Chicago. Said he, "when I arrived in Chicago I had no means at my command. Deprived of my home and business, I was sad and gloomy. As I retired to my room for the night and reflected upon my future prospects, the darkness of despair seemed to gather around me. In the midst of this gloom, something seemed to whisper to me, "This revolution convulsing our country is Liberty struggling for justice and right. The thought of my repinings made me ashamed of my selfish fears. I trusted in an arm of power; com posed myself to sleep, and awoke ready for action."

Surrounded by difficulties, which would have appalled a common mind, Dostie was cheerful and hopeful. For a moment a flash of despair, may have caused him to utter an expression of woe, but by an effort of his powerful will despondency was quickly cast from him. He was seldom heard to complain of any misfortune, but with a calm philosophical resignation, he could smile at woe; defy the powers of despotism, and look with contempt upon the indignities offered to himself and his friends by the enemies of his government.

In Chicago, he watched the progress of events connected with the revolution with intense interest. What hours he could spare from his business, were devoted to reading and correspondence with friends in different parts of the Union in relation to the great conflict agitating the nation.

In a letter at that time, he said, "I would gladly sacrifice my life if by so doing I could render assistance to the sacred cause of Liberty,"—little knowing that destiny had reserved his life for just such a sacrifice.

The following letter to Dr. J. C. Duell, expresses the patriotic love for the Union ever manifested by Dr. Dostie :

My Very Dear Friend,—Your letter, so kind towards me personally, and so loyal and patriotic to our grievously wronged country, was received in due course of mail. I might offer good and valid reasons for not having written sooner, but to do so would consume too much space, and I trust to your kindness to excuse the omission.

"You tell me that you and other friends supposed that 'most probably I was in the rebel army.' You and my other friends never more misjudged a character than in thus judging of mine. Ascribe to me, if you choose, all the crimes in the criminal calendar, but never the dark, atrocious and damning sin of treason. My manhood is immaculate against it. After my God, I love my country most—her freedom-breathing inspirations—the memory of her immortal defenders—their glorious battles for the achievement of man's liberty, freedom and equality. All personal considerations are rendered contemptible in the mere comparison. I have watched the progress of the great treason with the most painful interest. I saw it approaching when it appeared as but a little cloud, that a fearless patriot of Jackson's stamp might have dispelled before it assumed such great proportions. Such a man could have prevented the fratricidal war by exposing the deceptive and villainous schemes of demagogues and monsters, who would build up and agrandize themselves on the ruins of liberty, and visiting them with the traitor's punishment ere they had succeeded in beguiling the people so far in their treason.

"During the presidential campaign there was little or no disunionism publicly avowed. All joined in disavowing the criminal intent. Speakers were interrogated, and great and small either avowed that the election of Lincoln would not constitute sufficient cause for dissolving the Union, or they evaded the question. The mass of the people were as loyal to the old flag as they were anywhere in the North, until the few powerful conspirators sprung their *coup d' etat* upon them. Amazement and consternation ensued, and the terrific struggle began. Disunion and Union meetings were nightly held in the city of New Orleans. The Breckenridge politicians and their followers attended the disunion meetings. The union meetings were more attended by the moral and intellectual class of the community, including many who had been but little known, or not known at all, as politicians. The former were addressed by men of no standing or character, the latter by such men as Randall Hunt, Christian Roselius, Thomas J. Durant, and Pierre Soule. Unionism assumed a bold front, and little fear was entertained for the State of Louisiana until the Rev. Dr. Palmer sacriligiously preached disunionism from his pulpit. Then the parricides assumed a courage and confidence fearful in its influence for evil. At their meeting held in Odd Fellows' Hall, they substituted the bust of the great traitor, John C. Calhoun for that of Washington, the pelican flag for the 'ensign of the Republic,' and instead of the 'Star Spangled Banner' an imitation of the French 'Marseillaise' was sung by a young girl dressed and decorated as the Goddess of Liberty. The revolutionists themselves wore blue cockades.

"Their speeches were made up of wild invectives and denunciations against the North and everything northern. The union was cursed as a leprous sore. The gatherings of the Unionists continued until the 'Convention election,' when, having done their utmost to wrest the State from the conspirators, they ceased their meetings and active opposition. Unlike their adversaries they were unarmed and powerless. The official result of the election in the State was never published. That portion of the press which supported the cause of the Union contended that the result was opposed to secession and in favor of 'co-operation,' and demanded the publication of the official vote. But the demand was refused, and to this day the public does not know what the people's verdict was. The convention met at Baton Rouge, and with closed doors passed the infamous act. The event was announced by telegraph and the firing of cannon, and was variously received by the people. Some rejoiced, but thousands cried 'shame!' and foreshadowed in their faces the gloom that was to envelope them and that beautiful country.

"Down to this lamentable 26th of January, I scarcely knew a man possessing social or commercial standing, who did not mourn the posture the State had assumed, and feel the most unhappy forebodings. Soon a reign of terror was inaugurated; liberty of speech was proscribed. He was considered a bold and rash man who still advocated the cause of his country. There were still many who were thus bold. Men were daily arrested and imprisoned for expressing the Union sentiments of our fathers. My assistant, Dr. Metcalf, from Kalamazoo, Michigan, was incarcerated in a loathsome prison, as early as last April, for asserting that he believed 'Lincoln would shell Charleston and cut the levees of New Orleans, if necessary to the enforcement of the laws, and the maintenance of the integrity of the Union.' As soon as he was released he fled to the land of liberty. Thousands were driven away by the terrorism. Sojourners and citizens that had the means, left rather than compromise their manhood. Thousands there were who were anxious to leave, but had not the means to do so. Language cannot describe the mental and physical distress that existed in that community where a few months before they had been so happy, prosperous and contented. General bankruptcy of the business men, and destitution of the mechanical and laboring classes followed. Clerks, artisans and laborers were forced to join the rebel army for the support of themselves and their families, and thousands were kept from starvation by scanty supplies from the 'Free Market,' that was established as early as June last.

"The accounts published in our newspapers of the trials and persecutions of men and women who still have a lingering love for the Union are not overwrought pictures. These miseries are more than the pen can describe. I left last September; and if such was the condition of things then, you may imagine for yourself how much more aggravated their sufferings must be now. The great majority of the people in the South, in my opinion, love the Union, and the dear associations that cluster around it. They were deceived and cheated by designing knaves, to whom, for years, they had given their confidence.

"How fortunate was the escape of little Maryland from their clutches. The people of that State, protected by Federal arms, have, in their State election, spoken in tones of thunder for the old flag. Look at Missouri! How near the *villains* came to its possession! Yet the undaunted heroism of a Lyon, a Fremont, a Halleck, with the determined valor of its true sons, saved it; and now, letters to me from there, assure me there is a general joy felt and expressed for their deliverance. Look everywhere that our arms have reached for indubitable evidence of the loyalty of the down-trodden people.

At Nashville, Tennessee, on my way from New Orleans, I was imprisoned for expressions of loyalty. After my liberation many of the people grasped my hand in sympathy, and many of them openly told me that I was *not alone* in the entertainment of such sentiments, that thousands in Jackson's old State still loved and would yet offer their lives for the old Union. These were and are still the sentiments of many thousands in the South, deprived of the liberty of speech and of freemen's rights. These observations are the result of an intimate acquaintance and knowledge of the people of that section. General Houston, of Texas, is said to have gone after the 'strange gods.' I do not believe in the truth of the statement. He is an old man, the *protege* of Jackson, and in a speech uttered the undying sentiment,—'I wish no epitaph to be written to tell that I survived the ruin of this glorious Union.' I believe that he could not prove recreant, and must be, as ever, for the Union. His position illustrates that of thousands. They may be crushed to-day, but will rise in turn and crush the real invaders of their homes and despoilers of their happiness. They were constantly under the threats of imprisonment or of the bowie-knife and revolver, to intimidate and awe them into silence and submission. Those who would not submit to the despotism were shot down, imprisoned, or compelled to flee the country precipitately, leaving property, and in many instances, dear relations behind them. At the time of my departure, I was said to be the 'last publicly known Unionist in the city,' the thousands of others were crushed and made to *seemingly* yield to the powers that be. Disgraceful and discreditable as it is, many from the North were among the most noisy and bitter enemies Unionists had to contend against. Men, who a year or more before were 'Republicans' in the North, were now *spies* and *informers* against citizens of the South, both native and adopted. My persecutors were men who had been but a little while there. The dearest and nearest friends I had were natives or long residents of the South. They urged me to leave because of the personal dangers that environed me. But to the credit of Northern virtue and patriotic love for the Union, I was proud to witness that the great body of them left the country, and many are now heroically fighting the battles of Liberty. The feeling towards the Northern classes had been most cordially fraternal, until the election of Lincoln, when it became divided, but as the elections on the 'secession question' demonstrated, the great majority were still Union-loving and affectionate towards us. Only two of the seceded States, South Carolina and Florida, gave positive Union majorities. The rest, by treachery and the boldness of the despotism, were declared out of the Union. If the sentiment of the people there was not divided, but like that of our revolutionary fathers, united in a holy cause, mightier armies and navies than we now command could not conquer or subdue them. They had not sufficient aggressions nor wrongs from our beneficient and just government, and were not threatened with any. They knew at the time of raising the standard of rebellion, that admitting Lincoln would strive to encroach on their constitutional rights, Congress and the Supreme Court judges, were eminently conservative, and there were no cause for complaint or alarm. Had a score of men, whom I could name, been hung for treasonable speeches and acts, all the untold affliction which has since followed would have been obviated, and now we would be the same happy and great people we were. Having God and justice with our cause, and having never designed nor done them wrong, we can and will prevent a broken Union. We will again become a happy and united people, fulfilling our great destiny of establishing, not only on this continent but elsewhere, the liberty, equality and fraternity of mankind. Our armies and fleets will soon have reached the great 'Crescent City,' and I predict, its people will receive them with demonstrations of unaffected joy. The advices received from there are enough to satisfy any rational mind, that they are only kept under by power. Even now the intelligence has come, that the first and second brigades, including the *Gardes d' Orleans*, were called out and Gen. Beauregard's letter read to them, requesting reinforcements in Tennessee. They sternly *refused to go*. Reflect! The *Gardes d' Orleans* consists, in great part, of Creoles, and yet they dared refuse the call of the great Creole general, Beauregard. 'Straws tell which way the wind blows.' So does this refusal tell that the love for this good old Union is not altogether extinguished in that noble city. The war will scarcely last months longer. The leading traitors will flee and hide their heads or be brought to the halter, as they richly deserve, and this work will be done with the assistance of many of the good people they have oppressed and trodden to the earth.

"Andrew Johnson—God bless him—is now in Tennessee, commencing the glorions work of restoring the rights of the people and punishing the traitors by the vigorous arm of justice. Of my own trials and sufferings, I would rather not speak. Hundreds and thousands have suffered infinitely more. My property, my business, my happiness and contentment of life were wrecked. But I am happy in the consciousness that I never entertained a thought nor perpetrated an act of disloyalty to the Union and constitution of my country. I advocated the cause of the old flag on all proper occasions, and when asked if I would take the oath of allegiance to the government of Richmond to save my property and my liberty, I answered 'No, never!' Rather loss of liberty, life and all, before any portion of Washington's land should be severed from Union and liberty. I was then told I must go. I was given by that worse than Arnold, General D. E. Twiggs, a pass, of which the following is a copy:

'CONFEDERATE STATES OF AMERICA,
HEADQUARTERS DEPARTMENT NO. 1.
New Orleans, 21st August, 1861.

'Dr. A. P. Dostie, a citizen of the city of New Orleans, State of Louisiana, wishes to return to New York under the Alien Law. Allow him to pass through the Confederate States.

'D. E. TWIGGS,
Maj. Gen. Commanding.'

"Two days afterward I departed from what had been my beautiful and genial home, to come where I could once more see the old banner wave 'o'er the land of the free and the home of the brave.' For six months it had been shut out of my sight. I felt during that time despondent and gloomy, and almost ashamed of being an American and not with the battling hosts of my country, helping to raise that sacred ensign upon the parapets from which it had been so causelessly and ignominiously torn. I was resolved, if need be, to enlist, but thanks to the inborn patriotism of the people, I found on arriving here, there was no lack or need of men. They have gone forth in plentiful numbers, unfaltering in their determination to conquer back the Union, or die gloriously fighting for freedom's hope. We will not despair, the sky is brightening, the rainbow of happiness will soon appear. A little while and it will be visible, welcomed by the gladdened hearts of a glorious nation.

'May God save the Union, grant it may stand
The pride of our people, the boast of the land;
Still, still, 'mid the storm, may our banner float free,
Unrent and unriven, o'er earth and o'er sea.

'May God save the Union, still, still may it stand,
Upheld by the prayers of the patriot band;
To cement it our fathers ensanguined the sod,
To keep it we kneel to a merciful God.'

"Truly yours, A. P. Dostie."

CHAPTER IV.

NEW ORLEANS BEFORE GENERAL BUTLER'S ARRIVAL.

February 24th, 1862, General Butler said to President Lincoln, "We shall take New Orleans, or you will never see me again." The object of the expedition, headed by the brave Butler, was known to but few, yet its movements were watched by some who anxiously hoped its object was the taking of New Orleans from the grasp of treason. Among that number was Dostie.

New Orleans went more gradually into the vortex of Secession than other Southern cities. It contained more of the elements of Unionism than any other city. When General Butler arrived in New Orleans, few remained that had not been dragged into or become willing subjects to the poisonous influence, that made treason a power so dangerous. None who were suspected of loyalty to the United States government, could live in safety under its municipal government, unless they had been distinguished as aristocrats, slaveocrats, or politic men,—"men of chivalric positions"—"men of pre-eminent standing,"—"solid men of Southern States—men who had ever stood upon the broad platform of Slavery." These "were tolerated even with ostentation." Some of these privileged classes, cast a penetrating glance into the future of the Republic, and in that glance saw written upon the walls of their cherished institutions, "Death to Slavery;" saw engraved thereon with the pen of truth dipped in the blood of thousands, "UNION, LIBERTY, EQUALITY."

Poor patriots, who had dared to utter sentiments of loyalty, had been banished by Confederate law. A few remained who were reserved upon all political subjects —whose pent up devotions to the Union struggled for utterance, and who waited with trembling hope the arrival of the United States forces.

Pierre Soule, "the silver-tongued" and fluent Union orator of 1860, had stooped from his loyal eminence, and in 1862, was in the vile ranks of Secession, and in sympathy with the Mayor, Common Council and other city officials, noted for their rebellious acts.

Thomas J. Durant was classed among "the persons of pre-eminent standing who were tolerated even with ostentation." His wealth, aristocracy, and above all his policy, was in harmony with Southern chivalry. A prominent Slaveholder, his known sentiments on the subject of Slavery were a passport in his favor—even with those who suspected that he did not coincide with their disunion movements. Durant seldom committed an impolitic act. There was policy in retaining the friendship of Southern men of influence, wealth and position. His slave property was in danger. In the midst of the Rebellion he therefore complained for himself and his friends in a letter, which was sent to President Lincoln, "That in various ways the relation of master and slave was disturbed by the presence of the Federal army, and that this, in part, was done under an Act of Congress." Said President Lincoln, in writing of Durant and his letter, "The paralizer—the dead palsy of the Government in the whole struggle, is that the Durant class of men will do nothing for the Government—nothing for themselves except demanding that the Government shall not strike its enemies lest they be struck by accident."

Suddenly the politic Durant recognized the result of the Revolution, and became a Radical in Negro Suffrage; pointed to President Lincoln in the back-ground, represented himself as standing upon the pinnacle of Radicalism; denouncing the slow movements of his superior, in the great principles of Liberty.

In 1860–61, none perceived that Durant, who had "rested so calmly beside the throne erected to Slavery," would so soon become the champion of radicalism. He belonged to that class of men who, incapable of contending with aroused elements, model themselves upon the epoch in which they live; assume the individuality of the crisis, personifying the popular idea, whatever it may be.

Christian Roselius, was classed among "the solid men of Southern Status." Destiny had given him the experience of age, that he might dissect the rotten carcass which the Rebellion sought to vitalize. But he could not discern the corruption of Slavery, and with bold eloquence defended its principles. He became the learned advocate of slave aristocracy, and the relied-upon avenger of radical abolition. Enveloped in his cloak of conservatism, he feared no thrusts from treason's weapons. During the dark days of rebel power in New Orleans, his voice was heard exclaiming, "O, sirs, a fellow feeling makes us wondrous kind."

Conspicuous among the solid men of those times was

J. Ad. Rozier, whose antagonism to progress and liberty was more prominently exhibited than his patriotism. Said he, in one of his denunciatory speeches of radical measures, "President Lincoln has no right constitutionally to trample upon the rights of even rebels against the Government, and turn loose upon them four millions of slaves." Seizing the Constitution in one hand, he stamped bloody slavery upon it with the other, and vowed that "by the memories of Washington, Jefferson, and Madison, conservatism should palsy the heart of radicalism, if it attempted to subtract one iota from that Constitution." The history of Rozier is written by the radical pen of truth, who makes her foot-prints visible, although she wades through the blood of Revolution, massacre, and riot. Her record will mark the status of true Union men who were not stamped with the crimson stains of Slavery's curse.

These were some of the stars of the first magnitude that shone forth from the Union firmament in the Crescent City during the dark days of Secession. They were dark days indeed!

There were clusters of minor luminaries, which it were endless to delineate. There were some who, fearful of exposing their true principles, pretended to submit cheerfully to tyranny and oppression. Said one of that number, Michael Hahn, who ranked among the second of the classes described:

"During the war there were three classes of Union men in the South. Some left for the North as soon as they could after the commencement of the war, and before the military lines were drawn. The second class remained in the South as long as they could, and although their attachment to the Union was deep, and strong and heartfelt, and was known to each other, they nevertheless had the understanding that in all the mere outward displays, they would pretend an acquiescence in or approval of the Confederate Government. Some succeeded in this course of deceiving the rebel mobs and Provost marshals as to their real feelings up to the time when they were happily released from rebel bondage by the arrival of Federal troops. Others again, of the same class, were detected in their movements as sympathizers with the Union, before the loyal troops could come to their aid, and were sent out of the Confederacy, like Flanders, Hubbard, Tewell, and others, of New Orleans, or were hanged or made to mysteriously disappear.

"The third class consisted of such as never under any circumstances, or at any time even pretended to recognize the Confederate Government. I know of but one man in Louisiana who belonged to this class and who came up fully and completely to this home standard. This man was Dr. Anthony P. Dostie. One day he was seen making his way through an ante-room crowded with confederates, into the office of the traitor Twiggs, whom he addressed in this manner:

"'GENERAL: Your superior, Jefferson Davis, has issued a proclamation which is published in this morning's papers, notifying all Union men, or alien enemies, as they are called, to leave the Confederate States for the North within a time specified. I consider myself as embraced within that proclamation. I am a Union man. I do not recognize the Confederacy, and as your superior has ordered me to depart from your military lines, I expect I shall be protected in complying with this order; and I have come to demand of you a pass enabling me to go North."

"Twiggs eyed the man with wonder, and for some time hesitated about granting the request; but a perusal of the proclamation of Jeff. Davis, and of the Confederate law, on which it was based, convinced him that he had no right to withhold the pass. Armed with the paper furnished him by Twiggs, the noble Dostie left his home, his business and his property, and took the cars for the North. His trip was not one of the most agreeable character: for on the route on exhibiting his pass to the military, his status, of course, became known, and he frequently received insults from mobs, and was even thrust into prison, notwithstanding his pass from Gen. Twiggs. When he finally escaped from Dixie and reached Chicago, he wrote a letter which was published in a New York paper, giving a truthful account of what he saw and heard within the rebel lines. In this letter, speaking of the heroic efforts of the Union men of Tennessee to keep their State within the Union, he exclaims: 'God bless Andrew Johnson.'"

Fear did not, however, prevent Hahn on the 6th of May, 1860, at Lafayette Square, New Orleans, from offering the following resolution :

"*Resolved*, That we the citizens of New Orleans, regardless of all the minor differences of opinion that divide the people of this country politically, are of one mind and one heart, in support of the Union of these States, and that as long as the Constitution of the Republic and the laws enacted by Congress in accordance therewith can be maintained inviolate, as we confidently believe they can be, we shall regard with abhorrence all attempts to destroy the paternal ligaments which bind the sovereign members of this glorious confederation; and we here solemnly pledge ourselves, one to the other, and all to our country, to oppose all parties whose claims to public confidence are in any manner identified with disunion sentiments or designs, and to regard as enemies to Republican liberty all who attempt to separate these States from the Union."

The antagonism between slave aristocracy and liberal principles, was one of the conspicuous causes of the war. In 1860–61, the slave power ruled with a rod of oppression the entire South. Raising her potent hand she exclaimed in demoniac tones, "Behold the destiny of liberty crushed by the power of despotism: She shall be buried beneath the corner-stone of the 'Confederacy,' and upon her ruins shall rise an empire devoted to Slavery." The great mass of Southern aristocrats cried out in their madness, "Let us fall down and worship our idol—Human Bondage!"

Thuggery—offspring of the "pet institution"—scrutinized with a watchful eye all inovations, designated "reforms." Lucien Adams, chief of the Thugs in New Orleans, protected with the bowie knife and pistol the interests of the devotees to the ruling power, and marked with his murderous eye the man who dared to whisper "reform." The Police were all Thugs. "Assassination" was their watchword. Their record is marked by tyranny, outrage and murder. Monroe, the Mayor of the city, given up to the worst features of slaveocratic law was the personification of Thuggery. A man of no moral principle or intellectual culture, he was just the magistrate required to legalize the crimes of a people given up to intrigue and conspiracy. A lover of faction and anarchy, without the boldness to lead a mob, his forte was to accomplish by intrigue and cunning what he could not accomplish by his infamous treason and defiant manner. In his official capacity, he always had an excuse for crime, a smile for a traitor and a word of encouragement for his companions in rebellion. It was a class of men like Monroe and Adams, that the multitude followed. They possessed the true spirit of slavery. It was sufficient for these instigators of riot to indicate a spot on which to assemble, to create a panic, or infuse a sudden rage in the breasts of the populace, and prepare them for murderous action.

CHAPTER V.

BUTLER'S MILITARY RULE IN NEW ORLEANS.

May 1st, 1862, is a memorable day in the history of New Orleans. On that day, General Butler gladdened the hearts of a patriot nation, and struck terror into rebellion, by seizing the stronghold of Treason—the metropolis of the South. When Lincoln said to the noble Farragut, "Go with the fleet to New Orleans, and to the brave Butler; take your troops to that rebellious city;" he believed that the nation must be all free—that destiny had decreed the death of the national curse.

"Sweep from the waters of the Mississippi the foul works of traitor hands," was the command of Farragut to his brave men. Victory was theirs, and the Star-Spangled Banner floated in the breeze, and the national airs from an heroic band mingled with the music of the waters, in glad praises to freedom and loyalty. Farragut had struck the blow the Government required at his hands, and added a trophy to our naval laurels. Butler, as commander of the United States troops, was now to regulate the disordered elements, which had made New Orleans a tempestuous sea of revolt and anarchy. The harmonious action of the army and navy soon calmed the storms which threatened to destroy the riotous city. The news of the great Union victory over treason's stronghold, was received with emotions of gratitude and joy, by men like Dostie and his excited companions who had fled from their genial homes to escape death and oppression.

Men of secession principles like the Rev. Dr. Palmer, who had sacreligiously preached disunion and slavery from their pulpits, vowed revenge upon Farragut, Butler, and the United States Government; calling loudly upon the "Confederacy" to demolish the loyal army and navy, demanding the head of the "Beast" who had made their Monroe tremble before the law of justice—silenced the insults of rebel women, and made the outward signs of secession unpopular in New Orleans.

Mayor Monroe at first defied the commands of General Butler, but speedily brought to fear the iron will and just demands of his superior, he changed his course and sought by intrigue and hypocricy, to throw a veil over his duplicity, but the stern eye of the great criminal lawyer pierced his every motive. Laying his hand upon the traitor, he was conveyed to Fort Jackson, where he remained for months—not to repent of treasonable acts, but to plot future conspiracies.

The Public Schools, the Churches and the Rebel women of New Orleans, (all venomous in their treason) were made harmless for a time, by the firm rule of the subduer of traitors.

CHAPTER VI.

RETURN OF DOSTIE TO NEW ORLEANS.

The Star-Spangled banner waving under the command of Farragut and Butler, invited Unionists from all parts of the country to seek protection under its folds. Among the number who came, was Dr. Dostie. His arrival in New Orleans was thus announced in the *True Delta*, of August 20th, 1862:

"Among the arrivals by the steamer was Dr. Dostie, an eminent dentist of this city, who was compelled to leave, last August, on account of his bold expressions of Union sentiment. Dr. Dostie has been welcomed by a large circle of friends. He is a fluent and earnest speaker, and we hope, will be heard by our Union citizens at their meetings."

When Lafayette and the Baron de Kalb stepped upon Liberty's soil after a tedious voyage of months, they mutually swore to conquer or die in the contest upon which they were entering. That noble resolve was prompted by their true love of liberty. It was the same spirit which led the patriotic Dostie to exclaim, "I have come back after one year's absence from my loved home, to die for the cause of liberty, if by such sacrifice it shall receive one impetus." From that time his life was a continued series of patriotic deeds and self-sacrificing acts. Aug. 21st, 1862, just one year from the day he left the government of Jefferson Davis and the command of Gen. Twiggs, he addressed a Union meeting in New Orleans, under the Government, claiming Abraham Lincoln as its Chief Executive, and General Butler as its military commander.

The Rev. Mr. Duncan—President of the Union meeting addressed by Dr. Dostie, Aug. 21st, 1862—was to the cause of the Union, what Dr. Palmer was to the cause of Rebellion. Both were men of superior intellect. Both were in a position to exert an immense influence, either for good or evil—for a Republican Government, or a Slave Despotism. Dr. Duncan loving his Church next to his God, tore himself from its rebel influence, proclaiming amidst persecution and insult, his devotion to his Government, the Union, and Liberty. An exile from his Church, his family, and the society once dear to him, his mental anxiety and protracted labors were more than his delicate constitution and sensitive nature could endure. He died—a martyr to the sacred cause he had so cherished. A short time before his death he said, "There is no one who can appreciate my Union sentiments, and the sufferings I have endured for the beloved cause of liberty so well as my friend Dostie."

Dr. Dostie was never an orator. Yet he possessed the elements which constitute true oratory. He had never cultivated those powers, and never acquired that command of strong and appropriate language, which is an essential quality of a popular speaker. But he possessed the fire, spirit, the enchanting wildness, and magnificent irregularity of the true orator's genius, combined with judgment, imagination, sensibility, taste and expression.

Discipline would have made him an effective, graceful and popular orator. The enemies of Dostie have pronounced him a fanatical, reckless and thoughtless agitator. Yet his life proves him a deliberate, philosophic and thoughtful man—ever sincere, honest and truthful.

Said he to a friend, "I have always been in the habit of spending half my nights in reading, studying the works of philosophers, our standard poets, and best writers. It is one of the great pleasures of my life to commune in the silent hours of the night with those noble minds, who have left us their writings to cherish." His patriotism was based upon philosophical principles and profound reason—not upon fanaticism. The great purpose of his life, expressed in his every act, was to assist in upholding a truly Republican Government. Oppression, despotism and treason he dared oppose, even at the risk of life and property. His defence of humanity and freedom; his lowly birth, his poverty, and above all, his out-spoken hatred to the rebellion made him the object of marked dislike with the solid men of New Orleans, who like Roselius, Rozier and Barker, watched with jealous eye their superiors in patriotism, humanity and reform, and delighted to style them, "fanatic."

Surrounded by bitter enemies, determined to crush the fearless Dostie, we yet find him a power, rising superior to his enemies. At all the Union meetings, Associations and Leagues established in the Crescent City, he was a prominent worker in his beloved cause, braving every hatred and malice. In the midst of these labors he often received anonymous notes warning him to prepare for death, filled sometimes with scandal of the lowest order. To these he never paid any attention, so entirely absorbed was he in the great events by which he was surrounded.

CHAPTER VII.

PUBLIC SCHOOLS OF NEW ORLEANS.

Before General Butler's arrival in New Orleans, the virus of treason animated all the Public Schools of that city. The Board of Education, the Superintendent and Trustees, with but few exceptions, conspired to infuse the deadly poison of treason into the minds of the youth everywhere in their charge.

Wm. O. Rodgers was the Superintendent of the Public Schools in New Orleans, when the United States Government was treated with contempt by the scholars under his charge. Two months before General Butler's arrival in New Orleans, at a public examination in one of the schools, the black flag was hung upon the walls with the words worked in white, "We ask no quarters and grant none." A rebel paper in that city thus commented upon these emblems:—"Strangely appropriate emblems for our schools—the best in the Confederacy." Such were the institutions of learning under the secession epidemic. Treason had become a power which defied the United States Government, and the thousands, who daily assembled at the Public Schools, were taught to insultingly flaunt the flag of Secession in the faces of the United States officers, who were in New Orleans to protect Republican Government. These treasonable teachers soon perceived that their ship of rebellion must plunge beneath the waves of the contest in which they had so proudly embarked, and that the helm they had attempted to grasp, had passed into the hands of one fully capable of subduing defiant traitors. Butler quickly discovered the necessity of purifying the public schools from the corruption of rebellion.

Rogers fled before the stern justice of Butler into a confederate retreat. The Board of Education, which had favored the "black flag" in the schools expired, not to be revivified whilst loyal men governed New Orleans. Union men, among whom were Dostie, Heath, Hahn, Heine, Shupert, and Flanders were appointed to revolutionize the public schools. L. B. Carter was made the loyal superintendent. Dr. Dostie was the animating soul in that reformation, whose avowed work was to extirpate treason from those institutions. It was a settled plan in which all the loyal Board of Education harmonized, "That no symbol of treason should be permitted in the schools under their supervision." In March, 1863, the Board of Education adopted the following resolutions:

"*Whereas*, It is a rule of action in the education of youth, of universal acceptance that the inculcation of sound moral principle is no less important than intellectual culture: and,

"*Whereas*, The present lamentable state of our national affairs has lowered the standard of public morals, and to a certain extent created disregard for those high obligations which teach us to love our country and its beneficent institutions: and,

"*Whereas*, It is the duty of those to whom is entrusted the education of our youth to counteract the evil tendencies of the times, and to infuse into the minds of their pupils ideas in relation to public affairs which will be equally consistent with true patriotism and sound morality: therefore be it

"*Resolved*, That the teachers of the public schools be instructed, henceforth, to make the singing of patriotic songs, and the reading of appropriate passages from the addresses of patriotic men, a part of the business of each day, in the several departments of their respective schools."

A few days after these resolutions were passed by the Board of Education, an invitation was given to the public to assemble at the Madison School (where a few months previous the "black flag" had been displayed) to witness the interesting ceremony of presenting a beautiful United States flag to the school. Upon that occasion, hundreds of childish voices greeted their friends with the national air, "Star-Spangled Banner," after which, seven little girls stepped upon a platform and presented their flag to their school with the following address:—

"We dedicate to the Madison School this "Star-Spangled Banner," the emblem of our own dear native land, as a tribute to patriotism. Long, long may it wave over our school dedicated to union, science and liberty!"

Dr. Dostie, on behalf of the Directors, addressed the school as follows:

"Miss WHITBY, Principal; Ladies, Teachers; and you, Pupils of Madison School:

"The scene witnessed by the friends of thorough and correct education to-day is destined to be long remembered. There can be no occasion of deeper interest to the lovers of the human race, its progress in education and advancement in true loyal patriotic sentiments, than now appears in the brilliant and most encouraging spectacle you have, by your noble and indefatigable exertions, wrought for the hopes of *the* liberty and freedom of our land.

"Here the youths of our city have gathered for the culture and proper education of their minds and hearts in a correct knowledge of the various duties belonging to good and virtuous members of society.

"As we cast our eyes over this great Republic, bequeathed us by '*him* whom envy dared not hate,' and behold the causeless and furious civil war now desolating our once peaceful, happy and glorious land, filling, as it does, the patriot's heart with terrible apprehensions for the future of this most sacred of gifts—self-government—to whom are we to look for hope of salvation, but to you of this rising generation, educated as, we pray the Father of Nations you may be, in the just and beneficent principles of Republicanism, of unity, peace and fraternity. Then our dear country will not know the Arnolds, Burrs, Calhouns, or Davises any more.

"Be therefore zealous in the acquisition of useful knowledge that you may distinguish truth from error, virtue from vice, and labor assiduously in disseminating these virtues, these duties, and God will bless and reward you with felicity here and heaven in the hereafter.

"Trace thoughtfully the history of our immortal Washington's school days—remember he could not *lie*—that he lived and practiced all the pure and exalted virtues, thereby compelling the high eulogium from mankind of being 'first in war, first in peace, and first in the hearts of his countrymen.'

"The public schools of our nation should be the avenue to the education of all the various and manifold duties devolved upon the citizens of our great Commonwealth.

They should be treasured as the corner-stone of the Republic—they were designed for the education and enlightenment of the masses, in their duties to God, their country, and themselves; and where they prevail and are encouraged, treason, rebellion, and their atrocious attendants are not known.

"Had the youths of the rebellious portions of our country been the recipients of the blessings of this munificent institution, 'grim-visaged war,' with its concomitants—famine, pestilence and death, would not now be blighting our once happy and homogeneous people—the land had not been pierced by the murderous stabs of our brethren.

"Let us, citizens, be in future the careful and untiring guardians of this institution, pregnant with such vast promises of good; then the hydra-headed, execrable monster—Treason—will not again make parricidal thrusts at our dearest mother, who for eighty years has nourished us with the delicious milk of Liberty, Freedom and Fraternity.

"Now, in behalf of loyal Louisiana and of the loyal United States, permit me to introduce little Mary Murray, and through this pure patriot, her four hundred associates, in behalf of loyal Americans everywhere, to thank them for the gift of *that* 'gorgeous ensign of our Liberty Land.' That beautiful emblem of our glory and power! that a Washington triumphantly bore through the revolutionary struggles; that a Jackson won a halo of undying glory upon the Plains of Chalmette; that a Taylor so heroically bore aloft at Buena Vista; that a Scott reveled within the halls of the Montezumas; that a Farragut carried by Forts Jackson and St. Phillip in a flame of lightning; that Butler, the indomitable, unfurled from the ramparts of our treason-bound emporium; that will victoriously float over Liberty's Dominions, when the 'Stars and Bars' will be buried in oblivion."

This was the inauguration ceremony of a brilliant series of flag presentations, which ended in placing an American flag over every public school in New Orleans. The sight of the National emblem waving from the public institutions infuriated its enemies, who in their madness declared, "That their children should not be taught to love the United States Government."

Dr. Dostie, the chairman of that committee which had drawn up the resolutions requiring the introduction of national airs and patriotic sentiments in the schools, says, in his report to the Board of Education, "I have received communications from the principals of some of the schools, informing me that many of their pupils have risen in rebellion and refused to sing national airs as requested by their teachers. I am urged to use my influence in quelling this insubordination instigated by rebellious parents. Upon consultation with several members of the Board of Education, and finding that their views coincided with mine—that it was our duty to enforce the laws governing the institutions under our charge—I have informed the disobedient that the requirements were just, and therefore, irrevocable, and that if they persisted in their rebellion they must be expelled from the schools. Only three hundred of the eight thousand in attendance refused, and were expelled or withdrawn from the schools."

The following testimony relating to the noble labors

of Dostie in the cause of republican education, is worthy to be placed among the historical records of those eventful times when, in the hands of loyal educators, science, poetry, music, and flowers, combine to make Unionism and the United States flag popular in the halls of education in New Orleans. *The True Delta*, through a correspondent says:

"MESSRS. EDITORS: I ask the use of your columns to publish the following well deserved and highly flattering testimonial to the zeal and efficiency with which that pre-eminently earnest Union man, Dr. A. P. Dostie, discharged his duties while a member of the Board of Visitors of the First District Schools. The public generally, in common with the School Board, feel keenly the retirement of so earnest a votary of true education. They indulge the hope, though, that the work of regenerating the public schools from the moral leprosy of treason, so happily inaugurated by the Doctor during the past year, may be continued until there shall remain no youthful mind capable of retaining and receiving so unseemly a taint. * * * * *

"BOARD OF VISITORS OF THE PUBLIC SCHOOLS OF THE FIRST DISTRICT.

NEW ORLEANS, Sept. 15, 1863.

"At a regular meeting of the Board of Visitors of the First District Public Schools, held on the 14th inst., on motion of Mr. J. A. Noble, seconded by Messrs. Hahn and Graham, the following resolutions were unanimously adopted:

"*Resolved*, That the thanks of this Board be tendered to Dr. A. P. Dostie for his constant and well directed exertions in the cause of education, while a member of the Board of Visitors during the past year.

"*Resolved*, That the labors of Dr. Dostie have, in the

opinion of this Board, contributed more than those of any individual towards restoring the public schools to loyalty and patriotism, and that we regret his retirement from active co-operation with us in our official labors.

"*Resolved*, That the Secretary be instructed to forward a copy of these resolutions to Dr. A. P. Dostie.

"A true copy from the minutes.

"F. O. SCHRODER, Secretary."

Dr. Dostie's successful efforts in making treason odious in the public schools, made the enemies of the Union in New Orleans rampant in propagating slander against his personal truth and superior excellence. But his patriotic achievements will bear exposure to the scorn of rebellious spirits, whose tenacious calumnies not only followed him through his labors in the public schools, but in all the reforms wherewith his name was honorably associated. The extent of indignity to which Dr. Dostie was subjected, may be partially inferred from the following acrostic, one of the many low exhibitions of malice put forth to intimidate or prevent his exertions for liberty:—

"All hail to thee, Dr.! may'st thou always prove true,
Patriotic and proud of the red white and blue;
Do all that thou canst for the flag that once waved
O'er the land of the free and the home of the brave.
Stout hearts fight against it—they'll rally around:
The stars and the stripes they'll haul to the ground;
In the dust they will trail it, and thee they will hang,
Emancipating thy soul to where e'er it may gang."

In the midst of such enemies, the voice of a friend reached the ear of Dostie, breathing a spirit in striking contrast to the foregoing. In the columns of the New Orleans *True Delta*, appeared the following lines, a beautiful acrostical rejoinder to that of his enemies:

"Amid the stunted forest trees,
Perennial grows the stately oak,
Defying all the storm-king's power,
Or the fierce lightning's deadly stroke!
So thou, brave man, 'mid traitors' scorn,
Traced the white flame of loyalty!
In dangers oft, 'mid threats of death,
Ever the 'Friend of Liberty!'

"NEW ORLEANS, Sep. 2, 1864. UNA."

An inquiry into the private seminaries and schools of New Orleans instituted by a Commission appointed by Major General Banks, Commander of the Department of the Gulf—of which commission Dr. Dostie was an active member—reveals the following then existing state of things:

"In many of the schools in this city, persons are instructing our youth who avow themselves "rebels" or "rebel sympathizers!" And many others who show by their evasive manner of answering these questions, that their whole sympathies are with those now in armed rebellion against our Government and shedding the blood of our countrymen! And further, that these individuals are permitted to organize schools, teach our children and tacitly or openly instill the poison of rebellion and treason into their young minds! The thing would seem impossible, but there the record of facts stands, on their own confession—attesting to the impudent daring of a deed which is only exceeded in its violation of all that is right and honorable by the forbearance and magnanimity of the Government against which rebels and rebel sympathizers are waging a suicidal war, and under whose flag these teachers are or have been quietly pursuing their vocation."

Said Dr. Dostie, in referring to that commission to visit, examine and report as to the character of the private schools of New Orleans—"I knew that in that work I should meet some of my old personal friends, which the rebellion had made my enemies, and that the interview would not be a pleasant one. It was with no spirit of revenge or vindictive feeling that I approached my former friends, but I will never shrink from the duty of exposing the work of traitors—not if all my friends become my enemies." Dr. Dostie's unselfish acts often gained him the friendship of those who differred with him. Many of the most bitter rebels speak kindly of his benevolent acts. When Mayor Monroe was imprisoned in Fort Jackson; his wife, upon several occasions, requested Dr. Dostie to urge his influence with General Butler in her behalf. As she was left in destitute circumstances, he went several times to the office of General Butler to ask the favors she required. He also obtained a position in the public school for the daughter of Mayor Monroe. When told that he was rendering assistance to the family of a rebel, he replied, "Must the wife and daughter suffer for the acts of the husband and father? Bring me the proofs of treason and I will expose the perpetrators. They have assured me that they cherish Union principles, and I have no reason to doubt their word. The charge of treason, said he, 'when it has a just foundation is a fatal one, in my estimation, to personal character. In regard to that 'crime of crimes,' I must not act upon suspicion, but upon evidence."

CHAPTER VIII.

THE CHURCHES OF NEW ORLEANS.

The Churches of New Orleans are a strange part of the history of the rebellion. With the noble exception of the Rev. Wm. Duncan, the prominent clergymen of that city became Judases—betraying their Saviour, their Government. The names of Palmer, Leacock and Goodridge, are written with pens dipped in blood upon the tombstones of thousands of misguided youths, who listened to their eloquence in behalf of rebellion and slavery. The power of a Butler was again felt in New Orleans, when he laid his hands upon the heads of the Reverend traitors, and demanded of them obedience to the laws of the true Church, and the just laws of the Nation.

Upon the refusal of the clergy to pray for the President of the United States, their Churches were ordered to be closed, until loyal ministers could officiate in their places. The ecclesiastical institutions of the South were a dangerous power in favor of despotism and rebellion. It was necessary to strike the Church from its foundation by the earthquake advance of reform. It required men of the force of a Luther or a Cromwell, to blot out the disgraceful crimes which stained their statute books. Slavery had enveloped the consciences of its ministers, and treason lay like a dark pall upon their guilty souls. That power in the Churches of New Orleans, that defied the United States Government, was temporarily overthrown by General Butler. Loyal Christian ministers were invited to fill the pulpits of disloyal clergymen—men who would not advocate the divinity of slavery, but the charities of Christianity. Soon convened loyal congregations to listen to their prayers for the overthrow of Slavery and treason, and the preservation of their beloved President and the Congress of the United States. To men like Dostie, who watched with jealous eye every evil influence that opposed civil and religious liberty, the new turn in Church affairs, was a source of rejoicing. Every Sabbath morning he might be seen entering the Episcopal Church, formerly occupied by Dr. Goodridge, to worship with the reverence of a man of faith. His deep toned voice, which had a peculiar charm to his friends, upon these solemn occasions could be distinctly heard repeating that service to which he became deeply attached. Said he, "I always pray in faith for President Lincoln, for I feel in my inmost soul that the God of Nations will sustain the noble acts of our Chief Magistrate." From that time until his death, Dr. Dostie was a constant worshipper in Church. His religious views partook of his general character. They were broad and liberal, and not confined to any narrow creed. In a conversation with a friend, he remarked, "I believe that Christ died for all. I trust in God—the great Ruler of Events has placed before us his laws. If we are guided by them, they will lead us to happiness here and hereafter. That is my creed and my religion."

Upon the organization of a loyal congregation in Christ's Church, Dr. Dostie was chosen one of the wardens. Christ's Church! What a throng of associations gious home of the army and navy of the Gulf Department. cluster around that name! Christ's Church was the reli- There might be seen upon a Sabbath morning, the commanding General and his Staff; the officers of every grade of both the army and the navy; soldiers and sailor boys. Union citizens and loyal visitors from all parts of the country assembled in that sacred spot. What prayers have been offered by clergy and laymen for the preservation of the Union, and what heartfelt petitions have ascended to the God of Nations in behalf of President Lincoln and the Congress of the United States! That emblem of religious liberty—the United States flag—enveloped the altar dedicated to Freedom. That flag draped in mourning symbols, was wrapped around the biers of the patriots who fell by the hands of the enemies of their Government. It enclosed in its folds the pulseless form of the youthful De Kay, the gallant Cummings, the brave Dwight, and numbers of honored dead, who died for the Union and Liberty. How many weeping parents, wives, brothers and sisters, would have been comforted, could they have witnessed the tribute of respect, paid to their departed ones at Christ's Church, and beheld with what tenderness and sympathy, that friend of the loyal soldier, Dostie, and his brother officers in the Church looked upon the remains of those who fell in the cause of republican Liberty.

CHAPTER IX.

DR. DOSTIE'S ACTIVITY IN THE UNION CAUSE.

Dr. Dostie was a man of iron nerve and unceasing activity. Possessed of a strong constitution, a powerful will and an active brain, he could endure more physically and mentally than most men. It was not an uncommon thing for him to look after the interests of a dozen schools per day; work a few hours at his profession, receive not less than fifty calls; attend two or three Union meetings, and then spend half the night in reading and writing.

Not a Union Church or Sabbath School (white or colored), existed in the city in which he did not take a deep interest. Not an association or loyal gathering assembled that bore not witness to his exertions in the cause for which loyal men were battling. In many of these reforms, Dr. Dostie was the prime mover. Sensitive to the opinion of his associates; delighting in the approbation of his friends, and desiring the respect even of his enemies, no earthly power could induce him to swerve from what he considered duty. Where he could resist treason he never wavered. Said he, "It is the duty of loyal men who love their flag and their Government, to use every exertion to put down the signs of disloyalty." Wherever he observed an act or symbol of treason, it called down upon the offender his rebuke and bitter indignation.

Among the "fanatical acts" of Dr. Dostie that evoked the thundering anathemas of the rebel multitude was his noted performance at the Varieties Theater. A few determined Unionists, among whom were Judge Durell, E. Heath, and L. B. Lynch, headed by Dostie, resolved that the flag of the Union should float where it had been torn down by its enemies. The Varieties Theater had become somewhat notorious for displaying rebel emblems. It was decided by Dostie and his associates to make a demonstration of loyalty in that place to test the Union sentiment. With a chosen band, Dr. Dostie entered the Theater and displayed the "Star-Spangled Banner," requesting the orchestra to play a national air. Instantly the United States flag was displayed from all parts of the house, and the air of the "Star-Spangled Banner" demanded. This created a great excitement. The manager of the Theater appeared upon the stage and demanded an explanation of the demonstration. Dr. Dostie, standing by the flag he had unfurled, replied, "New Orleans is now a Union city. The audience have determined to hear the national airs; none but secession airs have been heard here during the season, and the present company intend to hear "Hail Columbia" before the performance proceeds." To this the manager replied, "That he had permission from the military authorities, and license from the city to conduct the Theater, and had received strict orders from those authorities to allow nothing of a political character." "'Tis false," arose from all parts of the house. The audience continued to demand the playing of the national airs, some, however, declaring that the airs would be in opposition to the orders of Mayor Miller. At this juncture, Major Foster of the 128th New York Volunteers, stepped upon the stage, and commanded silence, saying, "he would take the responsibility of ordering the orchestra to strike up "Hail Columbia." The order was reluctantly obeyed, and the old-time air was greeted with many cheers. General Bowen immediately issued an order of which the annexed is a copy:

"OFFICE OF PROVOST MARTIAL,
DEPARTMENT OF THE GULF,
NEW ORLEANS, April 22, 1863.

"Mr. Baker, Manager of Varieties Theater:

"It is reported to me that you have declined to cause the national airs to be played at your Theater at the request of the audience, for the reason that you have been forbidden by the Mayor of the city. No such order can be recognized or held valid in the presence of the United States army. You will, therefore, cause the national airs, "Hail Columbia," "Star-Spangled Banner" and "Yankee Doodle," to be played before the audience leaves your Theater this evening.

JAMES BOWEN, Brig. Gen., P. M. G."

It was from a few similar episodes in the life of Dostie that he acquired the name of "fanatic," "agitator," and "inovator." Yet he reverenced just law, order, and peace. "My principles were never law-defying, but I must oppose treason in all its forms," he replied when questioned as to his course in opposing the emblems of secession.

Those acts will bear scrutiny, for they did not often spring from sudden impulse, but from a settled purpose to attack injustice and disloyalty wherever found, and success generally attended his movements.

CHAPTER X.

DOSTIE'S POLITICAL VIEWS.

Dostie thus defines his political status: "I have always been a Jacksonian Democrat. When the great question came before the American people whether Slavery or Freedom should triumph in our nation, the Democratic party favored Slavery, and I trusted to the Republican party to save the country. Abraham Lincoln was the choice of that party for President of the United States. It had analyzed his character; had found him a friend of the working classes; an enemy to every form of Slavery—an honest man with qualifications worthy the ruler of a Republican people." In a political speech, he said, "From the moment I decided to support the noble Lincoln, I have watched with deep interterest his onward movements in the cause of Union, liberty and humanity. If he continues faithful to the principles by which he guides the nation, our hopes will be more than realized."

Dostie was never known to vote for any man who opposed the cause of President Lincoln. So strong was his faith in the great Emancipator, no argument could convince him that any other was so capable of securing the liberties of an oppressed race as Abraham Lincoln. In an address, he says, "I believe Lincoln was chosen by the Divine Ruler of Governments, for the purpose of liberating four millions of human beings from the tyranny of Southern despots."

Among the first to welcome General Butler to New Orleans, was Michael Hahn. He had combatted secession; had publicly announced his devotion to the Union until it became dangerous to give expression to his sentiments. Not willing to suffer martyrdom, he remained silent, patiently waiting the time when he could boldly proclaim his true sentiments. He had been a Douglass Democrat, but when he saw in President Lincoln, the preserver of the Union, he avowed his determination, publicly, "to stand by him as long as he stood faithfully by the Union." It was that avowal that first attracted the loyal heart of Dostie towards Hahn. It was the tie that united them until separated by death. A few days after publicly proclaiming his determination to stand by Lincoln, Hahn was elected to Congress from Louisiana. Among the crowd who assembled upon the levee to witness the departure for Washington of the newly elected congressmen, Flanders and Hahn, was Dr. Dostie. As the steamer left the landing he exclaimed, "Those men will stand by our good President and the true interests of Louisiana." Upon the return of Hahn from Washington, in an address before the people of New Orleans, he said, "If any man wishes to know my political position, I will inform him that I am ready to stand or fall upon the same platform with Abraham Lincoln. I have had opportunities of studying the moral and intellectual character of our present beloved Magistrate, and in my opinion a better man could not have been elected President of the United States. The preservation of the

Union is the great desire of his heart. When I first took my seat in Congress I thought it my duty to seek an interview with Mr. Lincoln, and state to him that I might cast votes that would displease him. The President took me by the hand and said, "Let the perpetuity of the Union be the prominent object of your official conduct, and you will not displease me."

Says Herndon, (the law partner of Lincoln), "Abraham Lincoln possessed originality of thought in an eminent degree. He was, however, cautious, cool, concentrated, with continuity of reflection, was patient and enduring. These are some of the grounds of his wonderful success. He was most emphatically a remorseless analyzer of facts, things and principles. When all these processes had been well and thoroughly gone through, he could form an opinion and express it, but no sooner. The mind of Lincoln was slow, angular and ponderous rather than quick and finely discriminating." When the good Lincoln did discern that the Union could no longer exist with the curse of slavery gnawing at its vitals, he struck the blow, and true Union loving men, such as Dostie, Lovejoy and Hahn, gloried in the salvation of their country.

Dostie, who had ever sympathized with such noble spirits as Clarkson, Wilberforce, Phillips and Garrison, could never for a moment stifle the sentiment that Slavery was the most atrocious of crimes. In the following address, delivered January 2d, 1864, in City Hall—the same spot where in 1860–61, speeches were made to secession crowds—after a few introductory remarks by Hon. Michael Hahn, and before an immense concourse of people, Dr. Dostie thus expressed himself upon the national situation:

Mr. President, Ladies and Gentlemen:

"We took our place among the nations of the earth in 1789. We were then a homogeneous, happy people. Our heroic struggle for independence was fought and achieved by the people of the colonies, cemented in a perpetual union. No single State could have thrown off the shackles of British tyranny. It was only by the fraternal bonds of union that our brave republican fathers freed themselves from monarchical despotism. Our recognition by the great powers of Europe, was as one nation and homogeneous people. The immortal Declaration reads: "United colonies," declaring themselves free and independent; and by the Constitution of the Confederation, the Continental Congress controlled and guided us to the haven of freedom and glorious nationality, and we have grown and prospered with a rapidity unequaled by any nation in the history of the world. The glorious Constitution that has enabled us thus to flourish, was adopted by the people, and not by State governments. Yes, it was by the people, in their individual and collective character, we were made one and perpetual. It was the people who, in their relation to States, yielded the power to levy taxes and impose duties, to regulate commerce, to make naturalization laws, to coin money, to regulate post-offices and post-roads, to define and punish piracies, to declare war, to provide an army and navy, to enter into any treaty, alliance or confederation, to issue letters of marque and reprisal, to emit bills of credit, to keep troops or ships of war in times of peace, and to enter into any agreement or compact, either with each other or with a foreign power. They placed all controversy that might arise between the States or individuals in the hands of the National Judiciary. After these concessions there remained no semblance of sovereignty, but simply the right of independent self-government in local or domestic affairs. Sovereignty the States never achieved. The people won their independence by their wisdom, their energies and their valor, after seven long years of struggle against British power and aggression. The Declaration of Independence sets forth the reasons and purposes of that revolution that achieved and established the freedom of our country. Not once does it mention the States, but it does mention the people in their united and national character. 'State Sovereignty,' 'State Supremacy,' 'State Rights,' and the cursed system of slavery, were ignored and repudiated by the consummate wisdom and goodness of the founders of this nation; and the latter by the enlightened voice of the world, as the crime of crimes against humanity.

"Permit me to ask you to listen to the voice of sages, Christians, patriots, statesmen, philosophers and philanthropists of this and other nations, concerning this hell-begotten wrong and outrage. Washington said it was his first wish to free America of the curse. Jefferson, the Apostle of Liberty, said he trembled for his country, and declared it was written in the Book of Fate, that the people should be free. Patrick Henry detested slavery with all the earnestness of his nature, and believed the time was not far distant when the lamentable evil would be abolished. Madison denied the right of property in man, and contended that the republican principle was antagonistic to human bondage. Monroe considered slavery as preying upon the very vitals of the Union. John Randolph detested the man who defended slavery. Thomas Randolph deprecated the workings of the evil. Thomas Jefferson Randolph classes the 'institution' among the abominations and enormities of savage tribes, and as tending to decrease free populations. Peyton Randolph lamented its existence. Edward Randolph, as member of the Convention that framed the Constitution of our nation, moved to strike out "servitude," and insert "service," because the former was thought to express the condition of slaves, and the latter the obligation of free persons. Henry Clay would never, never, never, by word or thought, by mind or will, aid in subjecting free territory to the everlasting curse of human bondage. The great Benton, in view of the peace and reputation of the white people—the peace of the land—the world's last hope for a free government on the earth, and because it was a wrong, condemned its extension and existence. Colonel Mason contended slavery discouraged the arts and manufactures, made labor disreputable, prevented immigration of whites, who enrich and strengthen a country, produced pernicious effects on manners, made the master a petty tyrant, and invited calamities to the nation. Governor McDowell says this people was born to be free, and their enslavement is in violation of the law of Deity. Judge Iredell, of North Carolina, would rejoice when the entire abolition of slavery took place. William Pinckney, of Maryland, considered it dishonorable and iniquitous. Thomas Marshall, of Virginia, said it was ruinous to the whites. Bolling said the time would come when this degraded and oppressed people would free themselves from their thraldom. Chandler calls it a cancer, and said it would produce commotion and bloody strife. Summers said the evils could not be enumerated. Preston said the slaves were men, and entitled to human rights. Birney, of Kentucky, said the slaveholder had not one atom of right to his slave, and that all peoples rejoice when they hear the oppressed are set free. McLane, of Delaware, said, I am an enemy of slavery. Luther Martin, of Maryland, said slavery is inconsistent with the genius of republicanism. An abolition society was formed in Virginia in 1791, in which slavery was denounced as not only an odious degradation, but an outrageous violation of one of the most essential rights of human nature, and utterly repugnant to the principles of the Gospel, and argued that all men are by nature equally free and independent. The heroic Marion said it reduced society to two classes —the rich and the very poor. Oglethorpe, the founder of Georgia, called it a horrid crime. Franklin called slavery an atrocious debasement of human nature. Hamilton said all men were, by nature, entitled to equal privileges. John Jay called it repugnant to every principle of justice and equity. William Jay contended the time had arrived when it was necessary to destroy slavery to save our own liberty. John Quincy Adams—the old man eloquent—said it perverted human reason and tainted the very sources of moral principle. Webster regarded it as a great moral and political evil, sustained by *might* against *right*, and in violation of the spirit of religion, justice and humanity. Noah Webster claimed freedom as the sacred right of every man. De Witt Clinton says the despotisms and slavery of the world would long since have vanished, if the natural equality of mankind had been understood and practiced. General Joseph Warren says personal freedom is the natural right of every man. England, through her Mansfields, calls it odious; her Locke, so vile that a gentleman cannot plead for it; her Pitt, that it should not be permitted for a single hour; her Fox compares it to robbery and murder; her Shakspeare said that heaven will one day free us from this slavery; her Cowpers and Miltons have, in immortal verse, execrated it; her Doctor Johnson says no man is, by nature, the property of another; her Doctor Price says, if you can enslave another, he can enslave you; her Blackstone tells us we must transgress unjust human laws, and obey the natural and divine; and her Coke, Hampden, Wilberforce, and many of her other learned and good men, endorsed this doctrine. Ireland's Burke said it ought not to be suffered to exist; her Curran demanded universal emancipation; her great O'Connell, speaking to his countrymen, said he would not recognize them, if they countenanced the horrors of American slavery. Father Mathew said slavery is a sin against God and man, and called loudly on all true Irishmen to help to move on the Car of Freedom. Scotland's voice is as potent in condemnation of this stupendous crime. Her Beattie said it is opposed to virtue and industry, and should be viewed with horror; her Miller said every individual, whatever his country or complexion, is entitled to freedom. France, speaking through her La Fayette, the friend of Washington and Liberty, tells the world he would not have drawn his sword in the cause of America, if he could have conceived that thereby he was founding a land of slavery; his grandson said the abolition of slavery commanded his entire sympathy. Montesquieu said the earth shrank in barrenness from the contaminating sweat of a slave. Louis X. said the Christian religion and nature herself cried out against the state of slavery, and demanded the liberty of all men. Rousseau said slavery and right contradicted and excluded each other. Brissot viewed it as a degradation of human nature. Schiller, Grotius, Goethe, Luther, Humboldt, and thousands of freedom loving Germans, have spoken deeply in condemnation of this monster iniquity. This noble people were the earliest to denounce the sin, and went so far as to declare the slave justifiable in the murder of his master who refused to let him go free. The greatest of Alexanders has declared, by a solemn ukase, the universal enfranchisement of his people, and sixty millions of human beings are thereby made freemen, to love God and the ways of justice and virtue. Cicero tells us all men are born free, and that law cannot make *wrong right.* Socrates calls slavery a system of outrage and robbery. Plato, that it is a system of the most complete injustice. The great Cyrus said that to fight, in order not to be made a slave, is noble. The churches of the world hold this sin as an abomination unto the Lord. The true interpretation of the Bible proclaims liberty throughout all the land, unto all the inhabitants thereof, and commands us to let the oppressed go free, to call no man master, neither to be called masters. Slavery is the black and loathsome sin that will not be forgiven in this world, nor the world to come. Thus the intelligent and great men of all nations denounce this foul system. The world—our own nation—all the States except atrocious South

Carolina and degenerate Georgia, deprecated and shuddered at this evil in the land. Through the pernicious influence of these States the system was recognized as a State Right, in permitting the importation of human beings for enslavement for twenty years, when the importation was branded and punished as piracy.

"Soon after the adoption of the Constitution, all the Northern States abolished and repudiated slavery, as a violation of human rights. The blighting influence of this curse caused the great flow of immigration to settle in the Northern States, hence followed the preponderance of population, wealth and power, and the vast advantages in all the avenues of happiness they now enjoy. Listen to facts to prove 'the earth is made to shrink in barrenness' from the malign influences of slavery.

"See the poverty, ignorance and desolation of the slave lands in contrast to great Freedom's onward and upward course. In 1790, the population of Virginia was double that of the State of New York. In 1850, that of New York was twice as great as that of Virginia. In 1791, the exports of New York amounted to about equal those of Virginia. Sixty years after, New York surpasses Virginia in her exports more than eighty millions. In 1790, the imports of New York and Virginia were about equal. Sixty years after New York surpasses Virginia more than one hundred million dollars. In 1850, the products, manufactures, mechanics and arts in New York amounted to more than *one billion* dollars more than those of Virginia. In the same year, the value of real and personal property in Virginia (including the negroes) is nearly one billion dollars less than that of New York. In 1856, the real and personal estate assessed in the city of New York was worth more than the whole State of Virginia. The value of the farms, farming utensils, mechanical and agricultural products in New York exceed those in Virginia in the same ratio. In 1850, the hay crop in the free States amounted to more than four times the value of the cotton, tobacco and sugar crops of the fifteen slave States. The total value of the property of the free States is more than three times that of the slave States. The bushel products, the pound-measure products, the gallon and the mining products of the Northern States are similarly ahead of the same products of the South, notwithstanding the superior advantages of the South in soil, climate, rivers, harbors, minerals, forests, and 245,000 more square miles of territory. In 1850 there were only eighteen hundred adult persons in Massachusetts who could not read and write. In the same year eighty thousand of the white adult inhabitants of North Carolina could neither read or write. The comparative intelligence in these States is presented to illustrate the ignorance, poverty and imbecility pervading the land of slavery in contrast with the land of freedom, where intelligence, wealth, prosperity, progress and happiness are everywhere visible.

"These statistical facts prove that when this nation commenced its existence, the South had the advantage of the North. Why has the South degenerated, and why is she to-day so far behind the North in all that relates to intelligent, civilized nations? In her commercial and business relations, why is she so far surpassed by the Northern States! Because the Goddess, Freedom, is working, speaking and running against the Demon, Slavery. This infamous monster is doomed to work out its own destruction. In aiming its deadly fangs at the nation's vitals, it has inflicted its own death wounds. Thanks to liberty, to republicanism, and the beneficent institutions transmitted to us by illustrious sires, it will thus ignominiously die, and pass from the face of the earth forever. We can but see that the 'institution' of slavery and the principles upon which our goverment is founded are antagonistic. Its constitution and laws are in direct violation of the spirit which our noble, self-sacrificing forefathers inculcated, which breathed only the aspiration of liberty and happiness to all men. We, as a State in this republican government, have departed from the principles and teachings of the signers of the Declaration of Independence, in declaring, by our constitution and laws, that all men are not created equal, and are *not* entitled to life, liberty and the pursuit of happiness. This atrocious crime of slavery assails the life of our State and nation—sows the seeds of discord and disunion, by destroying the principles of humanity, justice and good will toward men, by establishing this infamous curse, which is built upon the narrow grounds of pecuniary interest and sordid gain, embracing, in its constitution and code of laws, fraud, rapine, cruelty and bloodshed. Slavery is inconsistent with our dearest rights as a State. The Black Code of this State is a damning disgrace to our State records, and an outrage and robbery upon her citizens, and merits the contempt and detestation of all men. We ask and demand that this dead weight of human wrong be wiped from the escutcheon of our State, and that these laws and the aristocratic State constitution be destroyed, to give place to a free and truly democratic constitution and laws, based upon the inherent and fundamental principles of freedom and justice to all men.

"To show to you, friends of freedom, how the South has degenerated and relapsed to Egyptian barbarism, I will present a synoptical view of the pertinently named *Black Code of Louisiana*, and I am confident you will acknowledge it only worthy a Slaveocracy, for there is no other class on God's earth so brutalized and stupid in depravity and wickedness as to defend the diabolical rules and principles it inculcates. Well, thus saith the law that Mr. Davis and his compeers would restore and establish to Louisiana and the world, if they could command the power to do so. But, thank God, they will not be permitted to build a nation upon any such iniquitous 'corner-stone.' Any slave killing or attempting to kill, whether maliciously, or in defence of his family or self, shall be hung. If a slave strikes his master, or mistress, or their children, or any white overseer, he shall be hung, or be imprisoned at hard labor for ten years. If a slave shoot or stab any person with intent to kill, he shall be hung. If any slave or free person of color shall *attempt* to poison any person he shall be hung. Any slave guilty of encouraging an insurrection shall be hung. Any slave or free person of color who shall attempt to burn any building or outhouse shall be hung. Any slave who shall be guilty for the third offence of striking a white person shall be hung, *unless* the blow was given in defence of his master, some member of his family, or person having charge of him, when the slave shall be *excused*. Any slave forcibly taking goods or money from any person shall be hung, or as the court shall adjudge. Any slave who shall break into a place and attempt to steal, or commit any other crime, shall be hung. Any person cruelly treating a slave shall *not* be fined to exceed two hundred dollars. Any person who shall remove any iron chain or collar fastened to a slave may be imprisoned for six months. If any person shall, by words or action, advise any slave to insurrection, he shall suffer death or imprisonment. Whosoever shall attempt to produce discontent among the free colored or slave population, shall be imprisoned at hard labor, or suffer death. Any person from the bar, the bench, the stage, the pulpit, *or any other place*, who shall be guilty of discourses or signs tending to produce discontent among the free colored or slave population, or who shall bring into this State any paper, pamphlet or book having such tendency, may be imprisoned twenty-one years, or suffer death. Slaves accused of capital crimes shall be tried by two Justices of the Peace and ten owners of slaves. Any crime not capital shall be tried by a Justice of the Peace and *four* owners of slaves. One Justice and nine jurors shall constitute a quorum for the trial of slaves accused of capital offences. If a slave is convicted, the said Justice of the Peace shall sign the sentence. If the court disagree and do not convict, *it* shall have the power to inflict corporal punishment according to its pleasure. All slaves sentenced to death or perpetual imprisonment, shall be paid for out of the *public treasury*. A slave may be forced to testify against his fellow-slave, but he is not permitted to testify against a white man. Any slave accused of a capital crime in this parish shall be tried by the Judge of the First District Court and six slaveholding jurors. No slave can leave thė plantation without a written permission; and any person giving permission without authority shall be fined fifty dollars. Any person who shall mutilate a slave and render him incapable of work, shall be fined fifty dollars, and pay the master two dollars per day for every day lost; and if the slave be forever made unable to work, then the offender shall pay his value, or suffer one year's imprisonment. Any person, having been a slave, returning to this State without permission, shall be forced back to slavery. Any free person of color who may be ordered to leave the State and does not, may be imprisoned at hard labor for five years. Free persons of color are not allowed to land in the State without a legal permit. A master of a vessel must give a bond for the non-landing of free persons of color on board his vessel.

"This is the law of the chivalrous apostles of treason and rebellion; the rope, the stocks, the clog, the ball-chain, the gag, the vice, the "nigger dogs," are the humanizing aids for their enforcement, and conspicuously portray the religion, humanity and civilization of the slaveocracy of the barren and ruined land under their horrid and diabolical sway. Thank God, the Moses of this people has come, and is now bravely leading the sons of Africa from the land of bondage to the glorious heritage of freedom and human rights. Yes, the crisis which involves the question whether this accursed viper shall be suffered longer to gnaw at our national vitals, to destroy and overthrow our constitutional liberty and laws, or whether the cause of the stupendous affliction now upon this promised land of liberty shall be annihilated.

"There can be but one voice from the just, the good and the humane, and that voice is—perish slavery, perish its upholders, perish every power and obstacle to the disenthralment and liberty of the oppressed, whatever be his complexion or his condition. Hope beameth bright for the triumphant realization of freedom's jubilee. The battles fought, the proclamations from that best and greatest man, Abraham Lincoln—the man of liberty, of humanity, the people's man—the territory conquered, brothers reclaimed, those freed, show a future brighter and more glorious than the most generous ever conceived a hope for. How much more tenaciously should we cling to our dear country, now that she has been imperiled and made to weep tears of blood because of the unnumbered dead, the waste and desolation of her once fruitful fields and happy and contented culturers. Our forefathers were the instruments that have marked and explored the destiny of this land. The disciples of Calhoun have striven, and are still striving to pervert and destroy their lofty aspirations, and these oligarchs find sympathizers in the cold and withering aristocracy of the North; but the people have spoken in their strength and declared that these craven-hearted and weak-kneed traitors shall not succeed, but with their braver friends, fighting for their treason, shall go down in ignominy together. When treason and rebellion shall be crushed, and the great people, including us, Louisianians, shall realize nature's just law, that slavery is no longer to blight and curse the civilization, morality and religion of the nation, when man will be acknowledged 'for a' that;' that color and difference in complexion may still be 'endowed with power to discover, with sense to love, and with imagination to expand towards their limitless perfection the attributes of Him whose finger the heavens are the handiwork," then the blessings of Liberty, life and the pursuit of happiness, equality and all the other great human rights of civil, political and religious self-government will follow, to make glad the philanthropic heart, and bring happiness, prosperity and fraternity to unborn millions, who will rise up to revere and treasure our sacred bequeathment. Then that flag, acknowledged by every people, the emblem of all that is good, great and glorious, will dance over the oblivious graves of the parricides who trailed it in the dust of Fort Sumter; and when the names of the Arnolds of this struggle will only be sounded with execration and contempt. Then the people will feel and universally exclaim—

* * * * * * *

"Who would sever Freedom's shrine?
Who would draw the invidious line?
Though by birth one spot be mine,
    Dear is all the rest.

Dear to me the South's fair land!
Dear the central mountain band!
Dear New England's rocky strand!
    Dear the prairied West!

By our altars, pure and free!
By the laws deep-rooted tree!
By the Past's dread memory!
    By our Washington!

By our common kindred tongue!
By our hopes, bright, buoyant, young,
By the tie of country strong!
    We will still be one!

Father's, have ye bled in vain?
Ages, shall ye droop again?
Maker, shall we rashly stain
Blessings sent by Thee?

No! receive our solemn vow,
While before thy throne we bow,
Ever to maintain, as now,
'Union, Liberty!'"

Said Dr. Dostie, "I always cherished liberty, but I was led step by step, in the progressive movement of events, to perceive and acknowledge the truth that the Republic could no longer exist and withhold the sacred right of four millions of human beings. Events have proved the direct antagonism between Slavery and Republicanism, and that the one or the other must perish." Every event that unfolded the great plan of American freedom was embraced by him with enthusiastic joy. The arming of the negroes to fight against slavery and rebellion, was to him a source of rejoicing. The news of the fall of Port Hudson was received by the loyal people of New Orleans with great demonstrations of delight. The event was celebrated by thousands, both white and black, who assembled upon Canal Street around the statue of Henry Clay, to listen to addresses from the orators chosen for the occasion. Dr. Dostie being one of the speakers, addressed the audience as follows:

"On the 4th of July, 1776, our noble sires fought a great moral battle, and achieved a victory, proclaiming to the world the great truth, that all men are created equal, and are from God entitled to life, liberty and the pursuit of happiness. Under the influence of these inestimable blessings this nation has grown, prospered and flourished to rank with the first in the world's history.

"In 1860, traitors laid the corner-stone of slavery, and for more than two years struggled to erect a 'Bastile' on the ruins of liberty. But the men of the West, who had sworn with their swords to cut their way to the Gulf, met the enemy of man and free institutions at Visksburg, the Gibraltar of their power, on the eighty-seventh anniversary of Freedom's Day, and achieved a victory that has broken the back-bone of the monster rebellion. On the 8th of January, 1815, the iron-nerved Champion of Freedom—the immortal author of the words, 'the Union must and shall be preserved,' met the lion power of Great Britain on the plains of Chalmette, and drove the ruthless invader back, and taught him a lesson that he has never forgotten; showing to the world that freemen are mighty and cannot be bound by the power of despotism.

"Forty-eight years and six months thereafter the undaunted and heroic Banks fought a battle and won a victory vaster in its consequences than followed the brilliant achievement of the democratic Jackson. General Banks conquered the second stronghold of the rebellion, and now we are rejoicing that commerce will again flow uninterruptedly upon the bosom of the great Father of Waters, from its source to the Gulf. Let us, my fellow-citizens, devoutly thank the Great Disposer of all Good for these manifold blessings, and let us in all future prove ourselves freemen indeed, and firmly serve and uphold the flag of our fathers and make it what they designed, the emblem of liberty to all.

"Let us hold in hallowed remembrance the times that

tried men's souls, the souls of our fathers, and solemnly promise that treason and rebellion shall never eradicate the laws of justice, fraternity and liberty, that freedom of speech shall not be suppressed, nor rights molested, but that all may glory in being free and equal sons of America.

"SONS OF AFRICA, I am rejoiced to see you here in such vast numbers. In common with all mankind you love *liberty*. History accords you high soldierly qualities. Against the armies of the old world you have fought with a heroism unsurpassed by the bravest. In the struggle of American independence you are remembered with kindness and gratitude. In the darkest hour of that contest of "Liberty or death," you nobly and promptly came forward to help to turn the tide that eventuated in liberty and freedom to the land. In the war of 1812 you fought shoulder to shoulder with the white man in driving the British invader from our soil, and in this stupendous struggle to save Liberty, your daring exploits and desperate valor in South Carolina, before Port Hudson, and wherever else you have been *let loose* against the traitors, you have shown yourselves worthy sons of freedom; and, thank God, the precious boon is near you. Lose no time in coming to it. Urge, urge your brave brethren to enroll themselves in the *Union army*, that before another year rolls by, half a million of your people will join the white man in breaking down the rebellion and raise upon every foothold of treason the flag of Union and Liberty—and then one universal shout will go up to Heaven, proclaiming "Liberty to all."'

CHAPTER XI.

CHANGES OF MILITARY COMMANDERS IN NEW ORLEANS.

In December, 1862, General Butler left New Orleans, and General Banks assumed command of the Gulf department. One fact was ever apparent in relation to New Orleans—" that while President Lincoln lived, and the United States army and navy held possession of that stronghold of treason, Unionism was a power, before which the rebel masses trembled. The boldness and decision evinced by General Butler in his control of that city during the rebellion, marks him in future history the hero of the Gulf Department."

In revolutionary times decisive action is necessary to success. It was bold decision that subdued slavery, secession and rebellion. The decisive action of thousands of brave men who dared to plunge the moral and physical weapons of death into the heart of rebellion—saved our nation in the dark days of revolution. The Emancipation Proclamation and the Constitutional Amendment which forever abolished slavery in the United States, caused some strange developments in Southern politics. In New Orleans the agitations caused by those humane acts divided the political elements into numerous coalitions.

There was the bold radical party that denounced

everything opposed to the reforms of the age. Among the most prominent of that organization, were Dostie, Waples, Flanders, Hahn, Heath, Graham, Goldman, Durell, Lynch, Hire, Howell, Heistend and Durant. Then there was a class composed of men of the status of Roselius, Rozier, Fellows, Barker, Kennedy, Burk, men of conservative ideas, who had combatted the advance of reform, and attempted by every means in their power to preserve the flickering life of their beloved institution, Slavery. A third party consisted of the strong advocates of the rebellion. Their names were Legion. They kept themselves not openly defiant, but ever on the alert, watching with sleepless eye the movements of the other parties.

The dominant party were the radicals, whose political creed was based upon three prominent objects of Lincoln's Administration, viz.—the preservation of the Union; the abolition of Slavery, and the crushing of the great Rebellion.

Conspiracies, however, external and internal caused dissention in the radical Republican party of Louisiana.

The loyal portion of the State began to agitate the question of a Free-State Government.

At a Union meeting in New Orleans, March 6th, 1863, Thomas J. Durant said: "I have something practical to bring before the people. It is now ten months since the federal forces came to Louisiana, and no effort has been made to establish a State Government. The proposition I would make is, that this Association, as the only representative of the views of Union men of New Orleans, take steps towards the formation of such a Government. The city contains more than one-half the voting population of the State, and as loyal citizens are entitled to a government of their own choice, that portion of the country in the hands of the rebels containing but a minority of the white population. He submitted this resolution to the Association:

Resolved, "That the President of this meeting appoint a committee of three to prepare a plan for calling a convention of the people of Louisiana to be submitted to this meeting on Saturday evening next."

Said he: "If ten loyal men can be found in each parish to send a representative, they will be sufficient to save their parishes."

Durant's resolution was unanimously adopted by the Association. Among those who voted for the resolution were Dostie, Graham, and Waples. At a meeting of the Union Association in Lyceum Hall, April 12th, 1863, Durant read a letter from Hahn, which stated that in a conversation Hahn had held with President Lincoln upon the subject of organizing a civil government for Louisiana, the President heartily approved of the plan, and promised to send instructions to the military leaders in Louisiana to favor the movement. On motion of Dr. Dostie, the vote was taken, when the resolutions favoring the Convention were passed by 95 to 73.

The following letter from President Lincoln to General Banks in relation to Louisiana affairs is interesting as connected with affairs at that time.

EXECUTIVE MANSION,
Washington, August 5, 1863.

"My Dear Gen. Banks:—

* * * * * *

"While I very well know what I would be glad for Louisiana to do, it is quite a different thing for me to assume direction of the matter. I would be glad for her to make a new constitution, recognizing the emancipation proclamation, and adopting emancipation in those parts of the State to which the proclamation does not apply. And while she is at it, I think it would not be objectionable for her to adopt some practical system by which the two races could gradually live themselves out of their old relation to each other, and both come out better prepared for the new. Education for young blacks should be included in the plan. After all, the power or element of 'contract' may be sufficient for this probationary period, and by its simplicity and flexibility may be the better.

"As an anti-slavery man, I have a motive to desire emancipation which pro-slavery men do not have; but even they have strong enough reason to thus place themselves again under the shield of the Union; and to thus perpetually hedge against the recurrence of the scenes through which we are now passing.

"Governor Shepley has informed me that Mr. Durant is now taking a registry, with a view to the election of a Constitutional Convention in Louisiana. This, to me, appears proper. If such convention was to ask my views, I could present little else than what I now say to you, I think the thing should be pushed forward, so that, if possible, its mature work may reach here by the meeting of Congress.

"For my own part, I think I shall not, in any event, retract the Emancipation Proclamation; nor, as Executive, ever return to slavery any person who is free by the terms of that proclamation, or by any of the acts of Congress.

"If Louisiana shall send members to Congress, their admission to seats will depend, as you know, upon the respective houses, and not upon the President.

* * * * * * *

"Yours, very truly,

(Signed) Abraham Lincoln."

January 9th, 1864, the Union people of New Orleans assembled to endorse the action of the committe, and to give sanction to the request of Governor Shepley to order an election for delegates to the Constitutional Convention, with a view to making Louisiana a State, in accordance with the principles suggested by the proclamation of the President issued on the 8th of December, 1863. The President of that meeting was R. F. Flanders, Esq. Among the Vice-Presidents were Dostie, Shupert, Hire, Graham, Heath, Duncan, Howell, Waples, Shaw and Heistend. Mr. Flanders, in addressing the meeting said, "he thought the time had arrived for organizing a State Government in Louisiana. Six months before, a plan had been prepared by the Union men of the city for that purpose and presented to Governor Shepley. It was by him forwarded to the President, considered in a Cabinet meeting, approved and returned to Governor Shepley with the approval of the Administration endorsed upon it. Now it was necessary to appoint a committee to present resolutions to further the proposed plan." The following were the resolutions adopted:

"*Resolved*, That the future slavery of persons of African descent in Louisiana is a moral, legal and physical impossibility, and the proposed new constitution in declaring its non-existence within the borders of the State, will only assert a fact within the knowledge of all her loyal men.

"*Resolved*, That we cordially approve of all the proclamations of the President of the United States in regard to slavery in the insurrectionary districts, but more particularly the one recently issued under date of 8th December, 1863; that the means pointed out by him for the rebellious States to return to the Union are, in our opinion, eminently just and wise; and that the loyal men of Louisiana are now ready and willing to adopt them, and have nearly the required number of registered loyal citizens, good men and true, to bring back the State into the great nationality our fathers founded.

"*Resolved*, That the action of the "Free State Committee, in calling upon Brigadier-General Shepley, Military Governor of Louisiana, soliciting him to order, in the name of the people, an election for delegates to a Convention to form a State Constitution, is approved and ratified, and he is hereby authorized and requested to take all necessary steps to have such an election at an early day."

At that meeting Mr. Durant said, "It will be a glorious thing if we can make Louisiana the first State that declares for freedom among the late rebellious States."

Jan. 11th, the following proclamation by General Banks was issued:

"HEADQUARTERS DEPARTMENT OF THE GULF,
New Orleans, Jan. 11, 1864.

"To the people of Louisiana:

"I. In pursuance of authority vested in me by the President of the United States, and upon consultation with many representative men of different interests, being fully assured that more than a tenth of the population desire the earliest possible restoration of Louisiana to the Union, I invite the loyal citizens of the State qualified to vote in public affairs, as hereinafter prescribed, to assemble in the election precincts designated by law, or at such places as may hereafter be established, on the 22d day of February, 1864, to cast their votes for the election of State officers herein named, viz:

"I. Governor. II. Lieutenant Governor. III. Secretary of State. IV. Treasurer. V. Attorney General. VI. Superintendent of Public Instruction. VII. Auditor of Public Accounts; who shall when elected, for the time being, and until others are appointed by competent authority, constitute the civil Government of the State, under the Constitution and laws of Louisiana, except so much of the said Constitution and laws as recognize, regulate or relate to slavery, which being inconsistent with the present condition of public affairs, and plainly inapplicable to any class of persons now existing within its limits, must be suspended, and they are therefore and hereby declared to be inoperative and void. This proceeding is not intended to ignore the right of property existing prior to the rebellion nor to preclude the claim for compensation of loyal citizens for losses sustained by enlistments or other authorized acts of the Government.

"II. The oath of allegiance prescribed by the President's Proclamation, with the condition affixed to the elective franchise by the Constitution of Louisiana, will constitute the qualification of voters in this election. Officers elected by them will be duly installed in their offices on the Fourth day of March, 1864.

"III. The Registration of voters, effected under the direction of the Military Governor and the several Union associations, not inconsistent with the Proclamation, or other orders of the President, are confirmed and approved.

"IV. In order that the organic law of the State may be made to conform to the will of the People, and harmonize with the spirit of the age, as well as to maintain and preserve the ancient landmarks of civil and religious liberty, an election of delegates to a convention for the revision of the Constitution, will be held on the first Monday of April, 1864. The basis of representation, the number of delegates, and the details of election, will be announced in subsequent orders.

"V. Arrangements will be made for the early election of members of Congress for the State.

"VI. The fundamental law of the State is martial law. It is competent and just for the Government to surrender to the people, at the earliest possible moment, so much of military power as may be consistent with the success of military operation; to prepare the way by prompt and wise measures, for the full restoration of the State to the Union and its power to the people; to restore their ancient and unsurpassed prosperity; to enlarge the scope of agricultural and commercial industry and to extend and confirm the dominion of rational liberty. It is not within human power to accomplish these results without some sacrifice of individual prejudices and interests. Problems of State, too complicate for the human mind, have been solved by the national cannon. In great civil convulsions, the agony of strife enters the souls of the innocent as well as the guilty. The Government is subject to the law of necessity, and must consult the condition of things, rather than the preferences of men, and if so be that its purposes are just and its measures wise, it has the right to demand that questions of personal interest and opinion shall be subordinate to the public good. When the national existence is at stake, and the liberties of the people in peril, faction is treason.

"The methods herein proposed submit the whole question of government directly to the people—first, by the election of executive officers, faithful to the Union, to be followed by a loyal representation in both houses of Congress—and then by a convention which will confirm the action of the people, and recognize the principles of freedom in the organic law. This is the wish of the President. The anniversary of Washington's birth is a fit day for the commencement of so grand a work. The immortal Father of his Country was never guided by a more just and benignant spirit than that of his successor in office, the President of the United States. In the hour of our trial let us heed his admonitions!

"Louisiana in the opening of her history sealed the integrity of the Union by conferring upon its government the Valley of the Mississippi. In the war for independence upon the sea, she crowned a glorious struggle against the first maratime power of the world, by a victory unsurpassed in the annals of war. Let her people now announce to the world the coming restoration of the Union, in which the ages that follow us have a deeper interest than our own, by the organization of a free government, and her fame will be immortal!

"N. P. BANKS, M. G. C."

Who shall be Governor? was now the question asked by the loyal people of Louisiana. Said Dostie, in refering to that subject, "I will never vote for any man to fill that important office whom I do not know to be loyal to the Government, a strong opposer of slavery and a firm advocate of the just policy of President Lincoln." Durant, Hahn, Flanders, Fellows and Howell were among the most prominent names. February 1st, 1864, the State Nominating Convention met at Lyceum Hall. The delegates chosen by the several ward meetings in the city of New Orleans, and those from the county parishes within the Union lines, met for the purpose of nominating candidates for the State offices. It was soon discovered that the clouds were thickening in the political horizon, and apprehensions were felt by those assembled that their cherished plans might be broken up. Soon harmonious action gave place to faction. A disposition was shown by several members of the Convention to spend the time in angry dispute and selfish intrigue.

A motion was made that Durant be invited to address the Convention. Amid great confusion the question was put, and the chair declared it lost. It was then moved that Dostie be invited to address the Convention. The motion was put and declared lost. In great confusion the meeting adjourned. It was then proposed to re-organize the Convention and proceed with business. Mr. Wm. R. Fish was appointed chairman, and Dr. Wm. H. Hire, secretary of the meeting.

The Convention requested Dostie to address them. Said he, "In giving my opinion as to a suitable candidate for the office of Governor of Louisiana, I know of no better Union man—no better anti-slavery man—no better friend of the Administration than Michael Hahn. I believe him to be worthy the important trust the loyal people of Louisiana will place in the hands of their Governor."

A Committee on resolutions presented the following to the Convention:

"*Resolved*, That we solemnly believe the Union of these States handed down by our revolutionary ancestors, of infinitely more value than any falsely-termed State rights of any sectional institutions, and we deem it our most sacred duty as patriots to transmit it undivided to posterity.

"*Resolved*, That we as citizens of the United States, as well as of the State of Louisiana, know that the observance of the Union depends on maintaining the supremacy of the Federal Union, and do, on the part of Louisiana, utterly disclaim any pretension to any rights not subservient of that supremacy, and hold her primary allegiance as due to the Government of the United States. (Cheers.)

"*Resolved*, That, regarding the institution of slavery as a great moral, social and political evil, opposed alike to the rights of one race and the interests of the other, and inconsistent with the principles of free government, we hail and desire its universal and immediate extinction as a public and private blessing. (Great applause.)

"*Resolved*, That we desire the principles of this State to be based upon a surer and broader foundation than the operations of military order, and we will use every means in our power to hasten the day when they shall be embodied in a State Constitution that Louisiana is and shall forever remain a Free State. (Applause.)

"*Resolved*, That we heartily approve of the plan adopted by General Banks to ensure that result as well as to restore the voice of Louisiana to the councils of the nation. (Cheers.)

"*Resolved*, That we will support no man as a candidate for office who is unwilling to subscribe to and pledge himself to carry out the principles set forth in the above resolutions."

The resolutions were unanimously adopted.

Michael Hahn was nominated candidate for Governor. The roll of delegates was called, and he was declared the choice of the Convention. A committee was appointed to inform him of his nomination, and request him to state whether he accepted the resolutions adopted by the Convention. His address to the Convention was as follows:

"Free-State men of Louisiana:

"I have only to say to you to-night that the resolutions which I understand have been adopted by you, were read by me to-day, and I approve heartily from the bottom of my heart every sentiment in those resolutions. (Applause.) I have but one pledge to give you, and that is, if elected Governor of Louisiana, so far as it lies in my humble power, there shall not be a slave in this State after the 22d day of February. (Great cheering.)

"I thank you for the distinguished honor you have conferred upon me, and pledge you a faithful performance of the duties that will devolve upon me. I again thank you, and bid you good-night."

Many of Dr. Dostie's friends desired to see him a candidate for some State office. He had declined the nomination of Secretary of State, and State Treasurer at the convention. At a meeting of the Free State Executive Committee, Col. A. C. Hills said: "The name of Dostie I am desirous of having on the Free State ticket. It will add to its strength. We all know his pure record. I request that he be urged by the committee to accept some State office." To this request Dr. Dostie replied, "I regret that I can not comply with your wishes, but I sincerely believe that I can be more useful to the republican party by not having my name on the ticket. I am no office seeker. My mission is to assist in making Louisiana a Free State; I must request you to look elsewhere for a candidate for office."

The arguments of his numerous friends, at last prevailed upon the Dr. to accept the nomination of Auditor of State. He was unanimously nominated by the Free State executive committee for that office. The integrity, firmness, honesty and devotion to principle made the name of Dostie a power in his party. The annexed is an article from the pen of A. C. Hills, editor of the *New Orleans Era*—one of the Union papers of that city, and a fearless advocate of freedom. "We are gratified to learn that this unflinching champion of the Union cause has, at the earnest request of his numerous friends, consented to accept the nomination for one of the State offices. The State Convention, at its meeting on the 1st instant, named Judge Atocha for the office of State Auditor, but that gentleman has since declined the honor! and the duty of filling the vacancy devolved upon the Executive Committee.

There is scarcely a Union man in this city but fully appreciates and acknowledges the valuable services in the cause of freedom and patriotism of Dr. A. P. Dostie. He has been repeatedly urged by his friends to accept office, but has strenuously refused to consent. Every man who enjoys the confidence of the Doctor is aware that what he has done for the cause has been at much personal sacrifice, without a desire to be rewarded in any other manner than by seeing the glorious principles for which he is so sincere and efficient an advocate, triumphantly proclaimed in this the State of his adoption. The acceptance of office is another sacrifice asked at his hands by the friends of a Free State government. With this understanding, he has consented to accept the nomination for Auditor. There was no opposition in the selection by the Executive Committee.

We all know the thoroughness of Dr. Dostie's character. Whatever enterprise he undertakes, receives his earnest attention. Although reluctant to enter upon the political arena, he will labor zealously for the success of the ticket; his inflnence is great, and his name is an element of strength that must insure the success of the nominees of the Free State Union Convention."

February 10th, 1864, thousands assembled upon Lafayette Square for the purpose of ratifying the nomination of Hahn for Governor, and the other candidates for State Offices.

The following resolutions were adopted:

"*Whereas*, The State of Louisiana, placed by the act of traitorous men and the supineness of loyal ones in a position of hostility to the United States Government, is now by the success of the national arms and the clemency of the national executive, afforded an opportunity to resume her place in the Federal Union:

"*Whereas*, A proportion of her citizens, more than

equal to that demanded as requisite by the President's Proclamation of December 8th, 1863, comprising not only those who have always remained loyal, but many others who have returned to their allegiance, are anxious for the renewal of civil government and for that peace of which civil government is the proper representative and national unity the only security; and

"*Whereas*, The barbarous and odious institution of slavery, founded on injustice, fostered by pride and cupidity, a curse alike to the oppressor and the oppressed, has been for more than thirty years a cause of dissension between the different sections of this country, and has finally ripened into the bitter fruit of the existing rebellion; therefore, be it

Resolved, "That in effecting the reorganization of the civil government of Louisiana under the Constitution of the United States, we, the Free State Union party of Louisiana, heartily approve the plan adopted for that purpose by the Commanding General of this department as simple, practicable, and expeditious.

"*Resolved*, That we fully indorse the Proclamation of Emancipation and all other acts of the President and of the Congress of the United States having for their object the suppression of the rebellion.

"*Resolved*, That the mere setting free of slaves by the hand of the military power, we consider only the first step in that moral and political revolution which will not pause until the principle of universal freedom shall be embodied in the fundamental law of the land, and that we, the Free State Union party of Louisiana, recognizing this fact, will use every means in our power to bring about such a reform in the Constitution of this State as will insure to every human being within its borders the indisputable right of personal liberty.

"*Resolved*, That in the Hon. M. Hahn, the candidate of the Free State party for Governor of Louisiana, we recognize a man fully up to the requirements of the times, identified with the interests of this State, as his home, yet claiming the whole United States as his country, conscious of unswerving loyalty and unconditional patriotism, yet ready to extend the hand of fellowship to all who even at the eleventh hour are willing to resume their allegiance; a man of the people, deeply imbued with the progressive spirit of the age, and ardently devoted to the cause of liberty, his election will be a triumph in which every friend of loyalty and freedom will have reason to rejoice.

"*Resolved*, That we approve and ratify the nominations of J. Madison Wells, Esq., for Lieutenant Governor, S. Wrotnowski, Esq.; for Secretary of State, Dr. Belden, for Treasury, B. L. Lynch, Esq., for Attorney General, Dr. A. P. Dostie for Auditor, and John McNair, for Superintendent of Public Education."

The 22d of February, 1864—an ominous day for tyranny; an auspicious one for liberty—will be remembered, as the day which gave an impulse to the cause of freedom in Louisiana. It will be revered as the day when a monument was erected to the great Emancipator—the worthy successor of Washington. The events of that day decided the death of Constitutional Slavery in Louisiana.

March 4th, 1864, was the day chosen by the loyal people of Louisiana to express their gratitude for the prospects of enjoying constitutional rights. On that day—at early dawn, noon and nightfall—salutes of one hundred guns were fired by batteries of artillery, under the command of Brigadier General Arnold. The salute at sunrise was the opening note of the day's festivities. At the same moment, all the public bells rung out a merry peal in honor of the day. The military turned out in force. Representatives from almost every battle-field were there. Men who had served under Scott, McClellen, Pope, Meade, Grant, Banks, Sheridan and Sherman—men from the army of the Gulf and the army of the Potomac—the heroes of Chattenooga, Vicksburg, Port Hudson, Lookout Mountain, and Missionary Ridge, assembled together on Lafayette Square to witness the inauguration of the State officers of free Louisiana. The United States navy were there. The brave tars that gallantly stood by Farragut at Forts Jackson and St. Phillip's, rejoiced on that day in the remembrance of their struggles to redeem Louisiana from the power of treason. Flags of every nation were thrown out in every direction. Public and private buildings displayed the national colors. The ships and steamers in the harbor were decked in holiday attire.

From the circular stand, on which the solemnities of the day were held, the immense structure radiated in the form of a semicircle, seat after seat rising up step after step, until more than fifteen thousand seats were formed. At the base of this was the orchestra of five hundred performers, with the fifty blacksmiths that kept time on their anvils like so many real Vulcans. In front and on each side of the stand was another great platform, on which were seated invited guests, distinguished strangers, civil and military dignitaries. We are at a loss for words in which to convey to the reader a just conception of the magnitude of this structure. Nor can we do so in any other way than by remarking that a half million feet of lumber and a ton of nails entered into its construction.

From the centre flag-staff, long garlands of arborvitæ, hemlock, juniper, cedar, pine, and other evergreens reached to the circumference, forming a leafy canopy. Around the centre stand were evergreen wreaths enclosing the coat of arms of the several States richly emblazoned on heraldic shields. Across the front there hung like a veil a long line of signal flags, both those used in the naval service and the mercantile marine.

Around the outer circle fifty cannon stood in battery; from these, wires led to a telegraphic instrument on the music stand at which Captain Chas. S. Buckley presided. Not only did Captain Buckley fire the cannon, but by the same instrument he rang all the bells in the city that were required to keep in unison with the music. From the centre of the stage a large banner was displayed with the arms of Louisiana richly emblazoned thereon.

Each of the entrances to the Park was adorned with festoons of evergreens, and together the national colors wreathed in fantastic shapes.

An immense semi-circular amphitheater has been raised for the accommodation of the numerous schools, and the children began to arrive about 9 o'clock, and by 10 the vast space devoted to them was completely occupied by gay faces with smiling looks. In front of the children was placed a circular platform, for the Governor and those who were to surround him. From the centre of this platform arose a flag-staff bearing the national flag, and a ring suspended around the staff at about half-mast, from which was stretched, in circular form, ropes entirely covered with evergreens, the other extremity of the ropes being fastened to the surrounding trees. These ropes were profusely decorated with numerous flags, of various descriptions and hues, from the shipping.

ENTRANCE OF THE GOVERNOR AND SUITE.

The Governor and officers met at the City Hall, about

10 o'clock, and at a quarter before 11 proceeded to the Square in company with the distinguished military officers and others.

MUSIC.

HAIL COLUMBIA.

By eight thousand school children.

THE OATH

ADMINISTERED TO OFFICERS.

The oath of office was then administered to the Governor elect, in the presence of the Judges of the Supreme Court, by Hon. Judge Durell.

MUSIC.

STAR SPANGLED BANNER.

By eight thousand school children.

THE INAUGURAL

ADDRESS OF GOVERNOR HAHN.

MUSIC.

ANVIL CHORUS, FROM "IL TROVATORE."

Which was performed by the full band, accompanied by 50 time-beaters upon anvils and fifty pieces of artillery.

ADDRESS.

BY MAJOR GENERAL BANKS.

PRAYER.

BY REV. MR. HORTON.

" Almighty God, our Creator and our Preserver: We have too much to thank Thee for and too much to ask Thee for upon this present delightful occasion. Words are inadequate to express the gratitude that fills our hearts as we look upon this scene spread out before the gaze of these masses and before the eye of the God of the Universe, lighted by the effulgence of His glory.

"O God, we thank Thee that Thy love has abounded unto this people; that Thy good providence has been extended over this great nation. We thank Thee that Thou hast made our nation great and glorious among the nations of the earth. We thank Thee for all the past. We thank Thee even for this record of blood which Thou hast required of us; because we believe that from this baptism of blood we shall rise to a higher and holier position before Thee and among the nations of the earth.

"O God, we thank Thee for the pleasant auspices of this present occasion: that Thou hast permitted Thy most gracious smiles to fall upon us as here we have created anew the form and empire of the law over this State, with all its rich and fertile territory, with all its brave sons and fair daughters, to honor Thy service in the future.

"O God, we pray Thee to enable the officers that have been inaugurated to-day, faithfully to observe the obligations they have taken upon themselves. Aid and direct them in the faithful performance of their respective duties, and let Thy blessings rest upon them while they continue faithful to their several trusts.

"O God, we pray Thee now, as in the culminating of these exercises, we go out from this place to our respective abodes, that the present may prove only a fit symbol of that glory and that blessing that shall crown the history of this returning State.

"O God, we thank Thee for the blessings of the mild rule which we have received even at the hands of the military ruler that has been appointed over us. We thank Thee for the beneficent government of one who has been appointed over us in a semi-military position, whose rule has been one of integrity and patriotism.

"We pray that Thy blessing may rest upon these Thy servants, who have been charged with the performance, and who have assumed the trusts which a confident people have reposed in them.

"We pray, further, that under the shadow of the government which may be organized, free institutions, public education and religion may prosper and flourish for all future time, even until the coming of the Kingdom of our Lord Jesus Christ, with all its power and glory in this beautiful land that Thou has given to our common country.

"May Thy richest blessing rest upon those whose business it is to train the minds of these children and upon those little ones whose voices have given us the national anthems on this occasion.

"May Thy blessings rest upon the Executive of these United States in the further and future discharge of the onerous duties of his position, and grant that when another year shall have passed, and we are again called upon to place one in the highest position of authority and power in the gift of a free people that it may be to witness a complete and final destruction of the rebellion in every State, and that the whole people of the nation may feel that as a nation we shall be one and inseperable through all coming time.

"We ask it in the name of Thy dear Son, to whom, with the Spirit, we would ascribe all honor and power, world without end. Amen."

CHAPTER XII.

LOUISIANA CONSTITUTIONAL CONVENTION OF 1864.

Three things were evident to the reflecting minds of those who were interested in the political affairs of Louisiana in 1864. That the revolutionary movement advanced step by step to the complete restoration of the rights of suffering humanity; that it assailed tyranny and THAT aristocracy which sprang from despotic slavery, and that the social and political emancipation to which events pointed, would give to all the power to speak and act, according to the rights which emanate from true Liberty. It was a revolution in right—a revolution in ideas—a revolution in facts. The form of slavery was no longer visible, but it had left its foot-prints upon the Constitution of the State and the black code lay like a bloody pall upon it, a disgrace to the Nation and its Government.

On the 28th of March, 1864, an election was held, and delegates appointed to a convention to be held for the revision and amendment of the State constitution. On the 1st of April the convention met at Liberty Hall. Much has been said and written against the members of that convention. There were corrupt men in that Assembly. There was a Judas among the twelve Apostles; there was an Arnold among our Revolutionary patriots; a Davis in our National councils, a Johnson among the Presidents of our Republic, and there were traitors and conspirators in that Convention. Its objects were to amend the Constitution, and abolish the name of slavery in Louisiana. Those acts were consummated on the 11th of May, 1864. There are two names connected with this Convention, which it will be well to remember, as future events present them in strange contrast. Judge Howell first agitated the slavery question in that Convention. Said he: "I have not troubled this Convention so far with any attempts at speech-making, or presented any propositions; but I think it is time to go to work. With a view to that purpose, I offer the following resolution:

"1. *Resolved*, That a committee of —— members be appointed by the President of this Convention, to whom shall be referred the subject of immediate and permanent emancipation of slavery within the State of Louisiana, with instructions to report as early as practicable ordinances and provisions in relation thereto, to be incorporated in the Constitution of this State."

When the vote was called for upon the amendments of the Constitution, Judge Abell said, "I consider this one of the most tyrannical things I have ever seen. In the name of the people of Louisiana I vote, *no*." As Judge Abell is somewhat conspicuous in the history of Louisiana, it may be well to trace some of his movements in the Convention of 1864. May 2d, he says in defence of slavery, "It is both a Scriptural and historical institution, and should not be abolished. It only slumbers and will be called into life when the people have their will and are free from military law." On the same day he opposed the education of colored children.

May 4th, in a lengthy argument he attempted to prove the right to hold men as property. Said, " the idea of tearing property to the amount of 900 million dollars from slave-holders—the honest earnings of the people of Louisiana was a wrong he would fight on all occasions." Thus he labored in that Convention to carry his infamous doctrines against freedom, equality and education, foreshadowing his future murderous course. The friends of progressive freedom in that Convention looked with the same contempt upon the impotent assaults of Judge Abell upon the cause of Liberty, as did the majority of Congress upon the futlie arguments of a Davis or a Saulsbury, who opposed the Constitutional Amendment in the Senate of the United States.

An eventful and interesting portion of Dr. Dostie's life is associated with the Louisiana Convention of 1864. From the first day of the meeting until its close, he watched its deliberations with intense interest. In every important debate, he might be seen at Liberty Hall, watching its movements with pale and thoughtful countenance, his intellectual forehead flashing with emotion, and his penetrating eye lit up with patriotic fire as he noted the onward march of the principles of Liberty in the councils of his adopted State.

In the official minutes of the Convention of 1864, we find this interesting relic.

Mr. Abell rose to a question of privilege, and stated that he had received a communication of an extraordinary character, and believing it to be a breach of privilege, he wished to lay it before the Convention, and for that purpose asked that it might be read by the Secretary :

[*Confidential.*]

"New Orleans, July 15th, 1864.

"E. ABELL, Esq.,

"*Dear Sir:* I entertain so strong an aversion to the incorporation into the 'organic law' of the words 'white,' 'black' and 'color,' that I am induced in this confidential note, (accompanied by a proposed 'rider') to ask you to consider the propriety of altering the language of certain portions of the new constitution, so as to harmonize with the principle contained in this proposed 'rider.' Many members of the Convention have had the kindness to say to the governor and myself, that they will do what they can to expunge the obnoxious words from the militia and educational bills, before the question of final adoption, as a whole, comes up.

"Very respectfully, yours,

"A. P. DOSTIE."

This "extraordinary letter" was no doubt a criminal thing in the eye of Judge Abell, and his wrath, in view of the philanthrophy of Dostie, was treasured up for future action.

CHAPTER XIII.

DOSTIE AS AUDITOR OF STATE.

The business before Dr. Dostie as Auditor of State was foreign to his former habits of thought, yet after the first feeling of reluctance, he entered upon its details with characteristic energy. No man ever felt the responsibility of official business more than Dr. Dostie. He always defended his schemes for the public good upon the grounds of justice and economy, which sometimes brought down the denunciations of those selfishly interested, who accused him of guarding the public more carefully than his position required.

As Auditor of State he vigilantly watched and exposed abuses, which he considered in any way connected with his official duties. In his official relations he sometimes contended with the members of the Convention and Legislature. In those discussions he always maintained a respectful firmness, never yielding to conciliatory measures, or boisterous threats unless convinced of error.

Said Dr. Dostie, "In my official capacity I must be allowed to act according to my convictions of duty." The following correspondence illustrates the above sentiment:

"NEW ORLEANS, Nov. 12, 1864.

"Hon. B. L. Lynch, Attorney General of Louisiana—

"*Sir:* I respectfully call your attention to the following facts and request your legal opinion in the matter at your earliest convenience: Mr. E. P. Marrioneaux was elected on the 5th of September to represent the parish of Iberville in the House of Representatives, now in session, but declined to take his seat. On the 31st October an election was held to fill the vacancy occasioned by such declension, and Mr. P. L. Dufresne was elected. He took his seat in the House and was sworn in on the 2d of November.

"The House passed the following resolution:

"*Be it Resolved*, That the said P. L. Dufresne, member elect of the parish of Iberville, be, and he is entitled to the same per diem and mileage allowed other members of the House, from the 3d day of October, 1864."

"A warrant, in the usual form, signed by the Speaker of the House and Chairman of the Finance Committee, has been drawn on me for payment of Mr. Dufresne in accordance with the above resolution.

"Is the action of the House in accordance with the constitutional law of the State? Is it not positively unconstitutional? If so, have I the right, and is it not my duty as Auditor, to refuse to pay, except for the time since his election? Would it not be violating my oath of office to pay money from the State Treasury for services never rendered, and as per diem for an officer who did not exist, even though I had the sanction of the House to that effect.

"Article 32 of the new Constitution says: 'The members of the General Assembly shall receive from the public treasury a compensation for their services, which shall be *eight dollars per day during their attendance, going to and returning from the sessions of their respective Houses.* The compensation may be increased or diminished by law, but no alteration shall take effect *during the period of service of the members* of the House of Representatives, by whom such alteration shall have been made.' By this article of the Constitution, it seems to me plain that he cannot be paid from the 3d to the 31st of October, but only from the 2d of November to the 12th, inclusive, the time of actual membership.

"This is no donation to him for relief or charity, (the House unquestionably has the right to make appropriations for such purposes), but for per diem as the resolution expressly states.

"Hoping I may be honored with your opinion upon this important question as soon as practicable, I am, very respectfully yours,

"(Signed) A. P. DOSTIE, Auditor."

"NEW ORLEANS, Nov. 14, 1864.

"Hon. A. P. Dostie, Auditor of Public Accounts State of Louisiana—

"*Sir:* The resolution of the House of Representatives relative to the per diem of the Hon. P. L. Dufresne, is a flagrant violation of the Constitution of the State of Louisiana, and you are fully justified in refusing to audit the warrant drawn upon you under that resolution.

"'The members of the General Assembly,' says Article 32 of the Constitution, 'shall receive from the Public Treasury a compensation for their services, which shall be eight dollars per day, during their attendance, going to and returning from the sessions of their respective Houses,' and I cannot advise you to audit beyond the limits fixed by the Constitution."

"Very respectfully, your obedient servant,

" (Signed) B. L. LYNCH,

" Attorney General."

The following is a letter written by the Auditor to the Senate, after it had drawn up resolutions of impeachment against Dr. Dostie for refusing to audit certain claims.

NEW ORLEANS, Nov. 20th, 1864.

To the Hon. Legislature of Louisiana :

" Article 32d of the Constitution says: 'The *members* of the General Assenbly shall receive from the Public Treasury, as *compensation for their services*," &c. If it can be shown to the Auditor, whose sworn duty it is to 'audit, adjust, and settle all claims against the State, according to the Constitution and laws,' that the Senator was a member of the General Assembly from the 3d of October, and has rendered services, then it will become the Auditor's duty to draw his warrant upon the Treasurer in payment for such services from that date; but if on investigation of the claim it should be found that he was not a member, aud had not rendered any services up to the 24th October, then the Auditor, by making such payment, would be violating his oath of office, forfeiting his bond to the State, and rendering himself liable to fine and imprisonment.

"It is not, however, claimed by your resolution that the honorable gentleman was a member at the time in question, and as I have shown above, he was not an officer of the State until the 24th of October, therefore he is not legally entitled to compensation for services previous to this date.

"Complaint cannot be made, in justice, of the State

in adopting such rules, or of the Auditor for protecting the public treasury from unlawful demands. If the State did not, through her officers, correct errors of this character, her losses would sometimes be very severe, and her ability to maintain her credit materially lessened.

"For these reasons I must respectfully decline to draw a warrant in pursuance of your resolution. Honorable Senators—I desire to say in conclusion that this decision is from a conscientious conviction of duty, and not from any disposition to oppose your honorable body or clog the wheels of legislation. My history in the public affairs of the State establishes beyond a doubt my love and reverence for the new Government of Louisiana, and that my prayers are fervent and continuous for the progress, prosperity and permanence of the government under the Constitution of 1864.

"Let me pray that if you, in your superior wisdom, dissent from my views of law and duty, that you will, in your judgment, consider me honest and conscientious, and as not intending disregard or discourtesy towards the dignity of your body.

"I am, very respectfully, yours,

"A. P. Dostie, Auditor."

The position taken by the vigilant Auditor of State was decided correct, and an abuse, having no countenance of legality, was prevented.

CHAPTER XIV.

DOSTIE AND DURANT.

The names of Durant and Dostie are intimately associated with the political history of Louisiana during the rebellion. Both were natives of the State of New York. Both were self-made men. Dostie in his youth was a friend of liberty, and ever maintained its broad principles, which acted ever as a motive power and guiding star throughout his eventful life. Durant, in his youth, embraced the doctrines of slavery, and became an influential slaveholder. Dostie was by nature impulsive, large hearted and fearless. Durant was deliberate, politic and cowardly. Dostie was by nature a democrat —one of the people. Durant was an aristocrat—holding himself above the masses. Dostie drew the hearts of his friends to him by a magnetism which emanated from his honest, earnest soul. Durant repelled by his cold and studied manner. Dostie was a patriot; Durant a politician. Ambition was only a secondary consideration with Dostie. "Let us perish from the earth, if by our death equal rights and universal justice be promoted thereby," were the words of Dostie. "My slave interests must not be disturbed by the United States Government," were the words of Durant. Ay, and more! In every public act, even up to the eventful year of 1864, he expressed the sentiment, "No republican government must be established in Louisiana, wherein my fame is not conspicuous and my ambition is not gratified."

President Lincoln and his executive acts relating to Louisiana, and the established Free State government of 1864, were dear to the liberty-loving heart of Dostie, who regarded a word or an act against his authority in the light of sacrilege.

The following correspondence may not prove uninteresting as connected with the history of New Orleans in 1864.

"NEW YORK, July 26, 1864.

"Hon. Henry Winter Davis, Baltimore, Maryland:

"*Dear Sir*—The friends of freedom in Louisiana, thwarted in their efforts by the acts of the Executive at Washington, had placed their hopes on the bill guaranteeing us a republican form of government, which you reported to the House of Representatives, and which obtained such emphatic approval there and in the co-ordinate branch of Congress. We had watched its progress with anxiety, for we perceived it would give us relief from the incapacity, and, as too many had cause to believe, from the infidelity to freedom which had been the essential characteristics of Executive administration in our State. It is with the deepest mortification, therefore, we find a measure affording protection to loyal men by the only constitutional power known to the Government, defeated in its operation by the will of the Executive, seeking to perpetuate in Louisiana all that incapacity and selfishness can render odious to the citizens.

"The executive is 'unprepared to declare that the free State constitutions already adopted and installed in Arkansas and Louisiana shall be set aside and held for naught, etc.'

"As to the assertion that a Free State constitution has been adopted in Louisiana, the Executive has fallen into a grave error. *No Free State constitution had on the eighth day of July—nor as yet—been adopted or installed in the fragment of Louisiana held by the military forces of the United States.*

"On the 24th of December, 1863, the Executive, in a letter addressed to the Major General commanding the Department of the Gulf, constituted that officer the 'master.'

"Mr. Hahn was installed as Governor in New Orleans on the fourth of March, 1864, and on the fifteenth of that month there was addressed to him the following letter:

"'EXECUTIVE MANSION,
"'WASHINGTON, March 15, 1864.

"'His Excellency, Michael Hahn, Governor of Louisiana:

"'Until further orders you are hereby invested with the powers exercised hitherto by the Military Governor of Louisiana.

"'Yours, truly, ABRAHAM LINCOLN.'

"The missive is worthy of remark. It is signed by the incumbent of the Executive office, but not as President. It is not countersigned by the Secretary of State; and it bears not the seal of the Government. It is unofficial. Yet in effect it appoints an officer—Military Governor of a State—unknown to the Constitution and laws of the United States.

"The so-called Constitutional Convention now sitting in New Orleans was elected under the same usurped authority, and evinces the same aversion as the Governor to that principle, which in Louisiana can alone 'establish justice and ensure domestic tranquility'—equality of all men before the law—the failure to recognize which is, indeed, a defect in your bill, not pointed out by the Executive. The work of this Convention all the friends of freedom in Louisiana hope and trust, will be rejected by the Congress, as emanating from an usurpation of power by the Executive, no matter what may be its provisions.

"The journalists, politicians and public men of our country hold two sets of opinions, one for their private use, which they believe in, the other for public displays, so that what appears to be public opinion cannot be trusted as the opinion of the public. If this do not cease, the cause of liberty is in danger. Our leading men look too much to the law and the people:

"'Full well they laugh, with counterfeited glee,
At all his jokes, for many a joke has he.'

but in secret they deplore the calamity of a choice they dare not repudiate, from the unfounded fear that opposition would secure the success of an anti-national candidate. No nation will vote its own destruction, though the catastrophe may be accomplished by voting for incompetent men.

"There cannot be a difference of opinion as to the conduct of the Executive in stifling your bill, and thus prolonging arbitrary government over the loyal inhabitants of Louisiana, and defeating the will of the nation; and it is sincerely to be hoped that the Executive may yet be made to understand that the representatives of the people are the only power competent to organize civil government in the insurrectionary districts.

"I am, with great respect, your obedient servant,

"THOMAS J. DURANT."

"NEW ORLEANS, Dec. 29, 1864.

"Hon. Henry L. Dawes, Chairman Committee on Elections, House of Representatives, Washington, D. C.:

"*Dear Sir:* I see by the newspapers that the Congressional delegation from Louisiana has been met by a protest from thirty-one citizens of Louisiana under the leadership of Thomas J. Durant.

"The friendly spirit you manifested towards the Union men of Louisiana in your successful efforts for the admission of her Representatives to Congress in February, 1863, and the important official position you occupy with reference to questions of this kind, lead me to address you hurriedly some remarks with the view of enlightening you on the political antecedents of Durant.

"The insidious efforts of this man to thwart and defeat the restoration of Louisiana to the Union, make it highly proper, if not necessary, that some notice should be taken of his movements. He appears to have the reputation abroad of being identified with the Free State movement here and to have caused many citizens of other States, including members of Congress, to believe him to be the Magnus Apollo of our cause.

"During the reign of the Confederacy in this city he was one of its most obedient adherents. He conformed to the requirements for members of the bar and entered as one of the earliest and most active practitioners in the 'Confederate States District Court.' In doing this he showed much more readiness than after the arrival of the Union fleet when he refused to practice his profession for some six months on account of having to take the oath.

"Here is a specimen of Durant's practice in the so-called 'Confederate States District Court,' which may be seen in his own hand writing in the United States Court of this place:

"JOHN L. MANNING, &c., VS. ROMANTA TILLOTSON.— In the Confederate States District Court for the District of Louisiana.

"And now into this honorable Court, by counsel, comes Romanta Tillotson, the defendant, and pleads a peremptory exception to the jurisdiction of the Court, and for cause of exception he shows that this suit is brought by and on behalf of persons who are all citizens of the State of South Carolina, and that the defendant is a citizen of the State of Louisiana, and that this Court has no power or jurisdiction by the Constitution and laws of the Confederate States to entertain the cause.

"Wherefore, respondent prays that this exception may be maintained, and that the plaintiff's petition may be dismissed.

("Signed) DURANT & HORNOR,
"for Defendant.

("Signed) SINGLETON & SLACK,
"Attorneys.

"U. S. CIRCUIT COURT, SIXTH CIRCUIT AND EASTERN DISTRICT OF LOUISIANA,
Clerk's Office.

"I certify the foregoing to be a true copy of the original on file in this office.

"F. B. VINOT,
"Deputy Clerk.

"NEW ORLEANS, Dec. 27, A. D. 1864."

"When the hearts of the Union people of New Orleans were gladdened by the arrival of the Union forces, who among the citizens went out with rejoicing and welcome upon his lips? Was it Thomas J. Durant? no! He was invited to attend the first Union meeting, in Polar Star Hall. He did so. When the formation of a Union Association was proposed, he resisted it. Said

"It was now no time for such an organization, that our sons and brothers were upon the battle-field. That the result of Corinth was not yet known; that it behooved the people of New Orleans to await results; that Butler was enticing the negroes to the Custom-house and shielding them from the authority of their masters, and that it was best to know first whether our rights to our property were to be respected or violated. When the Assembly proceeded to organize the First Union Association, Durant withdrew.

"This man sets himself up as a sort of model upon the slavery question; in fact, his "I am holier than thou" sort of professions upon everything concerning the colored people—his refusal to give credit to the Free State movement for what it has done for their cause, make it necessary that I should analyze his antecedents strictly upon this question. I should not do so but for his unfairness and unjustness. Far be it from me to question any man's past, who is patriotically working for our country's future.

"That Durant has been no stranger to the system of slavery, the following document which may be seen at the Conveyance Office of this city will show.

"NINTH MAY, 1851—SALE OF SLAVES OF WIDOW PETER CENAS TO THOMAS J. DURANT. By act passed before W. Christy, Notary Public, dated the 28th day of October, 1845, Pauline Maria St. Jean, widow of the late Peter Censas, late of this city, deceased, has sold unto Thomas J. Durant, also of this city, the following named slaves, to wit: Rosanna, a negress aged about twenty-nine years, and her three children, to wit: Elizabeth, aged about seven years, Tyler, aged about three years, and Sally, an infant, aged about six months—all black.

"That sale was made for the sum of eight hundred dollars, ($800), for which said purchaser has furnished his note bearing eight per cent. interest from its date until final payment, drawn in favor of said vender, dated 28th October, 1845. New Orleans, 9th May, 1851.

"BERNARD MARIGNY, Register."

"Among the first notable propositions made by him as a Union man was to restore Louisiana to the Union by a Convention. He made several speeches in favor of immediate restoration by that method, and after most earnest and persevering efforts he succeeded in carrying one of the Union Associations in his favor. Those who opposed him believed in his views but deemed them premature. This was in February, 1863. He continued agitating the question in the district or local clubs. He became Attorney General under the military authority of Gov. Shepley, and commenced a registry system for voters of the city and country parishes. He had registers appointed in all the parishes within the lines. He got up a plan of a Convention upon the white basis, to consist of one hundred and fifty members apportioned among the parishas almost identically as was adopted in the calling of the Convention of 1864. It was understood that Durant was the active promoter of the scheme of a convention, but that Governor Shepley always found cause for delay. Excepting his *penchant* for delay, he left everything in Durant's hands; and with this Durant was well pleased. But a *certain letter* was received from President Lincoln, who, not pleased with Shepley's delays, placed everything in the hands of Major General Banks.

"Here was the beginning of Durant's hostility to the plan which has been substantially followed in the restoration of Louisiana. Before that time there was, according to *his own speeches*, *territory enough* and *population enough fully* to warrant such a proceeding. Taking the thing out of Shepley's hands was taking it out of Durant's hands. Although all the propositions and plans of Durant have been substantially, nay almost identically followed, his opinions have undergone a radical change. What caused that change to come 'o'er the spirit of his dreams?' Disappointment and ambition. He could not rule as 'master,' therefore he has striven to *ruin*.

"In his letter to H. Winter Davis he says:

"'No free State Constitution had, on the 8th day of July, been adopted or installed in the fragment of Louisiana held by the military forces of the United States.' On the 11th May the Convention, representing fully two-thirds of the entire population of the State, passed the Ordinance of Emancipation. Eighty-five members of the Convention were present and voted upon the great question. Of this number seventy-two voted in favor of the Ordinance, declaring slavery forever *abolished* and prohibited throughout the State, and inhibiting in their fiat the Legislature from making laws recognizing the right of property in man, and proclaiming that all children, from the ages of six and eighteen years, shall be educated by maintenance of free public schools; also, that all able bodied men in the State shall be armed and disciplined for its defence, and that the black man may receive the full rights of citizenship. Are not these jewels of liberty? With these invaluable jewels the Constitution was adopted in the hearts of the people. The form or ceremony of ratification had not been gone through 'tis true; but Mr. Durant, from his knowledge of the loyalty of his fellow-citizens, could scarcely help knowing it would be ratified by an immense majority, and if he was imbued with that patriotism and love of liberty his eloquent speeches in his saner and more generous moments portray, he would feel to thank those who stood by the helm of the ship when he was in the hold endeavoring to scuttle and sink her.

"Durant participated in the election for State officers in February, 1864; he was chairman of a committee which conducted the campaign for one set of candidates; he made numerous publications and speeches, and his partner, Chas. W. Horner, who now 'certifies' the protest, went before the people on Durant's ticket as a candidate for Attorney General! The Durant ticket obtained only about one-sixth of the entire vote cast. Finding the weakness of his party, and abandoning all hope of being returned to the Constitutional Convention, he suddenly came to the conclusion that he would not be a candidate, 'because the whole movement was irregular!' His partner was, however, again a candidate, and again unsuccessful. If Durant or his partner had been elected, it is fair to assume that we would have had none of their pigmy efforts to retard the great Free State movement in Louisiana. And if the President, in compliance with his wishes had directed General Butler to respect Slave property, Durant would not have sought in his published letter to H. Winter Davis to have ridiculed our glorious Lincoln.

"I have written more in a spirit of sorrow than in anger. My aim has been nothing to extenuate nor ought to set down in malice; but I have considered it my duty as a good citizen to unmask the conduct of one who has immodestly and unjustly sought to thrust himself before the country as the only consistent Union and Free State man of Louisiana, and thus sought to injure the glorious cause of loyalty and restoration, under our new Constitution.

With high regard, I am, very respectfully yours,

A. P. Dostie.

January 2d, 1865, Thomas J. Durant wrote to the editor of the "Anti-Slavery Standard:" "The citizens elected to fill the State offices in Louisiana have no confidence in the civil administration, and pronounce it powerless to punish offenders.

"Not long since, one Michael Gleason, a white man, was tried before a Court and Jury in this city, on an indictment for the murder of a negro boy, by wantonly and without the slightest provocation throwing him into the Mississippi river, from a steamboat lying at the levee, and thus causing his death by drowning. Four eye-witnesses, all of African descent, testified to the horrid crime; there was no countervailing evidence on the part of the accused, but he was at once acquitted by the Jury. Mr. Attorney-General B. L. Lynch, who was elected on the 22d of February, 1864, at the same time with Mr. Hahn, the Governor, had, under the same military order from the Major-General commanding the Department of the Gulf, prosecuted this case with an honorable zeal for the cause of public justice.

"In subsequently commenting on this deplorable result, Mr. Lynch said: "I spared no pains, I resorted to every legitimate means in my power to succeed in bringing upon the head of the murderer the punishment richly due to his appalling crime. I failed! and why did I fail? It was, in my opinion, on account of the color of the poor murdered youth! It was on account of the complexion of the four truthful witnesses, whom the Jury affected not to believe. It is enough to chill the blood to reflect on the horrid verdict of the twelve men, who swore they would 'true deliverance make,' and who, in effect, decided last Monday, in the First District Court of New Orleans, that colored people are outside the protection of the laws, for the maintenance of which they are gallantly baring their bosoms to the bullets and the bayonets of the enemy, on the battle-fields of the rebellion.'

"This official exposition of the condition to which, under this abnormal State government, the citizens of African descent are reduced, ought to arrest the attention of the friends of freedom throughout the nation. If the man of color is thus to be left to the despotism of rulers who have no sympathy with him, what a snare and a delusion is the pretended gift of liberty?"

The following communications prove that injustice to the colored man was not the fault of the State Officials of Louisiana in 1864.

"Office of Superintendent, Negro Labor, Department of the Gulf, New Orleans, June 17, 1864.

"CHARLES LEAUMONT, Recorder 2d & 3d District:

"*Sir:* For the purpose of ascertaining the exact legal status of the colored population of this city, particularly those who previous to the arrival of the United States army were slaves, I have the honor to respectfully solicit a reply to the following questions:

"I. Do you consider the laws of the State in relation to slavery in operation at the present time?

"II. Can negroes receive equal justice with white persons without reference to their social condition previous to the war in the court under your jurisdiction?

"I have the honor to be,
"Very respectfully your obdt. serv't,
("Signed) GEO. H. HANKS,
"Colonel and Superintendent of Negro Labor."

The Recorder evaded the responsibility of a legal opinion in reply, and sent the following note to Attorney General Lynch:

"RECORDER'S OFFICE, SECOND DISTRICT,
NEW ORLEANS, June 17th, 1864.

"To B. L. Lynch, Esq., Attorney General:

"*Sir:* The accompanying communication addressed to me by Colonel Hanks was this day received, and is respectfully referred to you for answer.

"Yours Respectfully,
("Signed) CHAS. LEAUMONT,
"Recorder 2d and 3d Districts."

The following extract is from the official opinion of Attorney General B. L. Lynch, rendered on the 18th of June, 1864, in reply to the communication of Colonel Hanks:

"On the 22d of September, 1862, a proclamation was issued by the President of the United States, setting forth, that 'on the 1st day of January, in the year of our Lord one thousand eight hundred and sixty-three, all persons held as slaves within any State, or designated part of a State, the people whereof should then be in rebellion against the United States, should then, thenceforth and forever be free.'

"Furthermore the President announced that, on the 1st day of January, 1863, he would, by proclamation, designate the States and parts of States, if any, in which the people therein, respectively, should then be in rebellion against the United States.

"The President, on the first day of January, 1863, *did* accordingly issue his proclamation, declaring the State of Louisiana to be one of the States then in rebellion, and proclaimed that all persons held as slaves within that State, with the exception of those in certain Parishes, were and should be thenceforth free.

"The Parishes exempted from the operation of the Emancipation Proclamation were the following: St. Bernard, Plaquemines, Jefferson, St. John, St. Charles, St. James, Ascension, Assumption, Terrebonne, Lafourche, St. Mary, St. Martin, and Orleans, which excepted Parishes were left in the condition as though the proclamation had not been issued.

"On the 11th of January, 1864, Major General Banks issued a proclamation, abolishing slavery in the above named thirteen Parishes, exempted in the President's Proclamation. This proclamation was not disapproved, and perhaps was suggested by President Lincoln.

"The present State Government was re-organized under the constitution and laws of Louisiana, *except so much of the said constitution and laws as recognize, regulate, or relate to slavery, which being inconsistent with the present condition of public affairs, and plainly inapplicable to any class of persons existing within its limits, was suspended and declared to be inoperative and void.*

"Whether the President and his subordinate, General Banks, in their action were warranted by the constitution of the United States upon military necessity, need not be enquired into here. I believe they were constitutionally empowered to issue and enforce the proclamations aforesaid. Be that, however, as it may, you and I, and loyal citizens of Louisiana have sworn to support those proclamations, and abide by them so long as they are not declared to be unconstitutional by the Supreme Court of the nation.

"I am, therefore, of opinion that all negroes and persons of color in the State of Louisiana are free *de jure*; that all negroes and colored persons in Louisiana, within the Federal lines are free *de jure et defacto.* I think they have a legal right to testify as witnesses in Courts of Justice, for and against white persons, as well as each other; that they may sue and be sued in all cases; that they are entitled to trial by Jury, to the writ of Habeas Corpus; in short, that they stand on the same footing before the law as white aliens residing in the country."

Although through politic motives on the part of Durant, there was no conflict between Durant and Dostie in many of the acts favoring the great movements of the cause of freedom in Louisiana, when the Free State government was attacked by Durant, the antagonism between the two men became most strongly marked.

CHAPTER XV.

LOUISIANA CANDIDATES FOR CONGRESS IN 1864.

August 13th, 1864, the friends of a free Constitution met in New Orleans to ratify the nomination of Abraham Lincoln and Andrew Johnson, and to express their approbation of the new Constitution which was to be submitted to the people of the State on the 5th of September.

A series of political meetings were proposed, for the purpose of obtaining a united support for the Free State condidates for Congress. On the 29th of August the delegates of the nominating Convention met at Liberty Hall, and proceeded to make choice of candidates for Congress which resulted as follows: First District, M. F. Bonzano; Second District, Col. A. P. Field; Third District, W. D. Mann. Judge Abell announced himself an independent candidate for Congress, in opposition to Mr. Bonzano. Said Dr. Dostie, in referring to the two last named candidates, at a republican meeting: "Gentlemen, you have now before you two candidates for Congress, both members of the late Convention, one in favor of slavery, the other the friend of liberty—which will you send to our National Councils to work for the people of Louisiana? Abell, the advocate of oppression, or Benzano, the lover of freedom." "Bonzano!" was the cry of the people.

In an address before a Union meeting, Dr. Dostie gives the following reasons for announcing himself an independent candidate for Congress against A. P. Field:

"For the first time in my life I appear before you under circumstances of embarrassment. For the first time do I stand before you voluntarily as an aspirant for office.

"You all know that I hold an office which I did not seek. I refused the office of Secretary of State, and twice was the Auditorship offered me before I consented to accept it. Before the war I followed a profession which yielded me every desirable comfort, and I never was an office seeker.

"But now I do ask your suffrages for the high and important position of a Representative to Congress. Not that I have the vanity to suppose myself more competent for that position than any other, but the Convention last night nominated Col. A. P. Field, whom you all know as the champion of the Masonic Hall clique—and as a foremost defender of Copperheadism—the friend of the Voorhees and the Vallandigham school. You know how I interrogated him a few nights ago, and how he evaded declaring himself for the new Constitution. How did he go to Congress? You all know how it was. And how, after Congress sent him home, they kindly gave him fifteen hundred dollars for his visit. I do not want a gentleman of such principles—allied to Copperheadism—to represent redeemed and disenthralled Louisiana in the Congress of my country. I am his equal in all the virtues of manhood—I am his superior in the advocacy of the God-given principle of liberty to all men. I do not wish Louisiana disgraced by sending a man of his Copperhead sentiments. Where have you ever heard his voice raised either in debate or on the streets in defence of the principles of liberty? He has vilified Butler and others to whom you owe so much. It is for these reasons that I have voluntarily acquiesced in the solicitations of my friends, and become a candidate for Congress."

Col. T. B. Thorpe, the same evening spoke in defence of the new Constitution and of the necessity of having good and loyal men to represent the State in the Legislature and in the Congress of the United States, concluding his eloquent defense of the Constitution as follows:

"Fellow-citizens, my name has been mentioned in connection with Congress. From causes to which I will not allude, a gentleman has been nominated in my place whom I have never heard of as practically sympathizing in this Free State movement, a gentleman, who, if his own language delivered on a recent occasion at the Jackson Railroad depot is to be believed, holds the Free State party, the Constitution, and the military representatives of the Federal Government in utter contempt. I respect Col. Field as a gentleman distinguished in the law, and I admired the boldness and power with which he assaulted the Free State party—with which he poured forth his utter condemnation upon our most cherished political principles. I was surprised, however, at his bitterness against the Federal Government, displayed in his sweeping denunciations of Federal officers and soldiers. Let the gentlemen who took the responsibility of the nomination bear the consequences, for it has either demoralized the party, or it will work a regeneration.

"But the Free State party of Louisiana, our Constitution, and our attachment to the Union, do not depend upon single individuals; and while I step aside in the great contest, another name appears, bright with every association of loyalty; a name so identified with every step in the regeneration of Louisiana that it will shine brightly in history for years and years to come. I mean the chivalrous, zealous martyr-patriot, A. P. Dostie. He has been announced as the Union standard bearer in this Congressional contest, as he will come out by your free and independent suffrage, the orator of the field. He has not to come before you at the last moment to attest his love for free institutions; he has not to get up endorsements to prove that his heart and soul are with us. When the rebel rule was in its height in this city, Dr. Dostie, in the impetuosity of his nature, could not control his hatred of the tyrants who had ruined his country, and his open defiance of the men who were guilty, led to his banishment from your midst. What Dr. Dostie has done for the cause of freedom since his return from exile, you know as well as I; for a more indefatigable, a more thorough, a more genuine apostle of freedom never enlisted in the great cause.

"Send Dr. Dostie to Congress—his earnestness in the national capitol will have a beneficial effect upon all who come in contact with him; his indefatigable industry will surprise the sleepy guardians of the national honor, his unflinching determination to carry through his cherished principles, will give strength to those who are despondent, and comfort those who like himself are in earnest. He has qualities that are eminently needed to carry on a reform, to assert and maintain our civil rights, to defend our new Constitution, and to get Congress to receive our delegation, and once more admit our State in full fellowship in the glorious constellation of stars. Elect Dr. Dostie to Congress, and in your devotion to him show the people of the North that the Free State men of Louisiana have no compromise with Copperheadism, no matter in what form it makes its appearance, that we want no candidates who make death-bed repentances, or become suddenly converted just before the meeting of a nominating Convention; that we will have nothing but tried men who have served in the field, fought our battles, and helped to win our victories, none in this Congressional election but men like Dr. Dostie."

The following from the pen of General Banks is expressive of the state of affairs during that Congressional contest:

"The events of the day show that a more general interest will be manifested in the coming election than has been anticipated. The *Times*, hitherto studiously silent upon the ratification of the Constitution, although unsparing in its censure of the Convention that framed it, now urges its readers to its support. 'We might,' it says, 'with reason, advance many objections to this Constitution, but we could, with still more reason and justice, advance many arguments for its adoption. Therefore, we shall vote for it, and urge upon all who, perhaps, would desire to do better, to do the best they can, and give in their adhesion and support.

"If the efforts for reconstruction of government in Louisiana are successful and recognized, peace is possible and proximative.

"The *Tribune*, a journal ostensibly devoted to the interests of the colored race, but apparently controlled by white men who seem to have failed in the struggle for leadership in the work of reconstruction, says, that of three alternatives presented to the people of Louisiana, all of which are elaborately argued, the true course is to vote against the Constitution. Its authors are unprincipled tricksters, it says, and their work must necessarily be detrimental to the public weal. The *Tribune* exhibits as much force in the expression, as the *Times* does in the suppression of its real sentiments, and puts the strongest point upon its avowed hostility.

"The canvass in the parish of Orleans is animated, and reminds one of the contests of 1860. Opposition more resolute and capable is the only aliment required to give to the political arena the interest once inspired by 'the contests of the fierce democracy.'

"We are informed that between nine and ten thousand legal votes are registered to the parish of Orleans alone. The vote of the State is likely to exceed that of the gubernatorial election some five thousand, probably presenting an aggregate vote of fifteen to seventeen thousand. This is certainly a sanguine, perhaps an over estimate.

"In the First Congressional District the contest will be animated, and the vote large. Abell and Bonzano are the candidates—the first opposing the Constitution and emancipation, and the latter (Bonzano) advocating the Constitution with emancipation and compensation for loyal slaveholders. Bonzano is the author of the article of emancipation as it stands in the Constitution to be voted upon, and Mr. Abell was its most persistent and able opponent.

"In the Second District, Dr. Dostie, independent, opposes Mr. Field, a supporter of the Constitution, but of strong Democratic proclivities. Mr. Field is known to the country as the unsuccessful claimant of a seat in the House of Representatives last winter. He failed in being recognized, on account of the fact that no opportunity was given for a general participation in the election, and the small vote given for the various candidates claiming membership to the House of Representatives. He is a strong man on the stump, and will make his mark in the councils of the nation if elected. But the faithful doubt him, and he has for an opponent Dr. Dostie, State Auditor. Dr. Dostie is regarded by his opponents as the Robespierre of the revolution without the passion for bloodshed with which his ancient Republican prototype has been charged, his defenders say falsely charged. Whatever is true of Robespierre of the French Revolution, his successor of the great American Rebellion is governed by a spirit of the purest benevolence. He is earnest, but not malevolent, 'he roars you as gentle as a sucking dove;' even in his anger. In former times when the city was decimated by pestilence, the Doctor was one of the leading men of the Masonic Order who dared death in every form, and carried to every stricken fellow-man, comfort and consolation, if not relief—the Garibaldi of the hospitals.

Between these contestants the struggle will be animated, not virulent. 'Let the winners pass!'

"It will not be strange if Louisiana becomes the pivot upon which the revolution will turn; at any rate, it already attracts a large share of public attention.

"The manifesto of recent date upon our state affairs has excited more discussion than any political paper for some years.

"We are informed upon very good authority, that the President has written a letter expressing his approval of the draft of the Constitution to be submitted to the people, and an earnest desire for its ratification by them. It is therefore an affair of moment in the minds of other people than our own."

From among the many cards sent to the city papers, expressing a desire to see Dostie, the friend of education, in Congress, we select the following, as expressive of the feelings of many of the loyal teachers in New Orleans in 1864:

"Although the political issues involved in the present Congressional canvass are of paramount importance, yet it may not be out of place to consider such other issues as are collateral to the main question: educational matters of vital importance will be placed in the hands of the next Congressional Representative. Louisiana has not yet availed herself of that bountiful donation of land offered by Congress to establish Agricultural Colleges. There are, also, we believe, vacant cadetships due to this State, both at West Point and at the naval schools and 'civil service.' Secretaries will without doubt be appointed during the present session. Three such prizes held out to our High School pupils would be glorious incentives to activity. Therefore, if other things are equal, it becomes the duty of all who love the youth of our schools and hope to see them enjoy the advantages procured for those of other cities, to vote for Dr. Dostie, the tried friend of schools and children. To him, more than to any other man, is due the loyal standing of our public schools. He is everywhere beloved by the young people of New Orleans.

"TEACHER."

The *Delta* of September 8th, in referring to the result of the Congressional contest, says:

"Dr. Dostie is justly regarded as one of the leading spirits in the cause of the people. A more devoted or disinterested champion of liberty has not appeared upon the political stage during the present century.

"The majority of the delegates to the Parish Convention, being satisfied with Colonel Field, presented his name as a candidate for that office. All the primary elections, so far as we can learn, were fairly conducted. The delegates were presumed to know the wishes of their constituents, and the Free State party was, in a measure, in honor bound to ratify their action. The moment the nomination was made known, every friend and supporter of the party and its principles became tacitly pledged to support the nominee.

"In such a light must be viewed the result of the recent election. To this must be ascribed the defeat (by a small majority) of Dr. Dostie, who is one of the most popular men in the Congressional District—one against whom not a breath of suspicion could be cast—a true patriot, an indefatigable worker in the Union cause, a tried friend and an honest man. Had Dr. Dostie consented to run in time to have had his name presented to the Convention, the result might have been different. With the party nomination, he would have kept pace with the vote in favor of the Constitution. As it was he received comparatively a large vote."

The election of September 8th, resulted in sending

Mr. F. Bonzano, and A. P. Field to Washington. The action of Congress in not admitting them to participate in the councils of the nation are recorded in the official documents of the National Legislature.

Dr. Dostie's only disappointment at his defeat in the Congressional contest, arose from an ardent desire to labor in Congress for the interests of Louisiana. He had watched with the discernment of a true reformer the developments in his adopted State; had gloried in the downfall of despotism and the elevation of the oppressed laboring classes, and studied diligently the advantages to which her wealth, strength and resources entitled her as a free State in the Union. He desired to be in a position where he could labor for the interests of the emancipated masses, made free by the acts of President Lincoln.

His public documents, private letters and sayings, all prove that his standard was elevated to the dignity of pure and true statesmanship. Judging from his record, his comprehensive and just views of the measures necessary to carry out republican laws, we can not doubt but that he might have maintained a high position among the radical members of the 39th Congress.

November 29th, 1864, the Union men of New Orleans, assembled on Lafayette Square to ratify the election of Abraham Lincoln and Andrew Johnson. Addresses were delivered by Governor Hahn, General Hamilton, Judge Heistend, and Dr. Dostie. The annexed resolutions were adopted:

" *Resolved*, 1st. That in the recent re-election of Abraham Lincoln to the Presidency of the United States, we behold one of the sublimest spectacles ever presented to the gladdened eyes of the lovers of liberty and Republican institutions. The doubtful are convinced, the hopeful assured, and the confident are elated; that, notwithstanding the outside pressure of a gigantic civil war, and a factious and fierce opposition from within, the great experiment of a constitutional Government, based on universal suffrage, has not failed. Clear above the din of battle and the clamor of faction was heard the low, but articulate voice of the people. Was it not the voice of God?

"2*d*. That we also rejoice in the election of Andrew Johnson to the next highest office in the Republic. It is fitting that he, a Southern man, alone 'faithful found among the faithless,' should preside over that august body, before which he raised—but raised in vain—his voice in thunder tones of remonstrance against the suicidal act of secession.

"3*d*. That peace, and not war, is the primal and healthful condition of nations. That we ardently desire peace on the basis of the integrity of the Union, and if the knot of our complications can be untied by the pen of diplomacy, while the sword is upraised to cut it. If possible let diplomacy arrest the impending blow."

CHAPTER XVI.

DOSTIE AND BARKER.

To his friends, in whom he reposed confidence, Dostie was all gentleness and good humor. His winning simplicity and kindness of manner, made him very popular with his numerous friends, but with Jacksonian temper he sometimes poured out his fury upon the heads of his enemies he believed capable of injustice, fraud and oppression. There has been, since the existence of slavery, a class of men in the South who have spent their lives jealously watching all who did not spring from Southern chivalry or Southern slave aristocracy. Their greatest pleasure has been to watch an opportunity to scandalize those they chose to brand as "political agitators, inovators, new comers, &c., always adding those who spring from the lower classes." Pre-eminently among this class in New Orleans stands the name of Jacob Barker, Esq., whose idol was money; a man in society without money, in his eye, had no rights in common with the wealthy aristocrat. Dostie who was born in poverty, and had been deprived of his honest earnings by rebels and aristocrats, had but little sympathy with the Barker class.

The following correspondence simply illustrates one of the many contests between the monied Goliah's of New

Orleans and "the son of a barber," who often smote the monied Philistines "with a sling, and with a stone."

"NEW ORLEANS, July 7, 1864.

"Major Gen. Banks:

"*Sir*—In compliance with your request for information relative to the receipt and disposition of gold in this city, I take pleasure in communicating all that I have been able to learn.

"The receipts of gold from New York from the 1st May to the 17th June were, according to published statements, as follows:

May 3	$23,000	May 30	$169,964
May 15	67,065	June 6	256,240
May 15	92,300	June 8	124,432
May 18	98,075	June 13	105,339
May 21	47,075	June 14	47,250
May 23	210,200	From Interior	9,000
	$537,715		$701,955
			537,715
Total			$1,239,670

"That this large amount of gold was not sent here for any honest purpose, or to satisfy the demands of commerce, seems very apparent.

"The large shipments received just previous to the publication of the bogus proclamation indicates quite strongly that the holders had a knowledge of its intended issue, and that it was a part of the conspiracy to sell that gold at an enormous rate in this market.

"The fact that the proclamation was telegraphed from New York to Cairo, and other points, after its falsity was known, favors this supposition.

"Of that received during June, the consignees naturally divide themselves into the following classes:

"First—persons claiming and receiving protection as subjects of a foreign Power.

"Many of these persons before the outbreak of the war, were considered citizens, and are believed to have voted, and accepted other privileges of citizenship.

"They are not known to have any attachment to the Union, nor is it believed they would forego an opportunity of profit because it might work injury to the Republic.

"The second class of consignees is composed of banks:

June 6—Citizens' Bank	$50,000
" 22— " "	50,000
" 8— " "	124,432
" 4—National Bank	10,000
" 22— " "	15,000
" 13—Bank of America	13,000
" 21— " "	17,000
" 21—Bank of Commerce	10,000

"At the beginning of the war the officers of these State banks were among the first to bestow substantial aid upon the rebel cause.

"Although corporations, having no souls, may not be guilty of treason, yet it is most certain that the individuals owning stock were, in secession, regarded as genuine rebels, and it is believed that they have exhibited no evidence of substantial repentance.

"Third—Persons having no feeling either for or against the Government, save as it may help their speculations.

"These are among the worst parasites preying upon

the country. The friends of neither combatants, they are ready to prey upon both parties.

"The fourth class is that of avowed rebel sympathizers, some of whom have taken the oath.

"These men are among us, but have neither part nor lot with us. They have not even the decency to hide or disguise their treason.

"I am persuaded that the great bulk of gold in this market, is in the hands of unscrupulous persons, caring for nothing but the money they make.

"I have not thought it within the compass of your inquiry to make any allusion to the measures necessary to be taken in this behalf.

"It is suggested that Order No.— having discouraged the speculation in gold within this Department, there is evidence of a combination to make breadstuffs the staple of this unholy object. It is believed that a systematic arrangement is now being made to enhance the price of articles of subsistence.

"I remain, very respectfully yours,

A. P. Dostie."

"*To the Editor of the New Orleans Times*, July 28th —The editor of the *True Delta* having declined to make the correction, the editor of the *Times* will be pleased to inform the public that the statement of A. P. Dostie, published in the *True Delta* of yesterday's date, is FALSE, so far as it represents the Bank of Commerce or its officers, as among the first to bestow substantial aid upon the rebel cause.

"Neither the said Bank nor its officers subscribed a dollar at that time, nor at any other time, to the Confederate loans in this city or elsewhere; nor has that

Bank or the proprietor thereof ever contributed funds in the formation of military companies or otherwise in aid of the rebellion, which the proprietor does now and has always condemned as uncalled for and ruinous to the whole nation, and particularly ruinous as it has subjected this community to the insult of being thus criticised by such a man.

"If A. P. Dostie has the merit of loyalty beyond what he considers likely to administer to his acknowledged appetite for gain, it must have arisen from recent and sudden conviction.

"Mr. Barker's loyalty was tested before the birth of A. P. Dostie.

JACOB BARKER."

"NEW ORLEANS, July 30, 1864.

"*To the Editor of the True Delta:*

SIR—The New Orleans *Times* of this morning contains a letter over the signature of Jacob Barker, violently abusive of myself, because in my letter to Major-General Banks, of July 7th, published in your paper of Thursday, I made the following observations: 'At the beginning of the war the officers of these State banks were among the first to bestow substantial aid upon the rebel cause. Although corporations, having no souls, may not be guilty of treason, yet it is most certain that the individuals owning stock were in secession regarded as genuine rebels, and it is believed that they have exhibited no evidence of substantial repentance.'

"That publication is my supposed cause of offence to Jacob Barker. In that communication, as will be seen, I did not name Jacob Barker, either directly or by necessary implication; but since he has seen fit to suppose himself one of the class of individuals referred to as having 'no souls,' of having been regarded while secession was rampant in arms in this city as a passable rebel, and as having since exhibited no evidence of substantial repentance, I am willing to avow and admit that he is, of all men in this city, one whom I should have placed in just that category. In that communication, for which I am thus personally and scurrillously assailed by Jacob Barker, I made no attacks on the private character of any stockholder or officer of any of the banks therein named; but I made allusion to them as a class of persons derelict in the performance of the duties they owed as citizens of the United States.

"I by no means regret that Jacob Barker has seen fit to make that publication the occasion of calling public attention to the manner in which *he* has performed *his duty* to the Government of the United States, under whose protection he has become bloated with the insolence of wealth, while that Government has been engaged in a life and death struggle with this hell-born rebellion. All good citizens in these 'times that try men's souls,' owe it to their country, in this her great struggle for national existence, to give active aid, by bearing arms, if fit for service, or by loan of their money if they have amassed wealth under the protection and advantages which that just and good Government has afforded them. 'Indifference or neutrality is a crime, and faction is treason.'

"Jacob Barker, by reason of his immense wealth, and the power of his position, owes it to his country, in these times of her national peril, to give more positive and substantial proofs of loyalty than merely to 'condemn the rebellion as uncalled for and ruinous.' Although too old, being a *nonagenarian*, to bear arms in person in her behalf, yet he owed it to his country to labor actively and boldly with his pen and voice to propagate and uphold sentiments of unconditional and zealous loyalty. He owed it to his country to sustain her credit by investing a reasonable share of his immense wealth in her bonds, for without the 'sinews of war' how can the loyal soldiers be armed, fed and clothed, and this diabolical rebellion be trodden under foot? And without the willing aid of loyal capitalists how can the Government effect its necessary loans to carry on wars?

"He asserts that his loyalty was tested 'before the birth of A. P. Dostie.' That may be so, and that loyalty might even then have been found, as in later times, to have consisted in selfish devotion to Mammon. Admitting that Jacob Barker's loyalty was 'tested' before my birth, and not found wanting at that remote period, I desire to know what 'test it has stood during the last eventful four years?

"It may not be known to many in this community—but it is a fact that should be made public—that Jacob Barker, the banker and millionaire, gave, among others, such striking proofs of active, unconditional loyalty to his country as these: When General Butler ordered the citizens of this city to renew their allegiance to the Government of the United States within a certain time specified, this same Jacob Barker made his appearance before the Provost-Marshal at the City Hall, just ten minutes before the expiration of the time limited, and reluctantly took the oath, and at that same time received for two members of his family 'registered enemies' papers.'

"To encourage or permit those of his own family to register themselves as enemies to their country, and to harbor them in his house, may perhaps be proof to some persons that his 'condemnation of rebellion' had always been terribly severe. When the Commanding General required a certain class of citizens to bind themselves with the 'iron-clad' oath he complied, but when and how? At the last moment, and very reluctantly. There was published in this city, for a short time, last year, a 'loyal traitor' sheet called the *National Advocate*, with Jacob Barker's name as ostensible and responsible editor and proprietor. That infamous sheet, during the period of its short and villainous existence, was commonly filled with all kinds of rebel dispatches via the 'grape-vine' line, terrific bulletins of Federal defeats, croakings and lamentations over the evils and burden of this 'cruel and unnecessary war,' all sorts of extracts from rebel-sympathizing papers, and with every kind of matter calculated to give aid and comfort to other loyal traitors in this city, until the nuisance became so intolerable that the publication of the *National Advocate*, edited and owned by Jacob Barker, was suppressed by Major-General Banks, out of complaisance, I suppose, to 'such a man's' mode of 'condemning the rebellion.'

"What public offences, or what kind of moral delinquency J. B. means to impute by styling me 'such a man,' I am utterly at a loss to know. He hints that I have an 'acknowledged appetite for gain.' Acknowledged by whom, pray? Even my worst enemies, among whom I am proud to include every man who does not love my country, will not accuse me of a sordid, money-loving spirit. What little money my labor has earned beyond supplying the wants of a frugal living, I have cheerfully given during this war to advance the glorious cause of our country. I wish Jacob Barker had done likewise in proportion to his resources. Then he would have lived for some useful purpose. I am willing to leave it to the public to judge whether my character for honesty will bear comparison with that of 'such a man' who issued and caused to be circulated in this city, thousands of dollars of notes purporting to be bills of the 'Bank of Commerce,' payable 'six months after the ratification of peace between the United States and the Confederate States of America.' I think that I perform my duties to my fellow-citizens and my country, quite as conscientiously as 'such a man,' who has devoted his whole power of thought to the sordid pursuit of acquiring and hoarding wealth, and who has not shown patriotism enough to give a single dollar to promote the cause of the Union, and of the benignant Government under whose favor and protection he has grown rich.

"I notice that J. B. gives as his 'particular' reason for 'condemning the rebellion' as 'particularly ruinous,' is that it has subjected 'this community' to the insult of being thus criticised by 'such a man.' What a lofty minded patriot! What a worthy millionaire! What a far discerning intellect, and what pure and noble impulses move the soul of this great and venerable banker and speculator, as shown in his statement of his 'particular reason' for 'condemning the rebellion!'

"No natural love of country, no profound perception of the intrinsic meanness and wickedness of treason and rebellion against our noble government, could furnish the mind of J. B. such a 'particular' good reason for 'condemning the rebellion,' as the insult to this community of being criticised by 'such a man.' Wonderful logic! Admirable consistency! Who compose the community which he asserts I have insulted? My communication to General Banks, which has provoked this irascible, superanuated old Copperhead to publish that scurrilous attack upon my character and motives, had reference to no other 'community' or classes of men than, 1st. persons claiming protection as subjects of foreign powers, some of whom were formerly considered citizens, and who are not suspected of any attachment to the Union; 2nd. the Banks among whom I placed J. B.'s Bank; 3d., those proverbial for having no patriotism; parasites, only coming to make money out of either party, and 4th., avowed rebel sympathizers.

"These classes compose the entire 'community' referred to in my letter on the gold question, and they alone are the 'community' to whom my publication was an insult, if insult it was to any. If that 'community' to which it would seem J. B. claims to belong, feel insulted by my criticisms upon their want of patriotism, they, and J. B. in particular, can seek any redress which they deem their 'wounded honor' demands.

"In the statement made by Mr. Barker of his paltry motives for condemning the rebellion, he discovers to public view a poverty of soul in striking contrast with the plethora of his money bags. Between the money and the man, the former has outweighed the latter and given him the position he now holds in society, '*Mene, mene, tekel, upharsin.*' His record as a citizen of a great republic is unworthy of his sires, and of the sublime lessons of Union and liberty transmitted by them to him. But let him come and labor side by side with the friends of the Union, and that immortal ordinance which forever abolishes slavery from Louisiana, and then I will call him honest, and believe him respectable. 'Principles demand support.'

A. P. DOSTIE."

"*To the Editor of the New Orleans Times.*—The *True Delta* having found room in that interesting sheet for a score more of falsehoods from the pen of one A. P. Dostie, the public will be pleased to excuse Mr. Barker for noticing a few of them.

"This man says, 'I did not name Jacob Barker.' That I am the sole proprietor and manager of the Bank of Commerce is as well known in this city as is my name; therefore to say, 'I did not name Jacob Barker' is a contemptible subterfuge, worthy of its author.

"It is false 'that Mr. Barker reluctantly took the oath before the Provost Marshal at the City Hall, just ten minutes before the expiration of the time limited.'

"Mr. Barker took the oath in court at the Custom House long before—not at the City Hall, and not just ten minutes before the expiration of the time limited; nor did he receive for two members of his frmily, nor for any other number, 'registered enemies' papers.' The allegation is therefore false, and Dostie is indebted for it to the *Delta*—a vile sheet which Mr. Barker's pen silenced long since.

"A. P. Dostie's prolific mind rendered it unnecessary for him to borrow falsehood from others.

"As to the iron-clad oath, he considered it harmless, as it could not increase the duty of a loyal citizen, yet he took it reluctantly, not liking to swear to support a proclamation he had not seen. The first law lesson he received was from General Alexander Hamilton, which was, never to form an opinion on a paper he had not read.

"The occasion on which Mr. Barker took that oath was preceding the first election, which required one-tenth of the population to vote to make the election valid, which General Banks considered important should be cast, and therefore requested Mr. Barker's co-operation, which was yielded with great earnestness, and which could not be done without taking that oath.

"This man, A. P. Dostie, not satisfied with denouncing Mr. Barker and his bank, assails the fair fame of the *National Advocate.* The dimensions of that paper having been taken by the community, and particularly by Mr. Barker's lady friends, he has not anything to say on that subject further than that he feels more vain of the fame it left behind than of the history of any other part of his life.

"The public will be pleased not to expect me to waste any more *ink powder* on this man, who should remember that 'our trees grow tar and our birds carry feathers.'

JACOB BARKER.

"New Orleans, July 31, 1864."

"NEW ORLEANS, August 1, 1864.

"*To the Editor of the True Delta:*

"SIR—'Mr. Barker,' having exhausted another charge of 'ink powder' in throwing empty bomb-shells at me through the *Times* of yesterday morning, permit me to trespass once more upon your columns.

"Jacob Barker asserts that my statements concerning him are false. Then, why does he not prove them so? He simply asserts them so without bringing forward any facts to substantiate his assertions.

"I am prepared to prove that on the 23d day of September, 1862, a few minutes before 3 P. M., at the City Hall, 'this man' appeared before the Provost-Marshal and *took the oath*, and at the same time received from that officer 'registered enemies' papers' for two members of his own family, remarking by way of apology, as he did so, 'that he could not control the members of his family in that respect.'

"Does the astute J. B. imagine that he has outlived the history of his earlier business career? Can he possibly drive himself into the belief that people have lost all recollection of the celebrated 'Washington and Warren Bank?' or what was worse, the 'Marble Manufacturing Bank?' Does not the ghost of his pitiable tool Malapart haunt his terror-stricken conscience, and warn him against the further misdeeds of the banker, broker and *breaker?* Or has he forgotten the time when he 'left his country (New York) for his country's good?'

"If he had not intimated that he would not waste any more 'ink powder' on 'such a man,' I should be tempted to inquire how he invested the large amount of 'Confederate money' he bought up in 1862? I think that transaction was one of the modes of his 'condemning the rebellion.'

"'This man' takes occasion to inform the public that 'our trees grow tar and our birds carry feathers,' intimating that if I persist in giving utterance to the truth against him, he will have me receive a *coat of tar and feathers*. If he expects to intimidate me by such puerile threats as that, he entirely wastes his 'ink powder.'

"If the chief object through 'Mr. Barker's' life of which he feels 'vain' is the '*fair fame*' of his defunct traitor sheet the *National Advocate*, he has very little now in his old age to look back upon with vanity or pride.

"The lady admirers of that paper, of whom he speaks, are well known in this community, and a season spent on Ship Island would be very beneficial to their moral health.

A. P. DOSTIE."

" *To the Editor of the Times:*

"Mr. Barker feels constrained to depart from his determination not further to expose the deliberate lies of one A. P. Dostie.

"In the *True Delta* of Tuesday he demands proof. Here it is:

'DEPARTMENT OF THE GULF, PROVOST COURT,
NEW ORLEANS, La., July, 19, 1862.

'Jacob Barker has taken the oath required by General Order No. 41 for a citizen of U. S. A.

'Witness: Major JOSEPH M. BELL,
Provost Judge.

'C. W. WOODBURY, Dep. Clerk.'

"The man Dostie avers that he has proofs that his vile falsehoods are true. If true they are matters of record, open to his inspection. Why not then give them to the public, in place of calling upon Mr. Barker to prove a negative.

"This traducer alludes to Mr. Barker's connection with the Bank of Washington and Warren, in the State of New York. That bank failed, after which Mr. Barker paid all its debts—a portion after his residence here, from his new earnings.

"Among the numerous falsehoods of the man Dostie, he asserts that Mr. Barker was connected with the Marble Manufacturing Bank, in New York, and its infamous proprietor, 'Malapar.' Mr. Barker never had any connection with either, or an account with that institution.

"There was a vile conspiracy in 1826 among certain Wall street gamblers and political aspirants to injure the fair fame of Mr. Barker, who hurled defiance at them in open court, and fought the battle successfully before he had read law.

"His Satanic Majesty has got them nearly all—only two or three have thus far escaped his vigilance. He will soon have the rest, with some additions from New Orleans, without the dishonor of meeting in single combat a man without position in society.

JACOB BARKER."

"NEW ORLEANS, August 3, 1864.

"To the Editor of the *True Delta*:

"'One' Jacob Barker having commenced and continued a most unwarrantable and scurrillous attack upon me through the columns of the New Orleans *Times*, I have been compelled, in self-defence, to reply to him through the columns of your valuable paper; and as he has again resorted to reply in similar language, though informing the public that he should not, I also am under the necessity of again requesting you to insert the following, which I trust will, for the future, silence the barker and render his bite harmless:

"*He* will soon have the rest, with some addition from New Orleans, without the dishonor of meeting in single combat a man *without position* in society.—*Jacob Barker.*

"And pray, Jacob Barker, what position have you *always held* in society?

"Hast thou not all thy life been an associate of stock gamblers, cheats and swindlers, and the chief of 'wild cat' banking houses? Hast thou not followed to the letter the advice of the Quaker mother to her son, 'make money, honestly if thee can, but my son make money!'

"Thou knowest, Jacob, that thou hast made money; but, Jacob, hast thou made it honestly? Let us see!

"Does Jacob Barker remember a certain book published in 1846, by Crook & Co., of Boston, entitled 'The Life and Times of Martin Van Buren?' If he does, he will recollect the following extracts:

"Page 38.—Warren Bank, a moneyed corporation, of two years standing, which the notorious stock jobber, Jacob Barker, has bought from the speculators who got it up. Barker could issue its bills at his Exchange Bank, New York, to mechanics and traders, who could find it no easy task to go North to Sandy Hill to get them cashed. With brokers and bankers he expected to hold his own.

"Jacob Barker being the sole, or almost sole, proprietor of the real 'wild cat bank.'

"Page 42.—In a card issued through the *Evening Post*, February, 1825, Barker said that $200,000 of the stock had been received from the debtors of the bank. Why was this done, when it was well known that the stock was worthless? Who beside Barker had $200,000 to pay in? Was it in this way that the securities for double its circulation went? If so, what could be a baser cheat? Stock was no payment of debts due the bank till its obligations to the public were met, and after that only its cash value in the market.

Page 169.—Copy of a letter from Benj. F. Butler to Lorenzo Hoyt, Esq., Albany:

"NEW YORK, Oct. 1, 1826.

Dear Sir:—Mr. Henry has gone home with an intention of preparing himself in the case of the Bank of Plattsburgh against Levi Platt, Wells and others, (the account case). I wish you would therefore * * * * I have but a moment and few details of the trial (Jacob Barker and others for a conspiracy to defraud). Must refer you to the papers. They bring down the details to yesterday at 1 o'clock. In the afternoon and evening we had a fine time of it, and when the court adjourned last night the case was left remarkably well for us. * * * Mr. Barker has done wonders. Truly yours,

"B. F. BUTLER.

"In another letter from Benj. F. Butler to Jesse Hoyt, dated Sandy Hill, November 16, 1819, and published on pages 161 and 162, are the following extracts:

"You are right in supposing that the late catastrophe (for I consider it the end of that drama) in the Exchange Bank, is a very common misfortune; to me especially it is a great one. I had cheerfully suffered the depreciation of *our paper*, that Mr. B. (Barker) might in the meantime bend all his efforts to the Exchange Bank, and in the resumption of payment then, hoped for the most auspicious result. The matter is past mending, and no doubt it is all for the best. We continue, paying daily in a small way, more to relieve the suffering community than for any other purpose. The credit of the paper is very bad in this country.

"Some of them, I hear, have the kindness and condescension to compassionate and pity me, while others consider me *full as bad as Jacob Barker*, which in these days is considered a pretty severe specimen of invective and reproach. 'So be it!'

"What does Jacob Barker think of these proofs? More extracts of a similar nature from this and other books of *auld lang syne* can be produced at any moment, but, for the present, I forbear.

"And now let me review 'this man's' oath, which *he* refers to and publishes in the *Times* of yesterday:

"DEPARTMENT OF THE GULF, PROVOST COURT.
NEW ORLEANS, LA., July 19, 1862.

"Jacob Barker has taken the oath required by General Order No. 41 for a citizen of U. S. A.

"Witness: Major JOSEPH M. BELL,
Provost Judge.

"C. W. WOODBURY, Deputy Clerk.

"He says: 'He demands proof. Here it is.' Yes, 'here it is,' Jacob, and just the proof I wished for. General Order No. 41 says:

"All acts, *doings*, deeds, instruments, records or certificates, certified or attested by, and transactions done, performed or made by any of the persons above described, from and after the *fifteenth of June instant*, who shall not have taken and subscribed such oath, are void and of no effect.

"This oath, Jacob Barker, you took on the 19th day of July, one month and four days beyond the time specified, thus making it 'void and of no effect.'

"General Order No. 76 then came to the relief of Jacob Barker and 'such men.' Ten minutes before the time expired rendering this oath null and void, you appeared before the Provost Marshal at the City Hall, raised your right hand and swore allegiance to the United States—to *save your property* from confiscation, I suppose. This was the oath I referred to, Jacob :

"There was a vile conspiracy in 1826 among certain Wall street gamblers and political aspirants to injure the fair fame of Mr. Barker, who hurled defiance at them in open court, and fought the battle successfully before he had read law.

"His Satanic Majesty has got them nearly all—only two or three have thus far escaped his vigilance. He will soon have the rest, with some additions from New Orleans, without the dishonor of meeting in single combat a man without position in society.—*Jacob Barker.*

"Who can Jacob Barker be referring to, except his venerable self?

"Oh, Jacob, Jacob, thy hairs are gray with the whitening frosts of nearly a hundred winters, yet thou retainest thy wickedness in spite of thy advanced age, and appear to think that his *Satanic Majesty* ceases to exist except in the person of thy august self. Oh, fie, Jacob Barker.

"A. P. Dostie."

Said a friend to Dr. Dostie, in referring to the above correspondence. "You have not reverenced old age in your attacks upon Mr. Barker." In reply, he said, "Mr. Barker is not too aged to strengthen treason and despotism. I shall never retain a vindictive feeling against any man—but a principle that aims to crush republican Liberty, I shall oppose."

CHAPTER XVII.

GOVERNOR HAHN.

On the 20th of January, 1865, Governor Hahn issued the following proclamation :

"*Whereas*, Our sister States of Missouri and Tennessee, assembled in Conventions representing the loyal people of their respective Commonwealths, have each passed Edicts of Emancipation, declaring the freedom of all slaves within their borders, and forever prohibiting slavery or involuntary servitude, except for crime, whereof the party shall have been duly convicted ; and

"*Whereas*, Said Edicts of Emancipation by our late slave-holding sisters, are acts of great historic significance, worthy all praise and commemoration, as indicating the progress of ideas, the courage, fidelity and humanity of the people, and the early establishment of the National Government upon the permanent basis of freedom and justice :

"Therefore, I, MICHAEL HAHN, Governor of the State of Louisiana, in the name of our free State and loyal people, do hereby extend to Missouri and Tennessee, and to the noble representatives in their respective Conventions, thanks and congratulations.

"And further, I do recommend that TUESDAY next, the 24th day of January, shall be observed and respected by our people as a holiday for recreation and festivity in honor of the memorable Emancipation Acts of the now Free States of Missouri and Tennessee ; which acts, with those of Louisiana and Maryland, are forerunners of the time when 'Liberty shall be proclaimed throughout the land to all the inhabitants thereof.'

"Given under my hand and seal of the State, this 20th day of January, A. D. 1865, and the Independence of the United States the eighty-ninth.

"By the Governor:

"MICHAEL HAHN.

"S. WROTNOWSKI, Secretary of State."

The 24th day of January, 1865, was observed in New Orleans, as a day of festivity in honor of the noble action of the citizens of the States of Missouri and Tennessee, who were determined to erect the standard of Liberty and Progress. All the State Courts were adjourned; Judge Durell dismissed the United States Court in the following manner:

"MR. CLERK:—Whereas, his Excellency Michael Hahn, Governor of the State of Louisiana, has set this day apart as a holliday in honor of the rapid progress now making in the cause of civil liberty on this continent, you will therefore enter upon the records of the United States Courts this most worthy cause for the adjournment of the same. Mr. Marshal, adjourn the Circuit Court; Mr. Marshal, adjourn the District Court.

Early in the morning the leading thoroughfares, were thronged with people, black and white, thousands of them arrayed in "red, white and blue." The public buildings were decorated with Stars and Stripes. The City Hall, the Headquarters of the Governor and Mayor were covered with the National emblems. The office of the State Auditor, A. P. Dostie, located at No. 17, St. Charles street, was decorated with National banners. In the evening a transparency was added to the other decorations, upon one side of which was a portrait of

Major General N. P. Banks, and upon the other, the motto.

"NEW GLORIES ARE BEFORE US."

Over the Public Schools both (white and black) the Stars and Stripes were hoisted. At noon a national salute was fired, and all the bells in the city rang a joyful peal. Thousands of the emancipated assembled upon Lafayette Square, where a battallion of the 11th Heavy Artillery, U. S. colored troops, and a Company of the 77th U. S. infantry, (colored) had assembled to listen to speeches and music. The National airs were popular on that day. The evening was spent by thousands in listening to speeches from Governor Hahn, Rev. Thomas Conway, Dr. Dostie, Judge Durell—and others.

January 9th, Governor Hahn was elected to the United States Senate. We annex his farewell Message:

"STATE OF LOUISIANA, EXECUTIVE DEPARTMENT,
NEW ORLEANS, February 27, 1865.

"To the Senate and House of Representatives of the State of Louisiana:

"*Gentlemen*,—I hereby resign the office of Governor, to take effect on the 3d of March proximo, so that my occupancy of the office may terminate with that date, and enable my successer to be inaugurated, if convenient to your honorable bodies, on the 4th of March.

"The one year of administration which I have had as your Governor, is a period to which I shall ever advert with pride and pleasure. Called to the office by a flattering vote of the people, I entered upon its duties with diffidence, and a full sense of its responsibilities. I leave it without self-reproach, and with pride at having performed a part however humble in the triumphs and glories which have marked the history of Louisiana the past year. At its commencement half the State—the portion excepted by proclamation—held slaves. By a vote approaching unanimity, every slave has been since set free; and slavery will never more have an existence in fact or a sanction in law in the State of Louisiana. Justice to a hitherto enslaved race has not ended here. The most extensive, as well as impartial and equal provisions have been made for their education; while our Constitution, keeping pace with the spirit of the age, has provided for their complete equality before the law, including the extension to them of the highest privilege of citizenship. I have no hesitation in saying that its terms will justify the adoption of universal suffrage whenever it shall be deemed wise and timely; and if the most devoted enthusiast shall complain that the doors have not been thrown open at once to all, he must admit, as we can claim, that our State has progressed further than three-fourths of the Northern States. We trust to vie in every noble and patriotic work with the best and foremost of our sister States. Our State has furnished, and is furnishing, in proportion to the able-bodied men in the State, a quota to the Union armies equal to that of any other State. Even in the parishes within the rebel military lines we are assured of the existence of a union feeling.

"I speak of these things as encouraging signs of the times. In Louisiana, which now, as at the outset of the rebellion, can claim to be fully as loyal as Missouri, Maryland or Kentucky, her inhabitants have passed the Rubicon of their trials. The power of secessionism is waning; its influence is now scarcely felt among our people.

"Our progress in civil reorganization has been equally auspicious. A constitution has been accepted by the people, which has swept away not only the last vestige of human bondage, but all the concomitant blemishes upon civilization which stood upon our statute books and were a part of our institutions. The Black Code, so long the reproach and regret of the humane and enlightened of the world, exists no more. The odious basis of representation, which gave to wealth and capital a leverage against the mechanical and industrial classes, and favored, as it was designed to, the establishment of an oligarchy among American freemen, is removed at once, without the necessity of a long and wearisome agitation, as would otherwise have been necessary for the attainment of the simple justice of equal representation. One voter is now equal to another, and entitled to the same privileges and proportional representation. Older governments and communities have had to battle for years without success for this plain, practical and essential republican measure. Our Constitution favors industry, secures the reward of labor, guarantees impartial education, invites immigration, and will be the basis of a prosperity hitherto untold in our annals.

"I leave your chief executive office in the hands of my constitutional successor, Lieutenant-Governor Wells. He has already received marks of the confidence of his fellow-citizens of this State, and is known to you for all his patriotic antecedents. I have full confidence that his administration of the government will have the support of our fellow-citizens, without distinction of party.

"For myself, I shall never forget the many and flattering marks of kindness which I have received from my fellow-citizens of Louisiana. That confidence which they have unwaveringly awarded me it will be my endeavor to merit and justify. Whether it be to serve her in the public or private station, her honor and her glory it will be my constant aim to promote, with all the humble ability I can command.

"I respectfully recommend the Legislature to take such measures as may be necessary to provide, in a fitting manner, for the inauguration of Lieut. Governor Wells into the office of Governor.

MICHAEL HAHN.

When Governor Hahn resigned his position, few doubted the firm loyalty of his successor. True Unionists believed he would defend their interests as his predecessor had done. His official acts had been in harmony with the measures of President Lincoln whose confidence he seemed to have gained. The following characteristic letter is expressive of that confidence:

EXECUTIVE MANSION,
WASHINGTON, March 13, 1864.

HON. MICHAEL HAHN:

MY DEAR SIR: I congratulate you on having fixed your name in history as the first Free State Governor of Louisiana. Now, you are about to have a Convention, which, among other things, will probably define the elective franchise. I barely suggest, for your private consideration, whether some of the colored people may not be let in; as, for instance, the very intelligent, and especially those who have fought gallantly in our ranks. They would probably help, in some trying time to come, to keep the jewel of liberty in the family of freedom. But this is only a suggestion, not for the public, but to you alone.

Truly yours, A. LINCOLN.

CHAPTER XVIII.

PRESIDENT LINCOLN.

On the night of the 15th of April, 1865, the loyal masses of New Orleans congregrated in Lafayette Square to express their gratitude on the downfall of the rebellion. Richmond had been captured, and Lee and Johnston had surrendered their armies to the United States forces under Grant. At that immense gathering, numbering thousands, the annexed resolutions were adopted:

1. *Resolved*, That the loyal citizens of New Orleans have learned, with the liveliest emotions of delight, that Richmond has been captured, and that the rebel armies under Lee and Johnston have surrendered to the forces of the United States, commanded by Generals Grant and Sherman.

2. *Resolved*, That next to that God who rules the destinies of nations, our thanks are due to the Army and Navy of our country, who have, through a protracted conflict of unexampled magnitude and fierceness, finally overthrown its enemies, and enabled us to anticipate the not far distant day when the National flag will once more float in triumph over every square foot of the National domain.

3. *Resolved*, That in the struggle thus determined we hail the realization of those ideas which furnished the main issue in the conflict—the issue between slavery and freedom—and that we pledge ourselves to sustain the

holy cause of freedom and equal rights as the claim of justice and the basis of future security.

4. *Resolved*, That the people of the United States, and the friends of liberty throughout the civilized world, owe to our patriotic Chief Magistrate, Abraham Lincoln, obligations of lasting gratitude for the patriotic courage and wisdom he has displayed under circumstances of unexampled difficulty, in vindicating Republican institutions from the aspersions of their enemies, for the invaluable services he has rendered the cause of human liberty, and for the successful manner in which he has brought the Ship of State through the rocks and shoals of rebellion to the haven of peace.

In connection with that memorable event, destined to live on history's page as the jubilee hour after four years of gloom, it is fitting to present the speech of the President, made to a vast concourse of people at the Executive Department in Washington on the evening of the 13th April, 1865—the last public address of the martyred Lincoln:

"We meet this evening, not in sorrow, but in gladness of the heart. The evacuation of Petersburg and Richmond, and the surrender of the principal insurgent army, gives hopes of righteous and speedy peace, whose joyous expression cannot be restrained. In the midst of this, however, He from whom all bounties flow must not be forgotten.

"A call for a National Thanksgiving is being prepared and will be duly promulgated. Nor must those whose harder part gives us the cause of rejoicing be overlooked. Their honors must not be paralyzed but with the others. I myself was near the front, and had the high pleasure of transmitting much of the good news to you; but no part of the honor for the plan or execution is mine. To

General Grant, his skillful officers and brave men, all belongs. The gallant navy stood ready, but was not in reach to take an active part.

"By these recent successes—the re-inauguration of National authority—reconstruction, which has had a large share of thought from the first, is pressed more closely upon our attention. It is fraught with great difficulty, unlike the case of war between independent nations. There is no authorized organ for us to treat with, no one man has authority to give up the rebellion for any other man. We must simply begin with and mould from the discordant and disorganized elements. Nor is it a small additional embarrassment that we loyal people differ among ourselves as to the mode, manner, and measure of reconstruction.

"As a general rule I abstain from reading reports of attacks upon myself, not to be provoked by that to which I cannot properly offer an answer. In spite of this precaution, however, it comes to my knowledge that I am much censured for some supposed agency in setting up and seeking to sustain the new Government of Louisiana.

"In this I have done just so much and no more than the public know. In the annual message of December, 1863, and the accompanying proclamation, I presented a plan of reconstruction, as the phrase goes, which I promised, if adopted by any State, would be acceptable and sustained by the Executive.

"I distinctly stated that this was not the only plan which might possibly be acceptable, and I also distinctly protested that the Executive claimed no right to say when or whether members should be admitted to seats in Congress from such States.

"This plan was in advance submitted to the Cabinet and approved by every member of it. One of them suggested that I should then and in that conjunction apply the emancipation proclamation to the———, except parts, of Virginia and Louisiana that should drop the suggestion about apprenticeship for freed people, and that I should omit the protest against my own power in regard to the admission of members of Congress.

"But even he approved every part and parcel of the plan which has since been employed or touched by the action of Louisiana.

"The new Constitution of Louisiana, declaring emancipation for the whole State, practically applies the proclamation to the part previously exempted. It does not adopt the apprenticeship for freed people, and is silent—as it could not be otherwise—about the admission of members to Congress so that it is applied to Louisiana.

"Every member of the Cabinet fully approved the plan. The message went to Congress. I received many commendations of the plan, written and verbal, and not a single objection to it from any professed emancipationist came to my knowledge until after the news was received at Washington that the people of Louisiana had begun a move in accordance with it.

"I had corresponded with different persons supposed to be interested in seeking the reconstruction of the State Government of Louisiana. When this message of 1863, with the plan before mentioned, reached New Orleans, General Banks wrote me that he was confident that the people, with the aid of his military co-operation, would construct substantially on that plan. I wrote him and some of them to try it. They tried it and the result is known.

"Such has been my only agency in the Louisiana movement. My promise is made, as I have previously stated; but as bad promises are better broken than kept, I shall treat this as a bad promise, and break it whenever I shall be convinced that keeping it is adverse to the public interest; but I have not yet been so convinced. I have been shown letters on this subject, supposed to be able ones, in which the writer expresses a regret that my mind has not seemed to be definitely fixed on the question whether seceded States, so called, are in the Union or out of it.

"It would have added astonishment to his regret, were he to learn that since I have found professed Union men endeavoring to answer that question, I have purposely forborn any public expression upon it. It appears to me that the question has not been and is not yet, a practically national one; and the discussion of it, while it remains practically unnational, could have no effect, other than the mischievous one of dividing our friends.

"As yet, whatever may become the question is a bad base of dispute, and good for nothing at all. We all agree that the seceded States, so called, are out of their proper practical relation with the Union, and that the sole object of the Government, civil and military, in regard to those States is to again get them into their proper relation.

"I believe that it is not only possible, but in fact easier to do this without declaring or even considering whether these States have ever been out of the Union, or whether finding themselves safely at home, it would be utterly immaterial whether they had been abroad or not.

"Let's join in doing acts necessary to restore the proper practical relation between these States and the Union to each other forever; after innocently indulging his own opinion whether, in doing acts, he brought the States from without into the Union, or only gave them proper assistance, they never having been out of it.

"The amount of constancy, so to speak, on which the Louisiana Government rests, would be more satisfactory to all if it contained 50,000 or 60,000, or even 20,000, instead of 12,000, as it does. It is also satisfactory to some that the elective franchise is not given to the colored man.

"I would myself prefer it were now conferred on every intelligent one and on those who serve our cause as soldiers; still the question is not whether the Louisiana Government as it stands is quite all that is desirable. The question is: Will it be wise to take it as it is, itself to improve or to reject and disperse?

"Can Louisiana be brought into her proper practical relation with the Union by sustaining or discarding the new Government? Some 12,000 votes in the heretofore slave State of Louisiana have sworn allegiance to the Union, assumed to be the rightful political power of the State, held elections, organized a State Government, adopted a Free State Constitution, giving the benefit of the public schools equally to the black and white, and empowering the Legislature to confer the elective franchise upon the colored men.

"The Legislature has already voted to ratify the Constitutional amendment recently passed by Congress, abolishing slavery throughout the Union, perpetuated freedom in the State, committed to the very things, and nearly all the things the nation wants, and they ask the nation's recognition and assistance to make this committal.

"We have rejected and spurned them; we do our utmost to disorganize and disperse them. We, in fact, say to the white man, 'you are worthless and worse; we will never help you, nor be helped by you.' To the blacks we say, 'This cup of liberty, which these your old masters held to your lips, we will dash from you, and leave you to the chances of gathering the spilled and scattered contents in some vague and indefinite when, where and how.'

"If this course of discouraging and paralyzing both the white and black has any tendency to bring Louisiana to her proper fractional relations with the Union, I have so far been unable to perceive it; if, on the contrary, we recognize and sustain the new Government of Louisiana no converse of all this is made true. We encourage the hearts and nerve the arms of 12,000 to adhere to their work, and argue for it, and fight for it, and feed it, and govern it, and repair it to complete success.

"The colored man, too, in seeing all united for time, is inspired with vigilance and energy, and doing to the same end. Grant that he desires the elective franchise, will he not attain it sooner by saving the already advanced steps toward it than by moving backwards over them? Concede what the new Government of Louisiana is only to what it should be as the egg to the fowl, and we shall sooner have the fowl by hatching the egg than by smashing it.

"Again, if we reject Louisiana; we also reject our vote in favor of the proposed amendment to the National Constitution. To meet this proposition, it has been argued that no more than three-fourths of those States which have not attempted secession are nececsary to ratify an amendment.

"I do not commit myself against this further than to say that such inference would be questionable, and sure to be persistently questioned, which the ratification by three-fourths of all the States would be unquestioned and unquestionable.

"I repeat the question; can Louisiana be brought into her proper political relation with the Union by discarding her new State Government? That which has been said of Louisiana will apply to the other States, and yet so great peculiarities pertain to each State, and such important sudden changes in the same State, and withal so new and unprecedented to the whole case, that no exclusive and inflexible plan can safely be prescribed as to the details of collaterals.

"Each exclusive and inflexible plan would surely become a new entanglement. Important principles may and must be inflexible. I am considering, and shall not fail to act when satisfied that action will be proper."

The news of the surrender of Lee and his army made the peace loving masses of New Orleans shout for joy as they united their voices in praise of their Leader, the army and navy. The Star Spangled banner floated from the public buildings of the city, and from many of the private residences. The leading Union men assembled upon Lafayette Square—which was almost enveloped with the emblems of Liberty and alive with the glad strains of the National airs—to speak in accents of praise and affection of Abraham Lincoln, who had carried the Nation safely through the dark waters of the rebellion, and landed it on the peaceful shores of Liberty.

At the close of the meeting Dostie stepped upon the platform and exclaimed,—"Let the air ring with cheers for Liberty—our glorious Lincoln—the Army and Navy." The enthusiastic crowd responded, and a shout of gladness arose from that vast multitude in honor of victory. Alas! at that moment the nation's martyr was silent in death! On the morning of the 20th of April, calmness had succeeded enthusiastic joy. New Orleans was quiet and peaceful, when suddenly the cry was heard in the streets, "President Lincoln is assassinated!" "'Tis false! It is a false report of our enemies!" was heard from every quarter. The morning papers, however, announced the telegraphic dispatch with their columns clad in the emblems of mourning. Joy was turned into woe.

Gloom hung over the city like a sombre pall. The public mind seemed filled with universal sorrow. All joined in condemning the terrible crime which had clad in mourning the Nation. Public business was suspended. The flags, at half mast, were hung with black. The Public Schools were closed, and their flags hung with the emblems of mourning. The military and navy headquarters, City Hall, Custom House, the principal hotels, churches, public buildings and private residences threw out the National emblems hung with the tokens of sorrow. Ships of all nations lowered their flags, which were draped in tokens of mourning for the Nation's loss. The bells all over the city—tremulous with sadness, tolled their funeral chimes. Lincoln had been snatched from the Nation's embrace, in the hour of universal joy. He had fallen gazing at the Star of peace, that appeared in the horizon as the clouds of the rebellion rolled away.

The great national bereavement fell with crushing weight upon the hearts of those in New Orleans who had cherished the noble acts of their liberty-loving leader. Said Judge Howell at a meeting organized to take some action for expressing in a public manner the feeling of the community: "Let us turn our hearts to the Almighty; may He in His wisdom look upon us and be with us in this great calamity." Said Mr. Waples: "This sad news is so shocking to humanity, that I feel that words can avail nothing. Let us endeavor to be calm under this terrible calamity." Said Judge Durell, upon being called upon to grant the motion of adjournment of the United States District Court: "This sorrow is so great and opens a future so vast, affecting not only ourselves, but those who come after us—affecting the whole framework of our Government, that I do not find this a fit occasion to speak of it." Said Dr. Dostie: "I can never cease to mourn the great and good Lincoln. Who in the nation can fill his place? My heart is full of woe when I attempt to look into the future."

Through the influence of Dr. Dostie and his co-laborers in the School Board, the Public Schools were closed for one week, in token of respect to the memory of President Lincoln. The following published notice from the loyal Superintendent of the Public Schools, appeared in the city papers:

OFFICE OF SUPERINTENDENT OF PUBLIC SCHOOLS,
NEW ORLEANS, April 21, 1865.

The Public Schools of New Orleans were reopened almost immediately after the revival of the national authority—in the midst of civil war—under the auspices of the good President whose melancholy departure our country now laments. That this cherished institution, therefore, may render grateful tribute to the memory of the illustrious dead, and that there may be due utterance to the unfeigned sorrow of all connected therewith over the parricidal act, by which a stricken people, yet in "the valley of the shadow of death," has been deprived of its faithful friend and guide, the flags of the respective schools will be appropriately displayed, and such other expressions of mourning observed as may be practicable, for thirty days from the morning of Saturday, the 22d inst.

JOHN B. CARTER,
Superintendent of Public Schools.

Upon the announcement of the death of President Lincoln, the officers of the Army and Navy of the Gulf Department assembled at the City Hall to make arrangements to attend Christ's Church, on the following Sabbath, to pay tribute to the memory of President Lincoln.

The following is a brief account of that solemn scene, taken from the columns of the New Orleans Daily *Picayune:*

According to previous arrangement, the officers of the Army and Navy stationed in this Department attended Christ Church on Sunday morning, in full uniform.

Gathering at the City Hall at half-past ten, they proceeded in a body to the Church, headed by General Banks and Admiral Thatcher. The display as they entered the sacred edifice and passed up the broad aisle to their seats, filling the entire central part of the building, was touching and imposing—the organ meanwhile giving forth a soft and solemn dirge.

The Church is superbly draped in mourning. The altar table is covered with black cloth, and behind it is a high screen, formed of heavy folds of black drapery, bordered at the top with white lace festoons. The desk and pulpit are fully shrouded in black, and the chancel rails are very tastefully hung with the same, and fringed with white. The marble font, which, on the previous Sunday (Easter), we saw so beautiful in its sumptuous array of spring flowers, is now hung with emblems of mourning. The columns are wreathed with festoons of black and white crape and lace, and the porch is literally canopied with flags. Over the main entrance to the Church there is a handsome display of appropriate mourning.

The services of the day were arranged to suit the solemn occasion. Of course, the Collect, Epistle and Gospel for Sunday after Easter, were read. But in saying the Morning Prayer, Rev. Mr. Chubbuck and his assistant Presbyter made some variations from the usual order. The first lesson was that touching portion of the first chapter of II Samuel, in which David lamented the death of Saul and Jonathan: "The beauty of Israel is slain upon his high places; how are the mighty fallen! Tell it not in Gath, publish it not in the streets of Askelon! How are the mighty fallen in the midst of the battle, and the weapons of war perished!" etc. The second lesson was that immortal argument of St. Paul to the Corinthians (1st Cor. XV) in support of the doctrine of the resurrection from the dead.

The Psalms selected, instead of those for the day, were the 31st, "In Thee, Lord, have I put my trust," and the 13th, "Out of the deep have I called unto Thee." The Prayers "For a sick person," and "For a person in affliction," the first being specially used with reference to the Secretary of State, and the last to the people of the United States and the family of the late President, were said in the proper place. The introductory sentences before the Exhortation, were those with which the burial service commences: "I am the resurrection and the life," etc.

The music was very touchingly performed by a well-selected choir. Previous to the commencement of Morning Prayer, that beautiful air of Paesiello, "Come ye disconsolate," was beautifully sung. Instead of the "Venite," the anthem from the 39th and 90th Psalms, from the burial service, "Lord, let me know my end," was sung to a plain chant with great expression. The canticle, "O all ye works of the Lord!" The Song of the Three Holy Children, which they sang as they walked in the midst of the fire, was chanted in the place of the "Te Deum," and the "Benedictus," instead of the "Jubilate." The introit was from the 86th Psalm, "Bow down thine ear, O Lord, and hear me," to which was finely adapted the beautiful music of the prayer in "Moise." The hymn was the 160th, "When gathering clouds around I view."

An address from the Rev. S. C. Thrall was then delivered, appreciated as expressed by the following letter:

NEW ORLEANS, April 27, 1865.

To the Officers of the Army and Navy in New Orleans:

Your Committee believing that the Address delivered at Christ Church, by the Rev. S. C. Thrall, D. D., on Sunday, the 23d instant, in memorial of the tragic death of your late Commander-in-Chief, the President of the United States, contains a truthful analysis of his character, and pays a just tribute to the admirable traits of his head and heart; and that you would desire to preserve a record in some permanent form, of the action you took in honor of his memory; and in order that your brother officers, who were unable to participate in the solemnities of the occasion, may in some measure enjoy the same pleasure in reading that you did in hearing the Address, have, at the suggestion of the present, and also of the former Commanding General of the Department of the Gulf, obtained a copy for publication as here printed.

The notice of the service taken from the *Picayune*, and the correspondence between your Committee and the Rev. Dr. Thrall, published with the Address, explains their action, and the deep interest manifested by the Rector, Wardens, Vestry, and Members of Christ Church, in an event that has drowned a nation and the whole world in tears—clad your country in the habiliments of sorrow. and your hearts in mourning.

E. B. BROWN, Brig.-Gen. Vols.
E. G. BECKWITH, Col. U. S. Army.
G. F. EMMONS, Capt. U. S. Navy.

CHAPTER XIX.

PUBLIC CONFIDENCE IN ANDREW JOHNSON.

"Who in the nation can fill the place of Abraham Lincoln?" was the great question of loyal people after the first shock of bereavement, feeling that no one, in truth, could fittingly succeed to a place consecrated by the Great Emancipator to loyalty and liberty.

Andrew Johnson was made President of the United States by the power of Conspiracy and Assassination. The people submitted to that decree and with sad, anxious hearts, the loyal masses endeavored to support his administration. Many with faith and hope looked to him as a guide and protector—as the Chief Executive of a Republic whose duty it was to make treason odious, and to frown upon rebellion and tyranny. The record of Andrew Johnson's official acts under the administration of Lincoln were those of a patriot. His record during the rebellion under the eye of the Just President was such as to draw the hearts of the loyal people strongly to him, who doubted not that his future course would harmonize with the beneficent policy of his Predecessor. With confidence in the administration of Andrew Johnson, the loyal masses of New Orleans met in Lafayette Square, August 17th, 1865, to give expression to their trust in the Chief Magistrate.

Dostie was one of the prime movers in organizing that meeting. He wrote to many of the prominent Union men of the city, urging them to speak in favor of Johnson upon the occasion. The meeting was called to order by A. C. Hills, Esq., who nominated Judge Durell for President of the meeting. Among the vice-presidents chosen were Dr. A. P. Dostie, B. R. Plumley, E. Heath, J. Graham, M. F. Bonzano, Wm. H. Hire, Rev. J. W. Horton, Alfred Shaw, H. C. Wamoth, Judge Heistend, Dr. E. Goldman, Ex-Gov. Hahn, John Henderson, and S. S. Fish. The following were some of the resolutions adopted at that meeting:

"*Resolved*, That the unity of this country is indispensable to the perpetuation of a truly republican government; that the freedom for which our forefathers fought can only be secured to us by a steadfast adherence to the great principles of liberty, equality and fraternity;

"*Resolved*, That to those who have promptly, honestly and in good faith, availed themselves of the Proclamation of Amnesty of President Lincoln, and who have by their countenance and support, aided the military authorities of the United States in their efforts to re-establish republican institutions in the insurrectionary States are entitled to the sympathy and regard of all good citizens, and to a full restitution of all political rights at as early a day as may be practicable.

"*Resolved*, That in our opinion, no man who has ever held any office of trust or emolument—civil, naval or military—under the rebel authorities, should be permitted to hold office under the United States Government.

"*Resolved*, That in re-establishing civil Government in the Southern States, our only safety consists in making all loyal men equal before the law; and that any government established that does not realize this principle, is neither just nor equitable, and consequently not a republican Government.

"*Resolved*, That while the loyal men of Louisiana were appalled at the brutal assassination, and sincerely mourn the loss of the wise, humane and noble President, Abraham Lincoln, they hereby express their confidence in the patriotism, ability and discretion of Andrew Johnson, President of the United States. That his long public career, unblemished by any stain of disloyalty, great in noble and successful devotion to the people's interests, especially marked by his earnest opposition to treason, has given him the right to our warmest admiration and heartiest support; that we pledge to him our constant aid in the work of re-establishing good Government and loyalty in the Southern States.

"*Resolved*, That J. Madison Wells, acting Governor of the State, who received the united vote of the Free State Party, has proved false to the high trust reposed in him, in appointing to office men who signed the ordinance of secession, and registered enemies to the United States Government; that his course as Governor has been reactionary, calculated to work injury to the Union cause, and that he is no longer entitled to our confidence."

Judge Durell addressed the meeting as follows:

"*Fellow-Citizens*—I thank you for the great honor this evening conferred on me. No greater occasion than this has offered itself during the past four years of battle than that which has called us together. When our great Republic has asserted its majesty and its power, beating down all the armies marshaled against it, and standing now in the morning of a new administration, called without respect to local divisions, but as equal lovers of our great country; called upon under such circumstances to come together and pledge our mutual faith—our mutual strength to the assertion of the unity of our country. This meeting is called to pledge to our nation at home and to the nations abroad our fixed de terminate will—fixed in the present as in the past—fixed in the future as in the present, to support the liberties and Government which our forefathers handed down to us.

"Gentlemen, I will perform the duties of this evening with pleasure. [Applause.]

Mr. Hills then read the following letters:

"New Orleans, May 17, 1865.

"Hon. A. P. Dostie:

"*Dear Sir*—I regret that prior engagements, which cannot be cancelled, will prevent me from complying with your kind invitation to address the meeting to be held this evening, by the friends of President Johnson, and of 'loyalty to national freedom and national Union.' It would afford me great pleasure to mingle with, and address the citizens whose names are signed to the call; for among them I recognize many who, during the reign of treason in this city, faithfully and wisely, though unostentatiously, adhered to the Union cause. Some participated with myself in the grand 'Union Rally,' on the same spot, on the 8th of May, 1860, when secessionism first reared its head in this city. The spirit of rebellion having been overcome by the courage and self-sacrificing efforts of the Union armies, it is right that the loyal people should meet and take counsel as to the principles to guide them in the future.

"The secessionists of Louisiana, the leaders who influenced and deluded the masses, the men who paraded our streets with blue cockades, and sneeringly denounced us as base 'submissionists,' who compelled Unionists like yourself to leave their homes, and who by fraud wedded the administration of our State Government to the cause of treason, aud thus sought to rob us of our proud nationality—have a terrible responsibility resting upon them. Many are now returning. Some have profited by their folly and their crime, and ask us to forget and forgive the past. Let our conduct towards them be marked by a calm forbearance, worthy of our triumph.

"The language of Andrew Johnson, addressed to the people of Tennessee, on the adoption of the Free State Constitution is equally and happily applicable to the condition of Louisiana.

"'The foundations of society, under the change in the Constitution, are in harmony with the principles of free government and the National Union; and if the people are true to themselves, true to the State, and loyal to the Federal Government, they will rapidly overcome the calamities of the war, and raise the State to a power and grandeur not heretofore even anticipated. Many of its vast resources lie undiscovered, and it requires intelligent enterprise and free labor alone, to develop them, and clothe the State with a richness and beauty, surpassed by none of her sisters.'

"Respectfully yours,

MICHAEL HAHN."

"NEW ORLEANS, May 16, 1865.

"Dr. A. P. Dostie:

"*Dear Sir*,—Your compliment to me is very gratifying. I have the highest respect for President Johnson. The American people will soon know how to appreciate his elevated qualities as a patriot and statesman.

"I would willingly take part in the demonstration to-morrow evening in the mode you suggest, but prefer on this occasion to take part as a spectator and listener. May all success attend you.

"Respectfully, J. S. WHITAKER."

"NEW ORLEANS, May 16, 1865.

"A. P. Dostie, Esq., Chairman, etc.:

"I aided the nomination of Andrew Johnson, and am to-day an ardent supporter of him. I shall be glad to do all that lies in my power at the meeting to-morrow night.

"Very respectfully yours,
J. P. SULLIVAN."

NEW ORLEANS, May 16, 1865.

Dr. A. P. Dostie, Committee of Invivation, etc.:

SIR: I have the honor to acknowledge and thank you for an invitation to address the meeting to-morrow night, in Lafayette Square, in support of our honored President, Andrew Johnson, and his Administration. I shall rejoice to add my little aid to the cause of Free Stateism and Johnsonian principles on that occasion.

Very truly yours,
RUFUS WAPLES.

NEW ORLEANS, May 15, 1865.

Hon. A. P. Dostie, Chairman, etc.:

DEAR SIR: Your note of this date, inviting me to be present and address a meeting of the friends of the United States Government who desire to sustain President Johnson, to be held on the 17th inst., on Lafayette Square, has just come to hand.

I had intended to be present as a citizen to hear what

might be said on the occasion, and had not thought of taking any part in the meeting. I prefer not to speak, yet, if desired, will do so.

Very respectfully,

L. A. SHELDON.

Many other letters were read from prominent Union men in New Orleans expressive of confidence in Andrew Johnson. Addresses were delivered on that occasion by Col. Thorpe, Judge Wamoth, Rev. Dr. Perne, Judge Heistend, and Dr. Dostie.

In the narration of these events, it will be necessary to go back to the 5th of March, 1865, when J. M. Wells was inaugurated Governor of Louisiana. At that time he was supposed to be in sympathy with loyal men and an enemy to the rebellion. In his first official acts he proved his opposition to the Unionists, who had elected him to office. Among his first recommendations was that of Dr. Kennedy to the office of Mayor of New Orleans. Dr. Kennedy was a strong advocate of the rebellion, a man who favored oppression, who believed in elevating the aristocracy and degrading the laboring classes. One of his first acts as Mayor was the issuing an order decreasing the wages of the city laborers, who were already suffering on account of their scant means of support. A call was made to the friends of the sufferers to assemble on Lafayette Square, for the purpose of denouncing the proceedings of the Mayor. At the hour appointed for the meeting thousands were seen going in the direction of the Public Square. Lafayette Square in New Orleans is considered as the property of the public. On the night of the laboring class rights meeting the anti-republican Mayor Kennedy ordered its gates locked. The meeting was held in the street, in front of the City Hall. The annexed resolutions were read and unanimously adopted:

Whereas, The present improvised and irregular Government has attempted to overrule the Constitution of the State by repealing the labor ordinance, thus removing one of the supports and guarantees due to labor.

Resolved, That this assembly disapproves and condemns this usurpation of power on the part of said city authorities.

Resolved, That said proceedings are without any justification or excuse, and utterly in violation of the fundamental law.

Resolved, That the administration of Acting Mayor Kennedy is a failure, and we call upon that incompetent functionary to resign.

Resolved, That we recommend like proceeding to Glendy Burke, Dr. Edward Ames, of the Bureau of Streets and Landings, and all others concerned in the movement against the interests of labor.

Resolved, That the city Government is now in the hands of Copperheads and notorious sympathizers with the accursed rebellion, which, thank God, our brave brothers have so well nigh crushed and destroyed; and that to the loyal citizen they are intolerable, and should be removed; that loyal and trusty citizens may be called to fill their places.

Among the speakers at that meeting was the Hon. John Henderson, a prominent opponent of slavery in the Louisiana Convention of 1864. From the New Orleans *True Delta* we extract the following in relation to the meeting:

"Mr. Henderson, in a very energetic speech, denounced the conduct and policy of Hugh Kennedy, the Mayor, and depicted him as an enemy to the free State of Louisiana, and inquired who appointed him. Mr. Henderson argued that the Government, by sending General Banks to this State, had virtually recognized us as a free State, but Governor Wells in his appoinements had shown himself unfaithful to the trust confided to him by the people, who believed him to be a good Union man when he came in the guise of a refugee. Mr. Henderson called on the people to seek proper redress."

Dr. Dostie was urged to address the assembly. He said he would only take a retrospective view of affairs. His remarks condemned the conduct of Governor Wells, and the proceedings of the Mayor as outrageous. He advocated law and order, but called on the people to seek redress.

He said the appointment of Mayor Kennedy was due to Governor Wells, whom he characterized as the John Tyler of the Free State party, who had sold out and turned over the party and its principles into the hands of the Copperheads. He said it was Governor Wells who had attempted to remove the Terrebonne officials, and appointed such men as Verret and McColium, signers of the infamous ordinance of secession. He proposed that the assembly, when it should adjourn, should proceed to the residence of Major-General Banks, and pay their respects as laboring men to the man who had risen from humble origin (having been a laboring man) to the high position he now enjoyed as a soldier and statesman, in command of the most important military Department, that of the Gulf."

There were men who had held human beings in bondage, who at the commencement of the slaveholder's rebellion gladly gave up their slaves and entered heart and soul into the great movement destined to revolutionize the Slave States. Such took no backward steps, and laid no impediments in the way of liberty. A policy based upon hypocrisy has ever been used by the despotic slaveholder to commit crimes of the darkest hue. It was that policy that led Governor Wells to conceal his true motives, until he could grasp the reins of power. Then, unmasked, he stepped upon the political arena to strike the blows of a despot. At first he timidly vascillated before the just policy of Lincoln, and trod lightly and stealthily upon the platform, which he feared might be resting upon a volcano of wrath. But over the grave of Lincoln he planted himself upon the rock which Andrew Johnson erected for despots and became his willing accomplice.

In September, 1864, General Banks was ordered North, and did not return until April, 1865, to resume command of the Gulf Department. Upon his return the few weeks permitted him to act in favor of loyalty were spent in bold decisive action. The following was one of his first orders:—

"DEPARTMENT OF THE GULF,
NEW ORLEANS, May 5th, 1865.

"*Special Orders, No.* 119.]

[EXTRACT.]

* * * * * * *

"5. Col. Samuel M. Quincy, 73d U. S. Colored Infantry, is relieved from his present duties, and is hereby assigned to the duty of Acting Mayor of the city of New Orleans.

"Upon the receipt of this order, he will proceed to the City Hall, and assume the duties of that office. The present Acting Mayor is directed to surrender to him all the papers connected with that office.

* * * * * * *

"By command of Major General Banks.

"J. C. STONE,
Capt. and Asst. Adjt. Gen.

Finding General Banks an impediment to his plans, Governor Wells hastened to Washington to unbosom his favorite theories to his friend Andrew Johnson, President of the United States.

At this crisis of political affairs in Louisiana, the friends of liberty looked to President Johnson as their future deliverer from rebel intrigue.

In a paper edited by colored men in New Orleans, at that time, we find the following article, expressive of that confidence:

"The removal of Hugh Kennedy from the office of Mayor and the appointment of Colonel S. M. Quincy to that place, has been the event of the week of most interest to our people. The appointment of Dr. Kennedy to the Mayoralty by the late General Hurlbut, through our departed Governor Wells, was the beginning of a new rule of Copperheads and rebels, out of which, if it were possible, slavery would be re-established, and all the old wrongs of the slavocracy would be again fastened upon us. Slavery never had a stronger advocate than Dr. Kennedy, nor a more practical supporter than Gov. Wells, who, owning three hundred of us in bondage, could not be expected to repent in a day, as indeed he did not; for instead of emancipating his slaves he had them brought near New Orleans, where he helped to support them, while he made political capital with the Radicals out of this professed humanity.

"Governor Wells was loud in his professions of radical politics, which secured for him the nomination and election for Lieutenant Governor. How much he must be wedded to the spirit, if not to the fact of the 'old evil,' may be known by his removal of Union Free State men, and his appointment of rebel sympathizers and registered enemies to their places, at the very time when our new President, the brave and loyal Andy Johnson, the liberator of our race in Tennessee, was speaking every day to delegations against just such men and such policy as our Governor was advancing.

"We cannot help being thankful to God, who all through this revolution for our freedom has sent us deliverance at the right time, that on this occasion the strong hand of our friend, Major General Banks, was present to protect us from the new rule of rebels and copperheads. Defeated here, Governor Wells and Dr. Kennedy, with a few of their friends have gone to Washington, to lay the last hope and the last prayer of the returning rebels, and the anxious Copperheads of Louisiana, at the feet of the heroic President Johnson, who, all his life, has been fighting to overthrow just such men as now ask him to restore them to power.

"May they have a good time in learning from our noble President that the scepter has departed from their hands, because they held it for evil, and henceforth there is for them only repentance and quiet submission to the true people whom the God of Freedom has appointed to rule."

Soon after the arrival of Governor Wells in Washington, the annexed order was sent to the excited city of New Orleans, from near the Executive Mansion:

WASHINGTON, D. C., May 21, 1865.

To J. S. Walton, Treasurer, City of New Orleans:

SIR: I hereby notify you as Treasurer of the city of New Orleans, not to pay at the peril of your securities any warrant drawn upon you for pay of individuals, material for public uses or other purposes whatsoever that may have been made or authorized by Col. S. M. Quincy, a colonel of a colored regiment of United States volunteer troops, or any other person acting or pretending to act under the appointment of Major-General Banks, Commanding General Department of the Gulf, as said General Banks acted contrary to law, and his proceedings are disapproved by the President of the United States, in suspending the civil authorities of the city of New Orleans and overthrowing the laws and ordinances instituted for its good government.

I have the honor to be, sir,

Your obedient servant,

(Signed) J. MADISON WELLS,

Governor.

To a greater length could testimony be extended, but enough has been written to show that never was reposed confidence more betrayed than the nation's trust in the successor of Abraham Lincoln.

CHAPTER XX.

GENERAL BANKS DISPLACED BY GENERAL CANBY.

June 4th, 1865, General Banks was removed from the Gulf Department and General Canby resumed command of the same. The acts of a Nero never created a greater consternation among his subjects than did the following order in the loyal ranks of New Orleans, who saw in it only the hand of Governor Wells and his advisers, Hugh Kennedy and Glendy Burke:

HEADQUARTERS DEPARTMENT OF THE GULF,
NEW ORLEANS, La., June 8, 1865.

Special Orders, No. 152.

[Extract.]

* * * * * * * * * *

17. Mr. Hugh Kennedy is appointed Acting Mayor of the city of New Orleans.

Col. Samuel M. Quincy, 73d U. S. Colored Infantry, is relieved from duty as Acting Mayor, and will rejoin his regiment. He will turn over to Mr. G. Burke, who is authorized to act until the arrival of the Acting Mayor, the duties of the office in which he is now acting.

By order of Major-General E. R. S. Canby,

C. H. DYER,
Capt. and Asst.-Adj.-Gen.

In league with the Chief Magistrate, with an armed police force at his command, and with the Nero qualifications of Glendy Burke to lead in municipal affairs until the arrival of "Lord" Hugh Kennedy, Governor Wells was prepared to instigate the hidden policy of the ruler who swayed his iron scepter over the poor oppressed people from the throne he had erected to the cause of the rebellion in the Capital of our Republic.

Loyalty in New Orleans was made odious; liberty was disgraced, and Union leaders and reformers were marked for rebel vengeance. Oppression and indignity was the fate of all who dared to resist the unjust decree of despots and tyrants.

To the proud spirit, patriotic heart, and iron will of Dostie this despotism was keen agony. Said a friend: "I went to Dostie's office to consult with him upon the strange state of affairs in the city. I found him in an agitated state of mind. I suggested 'that had Hahn remained Governor, things might have been differently conducted, and reflected upon Hahn's statesmanship in resigning his office. In his decided manner he remarked, 'Governor Hahn is no prophet; when he resigned his office as Governor, he could not foresee the murder of Lincoln. He acted, as he thought, in favor of the interests of his State, expecting to labor in the United States Senate for Louisiana. President Johnson is no traitor, but he listens to the advice of corrupt men who throng the Executive Mansion. The acts and sayings of Johnson have been my study too long to doubt his honesty. When he appreciates the condition of Union men in Louisiana our rights will be protected.'"

The finger of destiny plainly pointed to Dostie as the victim to be sacrificed to traitor hate and tyranny. His public acts and progressive movements made him a conspicuous mark for those who viewed with contempt his labors for liberty and exertions to protect the down trodden and the laboring classes. A true reformer, he bore a name worthy to be placed by the side of a Wilberforce, Lovejoy, Cobden or a Bright. His noble standard of radical Unionism upon which not a blot had been discovered was in direct antagonism to the prejudices of the aristocrats and rebels by whom he was surrounded. Jealous of the growing popularity and influence of Dostie, his enemies had cherished their wrath to pour it upon the head of their victim. "The proud spirit of Dostie shall be crushed," said a coalition who had conspired to plot his distruction. Governor Wells was the leader of that faction which had determined upon the downfall and death of the patriotic Dostie. The first blow was struck on the 13th of June, 1865. It was the seizure of the Auditor's office. As one of the many high-handed acts of despotism connected with the establishment of the iron rule of the Slave power and thuggery in New Orleans during the administration of Johnson, we present the following account of the seizure of the Auditor's office from the *True Delta* of June 14:

"Few of our citizens are now unaware that the office of Dr. A. P. Dostie, State Auditor, was yesterday entered by a body of the city police, and the Auditor forcibly and summarily expelled. We give below a plain, simple statement of the facts in the case, without comment of any kind:

"Between 11 and 12 o'clock, several policemen, headed by the Acting Chief of Police, Mr. John Burke, and accompanied by Mr. Julian Neville, entered the Auditor's office. Approaching Dr. Dostie, Mr. Neville presented a paper, after glancing over which the Auditor said, 'I shall probably be prepared to comply with this to-morrow morning.'

"Upon the Doctor refusing positively to vacate immediately, Mr. Neville turned to Lieut. Burke, and said: 'I now turn this over to your hands,' and left the place. Mr. Burke then informed Dr. Dostie that he was 'in charge of the office;' to which the latter replied that 'this is a State office, and I am a State officer, and it will require force to dispossess me.' Mr. Burke replied: 'My orders are to take possession, and I shall certainly do so.' Dr. Dostie asked if he had written orders. Mr. Burke said he had. Dr. Dostie asked to see them, and they were shown him. He then asked for a copy, but Mr. Burke replied: 'I have no orders to let a copy be taken.'

"For a moment Dr. Dostie went to his private room, and returning, instructed Mr. Kruse—one of his clerks, to take charge of his private papers. He then again protested against the proceedings, and said he would be expelled only by force. In a loud tone of voice he then exclaimed, turning toward the latter gentleman, who was in the office on business: 'If I must go, I wish first to say a few words in presence of Mr. Kruse and Mr. Blake, ——'

"Here he was interrupted by Mr. Burke, who addressed one of his subordinates, as follows: 'Bhome, put the Doctor out!' The policeman advanced and seized Dr. Dostie by the shoulders, with the remark: 'I can handle you like a book.' The Doctor, seeing further resistance useless, thereupon left the office.

"The police remained in possesion of the office, retaining the private letters and papers of the Auditor and his clerks, and even some of Dr. Dostie's wearing apparel. Lieutenant Burke went in search of Mr. Neville, to whom he gave the keys, with the exception of that belonging to the safe, which he retains, and which he will refuse to give up. The Doctor locked the safe while the officers were in the outer office.

"Dr. Dostie received no notification of his expulsion prior to the arrival of the police. The following is the authority upon which Lieutenant Burke acted:

"MAYORALTY OF NEW ORLEANS,
June 13, 1865.

"*Lieut. J. Burke, First District Police:*

"*Sir*—You will proceed immediately to the office of Auditor of Public Accounts, now in the possession of Mr. A. P. Dostie; and declared vacant by His Excellency, Governor Wells.

"You will take possession of the office and the records, and deliver the same at once to Julian Neville, Esq., appointed by the Governor, Auditor *pro tempore.*

"You will see that Mr. Neville, is placed in secure possession of the office.

"If physical force is needed, you will use it, and you will commit to prison any individual or party who interferes in any degree, in the execution of this order.

"(Signed.) G. BURKE,
Acting Mayor.

"After executing the above, Lieutenant Burke made the following report:

"OFFICE OF THE CHIEF OF POLICE,
NEW ORLEANS, June 13, 1865.

"*Hon. Glendy Burke, Acting Mayor:*

"*Sir*—I have the honor to report that in obedience to your order of this date I proceeded, in company with Julian Neville, Esq., to the office of the Auditor of Public Accounts.

"Mr. Dostie positively refused to vacate the office,

whereupon I called a policeman to eject him in as gentle a manner as the circumstances of the case admitted of.

"I securely closed the doors, delivered the keys to Mr. Neville, and placed a guard of policemen on the office, with instructions that none but Mr. Neville or his deputies should have access thereto.

"Very respectfully, your obedient servant,

(Signed) J. BURKE,
Lieut. and Acting Chief of Police.

"The following is the order of the Governor referred to by Mayor Burke:

[BY THE GOVERNOR.]

STATE OF LOUISIANA,
EXECUTIVE DEPARTMENT,
"NEW ORLEANS, June 13, 1865.

Whereas, The General Assembly of the State of Louisiana, at its last session, did adopt a joint resolution in the words following to wit:

[No. 38.]

Joint Resolution, Requesting the Governor of the State to see that all laws are enforced in the case of all persons holding civil offices under the State who are required to furnish bonds for the performance of their official duties.

Whereas, Persons are holding and exercising the duties of civil offices in the State who have not furnished bonds as required by law.

Resolved by the Senate and Houes of Representatives, in General Assembly Convened, That the Governor of the State be and is hereby requested to take immediate measures to compel all such persons to furnish bonds according to law, and in default thereof to remove such persons from office.

Resolved further, That where bonds have been given, subject to the approval of the Governor of the State, he be and is hereby requested to investigate the solvency of all such bonds, and if he shall deem the bond or bonds insufficient, to require new bonds to be furnished satisfactory to him.

(Signed) SIMEON BELDEN,
Speaker of the House of Representatives.

(Signed) LOUIS GASTINEL,
Ex-Officio Lieutenant Governor and President of the Senate.

Approved March 29, 1865.

(Signed) J. MADISON WELLS,
Governor of the State of Louisiana.

A true copy:

S. WROTNOWSKI,
Secretary of State.

And Whereas, Acting in pursuance of the special authority conferred on me therein, as well as by my constitutional obligations to see the laws enforced, I deem it my duty to address the said A. P. Dostie, Auditor of Public Accounts, by letter, requiring him to furnish a new and sufficient bond, as will appear by copy herewith, viz:

STATE OF LOUISIANA, EXECUTIVE DEPARTMENT,
NEW ORLEANS, April 15, 1865.

A. P. Dostie, Esq., Auditor of Public Accounts:

"Under authority of joint resolution of the General Assembly, (copy of which is herewith annexed,) and regarding your bond on file in the Secretary of State's office as insufficient, not one of the sureties being assessed for real estate, you are hereby notified that you are required to furnish a new bond, 'with not less than five good and sufficient securities,' satisfactory to me, within thirty days from the date hereof.

J. MADISON WELLS,
Governor of Louisiana.

And, whereas, The said A. P. Dostie has failed to furnish the required official bond within the time prescribed by law, and the consequence is that the State is without adequate security for protection against any illegal acts that may be committed by him:

And, whereas, The second section of the act of 1855, entitled "An act to regulate the office of Auditor of Public Accounts, provides "that, should he [the Auditor] fail to give such bond and security within the time required, the office shall be considered vacant, and the Governor shall immediately order a new election;"

Now, therefore, in view of the foregoing premises, I, J. Madison Wells, Governor of the State of Louisiana, do hereby declare the office of Auditor of Public Accounts to be vacant, and by virtue of the 26th section of the act of 1855, before quoted, I do hereby appoint Julian Neville, Auditor of Public Accounts, to fulfill all the duties and enjoy the emoluments of said office, as provided by law, until after an election shall have been held throughout the State to fill the vacancy, and the Auditor so elected be duly commissioned and qualified according to law.

Given under my hand at the city of New Orleans, this 13th day of June, A. D., 1865, and of the year of the Independence of the United States the eighty-ninth.

J. MADISON WELLS,
Governor of Louisiana.

The following letter from Dostie gives the true explanation of the non-renewal of bond, showing the falsity of the charge:

NEW ORLEANS, June 13, 1865.

"*To the Public.*—I was to-day waited upon by Julian Neville, Esq., accompanied by the Acting Chief of Police, Mr. Burke, and two other police officers. The former presented to me an order, issued by Acting Governor Wells, requiring me to turn over the archives of my office to him as Auditor *pro tem.* Refusing to obey the illegal mandate, I was seized hold of by Acting Chief Burke and one of the policemen, and taken from the room by force. Returning subsequently, I found the office closed and in charge of the police. The ground alleged by the Acting Governor was the non-renewal of my bond, which was sometime ago demanded of me on the ground that my securities were not assessed for real estate.

"After the demand was made, Acting Governor Wells, unexpectedly to me, left the State, and did not return again within the thirty days allowed me. Otherwise I should have responded to him, as advised by legal counsel, arguing that the demand was illegal, good and solvent security only being required by law; or I would, if insisted upon, have complied with the demand, illegal as it was, either of which I was fully prepared to do. My bonds had not been objected to on any other ground. The securities were perhaps not assessed for real estate within the Parish of Orleans, but they were fully competent and possessed of ample means to secure the $10,000, or several times that sum, if necessary. I was elected by the people, and had within thirty days after being notified of my election duly given bonds, which were approved according to law. No man can say the securities were not good, solvent and sufficient, or that they are less so now than they were then.

"Be that as it may, I was yesterday violently ejected without other calling of my attention to the subject, or preliminary warning or notice than the appearance of the policemen with the order alluded to.

"The proclamation with the reasons assigned, was published at a subsequent hour in the Picayune, and was only seen or known by myself or the public after these violent proceedings had taken place.

"When securities to bonds are required to be freeholders

the bond expressly so states. Such is the case with the Treasurer's bond. But there is no such requirement of law in the case of the Auditor. The joint resolution passed by the late Legislature required the Governor to investigate the "solvency of bonds." He never objected to my bonds, nor called my attention to it for any want of "solvency" which would have given a color of law to his original demand, but only for the securities not 'being assessed for real estate,' which is no legal ground whatever.

"I am a civil officer, a co-ordinate member of the Executive Department of the State, and Acting Governor Wells is also a civil officer. There was a way of testing my right to the office by law, through the agency of courts of justice. Every respectable lawyer knows the means and the way. If civil law is to reign in our State, instead of usurpation, that means should have been pursued to test the question. The use of the City Police to obtain violent possession of the office was not a legal means, but an outrage against the law.

"Mr Julian Neville was a candidate against me for the office of State Auditor. I was elected by a majority, I think, of nearly three to one. He was not a candidate on either of the tickets upon which Acting Governor Wells ran, but against them; and it is saying nothing in disparagement of Mr. Neville, to characterize his appointment as a pure John Tylerism on the part of the Acting Executive.

"I make no vauntings of what I shall do, as time has not been afforded me for legal consultation or advice under the circumstances. But I make this early statement of facts to a public who know me well, and will judge between me, a poor man, possessed of no means but my legal rights as a citizen and an officer, on the one hand, and the great defaulter of Rapides, whose name has stood on the Auditor's reports of the State for more than twenty years for $12,678.67, with accumulated interests, now amounting to $28,209.95 on the other. He has lately declared himself, on several occasions, to be worth his hundreds of thousands. With his great Red river operations on the cotton market, and the means realized by his grand tax-sale proceedings, he may succeed in crushing me, so far as success in this usurpation against me is concerned. But while my voice or my life do not fail me I shall not cease to vindicate my manhood or my rights as a citizen and a freeman.

A. P. Dostie,
State Auditor.

It was the illegal despotic manner in which Dr. Dostie was removed from his office that made the hand of the tyrant visible, marking him the despot, aside from a desire to show his power. Governor Wells, in this unjust act, was influenced by personal animosity, and stooped from his high position to low acts of revenge. Dostie had pointed out his traitorous course, and exposed his dishonesty to the world. Not with a spirit of vindictiveness but with his characteristic fearlessness and contempt for treason and dishonesty. Governor Wells had betrayed the Union party, and had been proved a defaulter. The following letter was probably one of the causes of the removal of the Auditor of State by the Governor:

AUDITOR'S OFFICE, STATE OF LOUISIANA,
New Orleans, May 18, 1865.

Hon. Chas. Leaumont, Judge of the Fifth District Court, New Orleans.

"*Dear Sir:* I beg leave to call your attention to section 1st, page 181, of the Revised Statutes of the State, which provide that the Judges of the District Courts shall require the District Attorneys to proceed by rule for the removal from office after ten days notice of any person holding office who shall at any time have been a defaulter to the State.

"His Excellency, J. Madison Wells, acting Governor of Louisiana, became a defaulter to the State in 1840, in the sum of $12,680—as will be seen by the reports of the Auditor of Public Accounts for succeeding years, a proof of which defalcation will be furnished on the day of trial of the rule. Article 35 of the present Constitution, the same as Article 28 of Constitution of 1852 and Article 30 of the Constitution of 1845, says as follows: 'No person who at any time may have been a collector of taxes, whether State, parish, or municipal, or who may have been otherwise entrusted with public money, shall be eligible to the General Assembly, or to any office of profit or trust under the State Government, until he shall have obtained a discharge for the amount of such collections, and for all public moneys with which he may have been entrusted.'

"Your immediate attention to this important question is earnestly solicited.

"Very respectfully, yours

(Signed.) "A. P. DOSTIE, Auditor."

The personal indignities offered to the Auditor of State through the scurrilous remarks of the city press in sympathy with the Governor and his friends; the criticisms upon his wardrobe and private letters, which were dragged through the streets of New Orleans by the tools of the Chivalry of that city—the half column devoted to remarks upon his razor and toothbrush—the allusion made to his once having been a barber and a dentist, with the suggestion that he had better return to "his plebian accomplishments" would have been somewhat annoying to a mind less philosophical than that of Dostie's.

Firmly defending his rights, until overpowered by his enemies, he yielded to despotic power, and hopefully looked to future events for the triumph of justice.

On the 17th of June a mass-meeting was called, and the citizens of New Orleans assembled on Lafayette Square for the purpose of honoring Governor Wells, and upholding his administration. The following letter from one of the vice-Presidents of that meeting is in harmony with the principles there expressed:

NEW ORLEANS, June 18, 1865.

Hon. A. P. Field, Chairman:

" *Sir*—I have the pleasure to acknowledge the receipt of your note, appointing me one of the Vice-Presidents at the Mass Meeting to-morrow evening, to receive our Governor. Reluctant as I am to appear amidst the hurly-burly of politics, I thank you for this honor and accept it. The man and the occasion demand an expression of opinion from the Conservatives of this beautiful State:

"Where grows the orange, and pomegranate, and fairest of fruit,
And the song of the nightingale never is mute."

"We have beheld the pitiful spectacle of the successor of Chief Justice Marshall soiling his ermine by making electioneering speeches—prostituting his almost sacred office as a political huckster—pandering to the most depraved appetites to effect his unholy ambition; placing the ignorant horde on a level with the intelligent. You, sir, as a former Secretary of State of Illinois, know what the poor African suffered, until very recently, there. That, so far from granting him the privileges of *a voter*, he was sold to the highest bidder. In New York, it requires double taxes and twice the time of residence, to enable the colored man to vote; yet these radicals would fain make voters of millions of men who could not read their ballot! But such are the debris of civil war. Addison truthfully puts into the mouth of Cato, and we are but repeating the history of all Republics:

"When the kettle of sedition boils,
The scum arises to the top."

"Very respectfully, yours, &c.,
"S. F. GLENN."

The following we quote from the address of Governor Wells, delivered on that occasion:

"Not being myself a candidate for re-election to Gubernatorial honors, I hope I shall be acquitted of any attempt to favor party politics for political purposes. In regard to National affairs I have but little to say. The war that has but recently so happily ended, has left us almost without resources and without government, and in our attempt to resume our relations with the General Government, we will have many obstacles to meet. A party unscrupulous and exacting will insist upon our utter humiliation as a means by which we may learn to love our country better, and as the ultimatum for our return to the folds of the Union, but happily for us this party has lost much of its prestige.

"It must be perceptible to every one, who is at all consistent with the political history of this country, that the Radical Abolition party is broken up, disorganized, and demoralized, despite their apparent success during the present war.

"Their official corruption, unequaled by any party which has ever preceded or may ever succeed it, has rendered them obnoxious to the American people.

"The heavy taxation which must necessarily follow to pay the enormous debt of this war, and which must continue for the next half century, fixes an odium upon the party which will outlive the party itself. Then to whom are we to look for the healing of the National wounds? Is it not to those who have taken National Conservative grounds, and who have ever, during this war, advocated conservative principles—those principles advocated in past years by the old Whig party, and more recently, by the Conservatives of the Republican party, and of the Democracy, and under whose benign teachings we have grown and prospered as a nation?

"Our President, Andrew Johnson, has ever been a Conservative Democrat. In his hands is placed the destiny of this Nation, and from him we have nothing to fear, but everything to hope. I speak for his Administration one of the brightest pages in our history: and under his Administration, fellow-citizens, looking to him for protection, and taking his policy as our guide, must we organize our State Government.

"Every effort will be made by the Radical Abolition party to prevent the return of power to the Conservatives of the South, and all the elements of opposition will combine to prevent their success, and one of their most formidable anxiliaries, as they suppose, is to extend the benefit of suffrage to that numerous class of persons recently put in possession of their freedom. This has been too clearly fore-shadowed by the political adventurers who have come among us to have escaped your attention.

"This, then, will be a question for your future action, and if, after having taken this continent from the red man, and holding it for more than a century, you have become so charitable as to give it to the black man, I can only submit, and bow to the will of the people."

The following letter from the pen of J. Ad. Rozier, was read at the meeting:

NEW ORLEANS, June 16, 1865.

"Hon. A. P. Field, Chairman of Committee of Arrangements for the Reception of Governor Wells:

"I embrace this occasion to say that I regard with no little concern, the strides made by Governor Wells in the right direction of maintaining the true principles of government. I take it he means to follow in the footsteps of President Johnson, with regard to the reorganization of civil government in the State of North Carolina. Louisiana is as much entitled to self-government, subordinate to the Constitution of the United States, as North Carolina.

"Governor Wells is giving us unmistakable evidence of his intention to purify the ballot-box, to rid himself and the country of so many obscure and fifteenth-rate men who have swarmed in the public offices; to allow the good and the honest to be heard in the public councils; to purify the political atmosphere; to make the judiciary independent, in all cases, and not to reverse the decision of a duly constituted Judge in the Governor's Office, at the same time kicking the Judge out of office to the great scandal of the people. In a word, he is endeavoring to restore the people of Louisiana, as his friends assure us, to their civil rights.

"If this be his programme, or that of any other man, I say, God speed him! The country needs repose. Conservatism will be the balm to all political wounds. Let us eschew all intemperate men; let us detest the sanguinary.

"Radicals instil venom in the body politic; they always have and always will. They quote Christianity, but act like heathens.

"It is very evident that the masses of the Southern people are fast returning to their allegiance in a *bona fide* manner—they have gone to work to repair their fortunes, they recognize a great change as a fixed fact—like the rest of their countrymen, their characteristic trait is law-abiding, promises will be held sacredly obligatory. The arts of peace will be cultivated by them.

"Now, at the glorious close of this bloody civil war, let us imitate the Romans, who, in similiar circumstances, went into mourning for the precious lives lost. Let confiscations, and other pains and penalties, be blotted out of the statute book—let the era of good feeling return and be perpetual—let us not be Christians in name, but also in our hearts and our acts, toward our erring brethren. Very respectfully,

"J. AD. ROZIER."

The following resolutions were then read and adopted.

1, *Resolved*, That we welcome among us again our distinguished fellow-citizen, J. Madison Wells, Governor of the State, and extend to him our thanks, cordial and heartfelt, for the interest he has manifested in the welfare of the people of the State, as exhibited by his recent hurried journey to the National capital, and by his action since his return, in removing from places of trust and power corrupt and venal officials, in the correction of abuses, in purifying the ballot—the only palladium of our liberties as a people—and in preparing the way by which the people of Louisiana can safely and harmoniously take part in the restoration of civil government, and return to their proper place in the councils of the nation. We pledge him our countenance and support in all his endeavors to restore to Louisiana a loyal and constitutional State Government.

2. *Resolved*, That in the policy of Andrew Johnson, President of the United States, as exhibited in his administration, and especially in those great acts of his, the proclamation of amnesty and for the restoration of civil government in Virginia and North Carolina, and in his pledged support of a similar policy in Louisiana, we hail a return to peace and prosperity, and that good feeling which should ever exist among citizens of a common country, and to him we pledge our hearty and active support.

It had been reported that Dr. Dostie would attempt to speak from the platform erected upon Lafayette Square on the night of June 17th. An armed police force was ordered to be stationed around the stage and in different parts of the Square.

Dostie was called upon to address the assembly, whereupon several policemen sprang from the side of Governor Wells and seizing a number of peaceable citizens, conducted them to jail, and as there were two hundred policemen (faithful to the powers that ruled) within calling distance, resistance was useless.

The following statement is from the pen of Wm. Baker, appointed Street Commissioner of New Orleans under the administration of General Sheridan, Military Commander of the Gulf Department:

" *To the Editor of the True Delta:*

" The conduct of the police at the meeting on Lafayette Square on Saturday evening is a matter of general comment. It would seem from their numbers that the meeting was held for their special benefit, for nearly all the police in the city were there. They behaved themselves in a scandalous manner. Had the meeting been held in the capital of Austria or under any other despotic government their conduct could not have been worse. I saw several citizens dragged off and ordered to be locked up for expressing their opinion to their neighbors and acquaintances. In some cases one or two policemen were set to watch quiet and peaceable citizens with orders to arrest and lock them up if they dared to speak. Had they been known to be thieves or pickpockets they could not have been treated worse.

" It may be pretended that they were disorderly or making a disturbance. It is not true. Of the five or six whom I saw arrested not one was making any disturbance. One policeman went up and pointed out a prominent citizen whom I saw standing a few feet from me, and told a policeman to arrest him if he opened his mouth. And this without any kind of an excuse.

" If the police force is to be used to suppress public sentiment, as they were a short time ago used for political purposes at the ballot-box, the quicker we have a military government, pure and simple, the better. Were the men at the head of our affairs elevated to power to crush out the liberties of the people, prevent the free expression of opinion, and once more enslave both black and white? Are we to have the old thug rule—the brass knuckle, knife, pistol and slung-shot?

"The talk which I heard in the Square on Saturday evening about establishing law and order is a cheat. The very men who we are told are going to do these most desirable things, give the lie to their flattering, fawning sycophants. Within the last two weeks we have had several instances. The forcible ejectment of the Auditor from his office, in violation of all law—the breaking open a safe—the expulsion of a man from his property and place of business, he having paid a license (and a large one at that) for the privilege, is an outrage, in violation of law, and if such acts can be committed by mere brute force, without hindrance, no man is safe."

"It is time that this community ask itself what manner of men we have among us? And now, forsooth, men must go to public meetings and hold their tongues, by order of a set of hired bravos and ruffians, called policemen. Is it for this our 'erring brethren should be invited to participate in the management of our affairs?"

"Wm. Baker."

On the evening of the great demonstration in honor of Governor Wells, Dr. Dostie walked to Lafayette Square with his friend, Alfred Shaw, Esq., stood in front of the platform, and listened attentively to the remarks of the Governor of Louisiana. He heard his party defamed by that gentleman; saw liberty disgraced by the police organizations; the policy of Abraham Lincoln, and the Free State Government of his beloved Louisiana pointed at with derision and scorn, yet viewed it all with the heroic firmness and hopeful calmness of a true philosopher. He believed that the progress of corrupt men would be impeded by the action of that man who as Governor of Tennessee had declared that "Treason should be made odious."

On that night Dostie was surrounded by enemies, who had decreed that he should perish politically; that he should never succeed in business; that he should finally be the victim of conspiracy.

Surrounded by gloom and poverty; struggling with a power destined to crush him, he was yet comparatively a happy man, such was his philosophy. A friend who called upon him a few days after his expulsion from his Auditor's office, was surprised to find him in excellent spirits. Upon denouncing Governor Wells, Dr. Dostie replied: "I don't think of Wells as my personal enemy. I could take him by the hand to-day if he would reform in his principles. I care not for my own sufferings. What are they compared with many others?"

Taking the Life of Governor Brownlow from the table, he said, "I have just been reading of Brownlow's sufferings, caused by rebel rule. I look into the future, bright with hopes. Events point to victory, peace and unity. Man may decree, but there is a Ruler of events whose divine laws conflict with injustice and oppression. That Infinite power rules the nations of the earth." Such was the heroic, unselfish philosophy of Dr. Dostie.

CHAPTER XXI.

DOSTIE'S CONFIDENCE IN JOHNSON.

The eighty-ninth anniversary of our Independence was an event in which thousands of emancipated human beings desired to participate with heartfelt gratitude. The committee appointed by the constituted authorities of the city of New Orleans resolved to celebrate the day. That committee was principally composed of citizens who had been in league with the rebellion and slavery. The Republican party was almost entirely excluded from acting with that committee in making arrangements to celebrate our day of Independence. The speaker chosen to deliver an oration upon the occasion was an ex-colonel of the Confederate army, who had never avowed his conversion to the principles of republican liberty.

Dostie and his radical brethren decided to draw up another programme, in which they invited the true friends of loyalty and independence to participate in the great national jubilee of Freedom which the 4th of July, 1865, was to the Emancipated of the South. The annexed is the announcement of that celebration:

CELEBRATION OF THE FOURTH OF JULY.

At a meeting of the National Republican Association, held on Friday evening, June 30th, it was unanimously resolved that the following committee be appointed and announced to provide for a celebration of the coming 4th of July, at such place as shall be hereafter announced:

General Committee.—Dr. A. P. Dostie, Rufus Waples, James Graham, Judge E. Hiestand, Ed. Heath, Rev. Dr. J. P. Newman, W. H. Pearne, Dr. W. H. Hire, Judge H. C. Warmoth, Jos. T. Tatum, Jno. Purcell, Tho. M. Conway, S. Wrotnowski, B. R. Plumley, Danl. Christie, N. W. Travis, Geo. S. Dennison.

All Civic and Benevolent Associations, officers and men of the Army and Navy, teachers and pupils of the Public Schools, and the public generally, are cordially invited to participate in this celebration.

Seats will be provided for ladies.

A. P. Dostie, President.

Jos. T. Tatum, Secretary.

The Custom House was chosen by the Republican Committee, as an appropriate place in which to celebrate the joyful Anniversary of American Independence. The Custom House of New Orleans is a historical place. It was in that building that the United States troops under General Butler shielded slaves from their cruel masters!

On the 4th of July, 1865, those same slaves made the walls of the old Custom House ring with shouts of freedom. General Banks was the orator of the day. In his able address, he argued that "those who had been in rebellion could not safely be permitted to assume the political rights they had abdicated; that the emancipated were entitled to enfranchisement, and for the public good should enjoy their rights; and that the policy of President Lincoln embraced that event."

The loyal people of the South—surrounded by a dangerous foe, naturally looked to the successor of President Lincoln for protection. They reposed all confidence in his Executive power, and looked upon the anarchy and disorder around them as a natural result of the great Revolution, not suspecting the workings of his hidden policy. With dismay they witnessed the high-handed acts of disloyal men in high positions, but, with faith and hope, waited with patience for the President to form his policy, believing that his firm loyalty and his avowed aversion of traitors when Governor of Tennessee, would be embodied in his executive plans for a just reconstruction whtch they vainly hoped would bring peace and unity out of chaos. Never did a people trust to human power with more perfect confidence than did the loyal masses of the South trust Andrew Johnson, never were a people more cruelly deceived.

Had the policy of the President been boldly announced, sufferings, oppressions, and mental agonies might have been avoided! Loyal men might have escaped the clutches of tyrants and murderers. Conspiracy, rebellion and treason are best conceived in secrecy. The policy of Andrew Johnson in his restoration measures and movevents was a combination of the above elements, and for a time he moved on in his plans, so secretly that the most scrutinizing did not discover the lurking venom of "My Policy," Said General Butler in a speech delivered in New York, "I am glad to say to you what I know to be the sentiment of the President who has succeeded Abraham Lincoln by the dispensation of Providence to the highest place on earth—I know that Andrew Johnson feels as you and I do upon the subject of the rebellion. He has had a nearer view of it than we have, and is able to deal with it as we would have it dealt with." Said General Banks, in New Orleans, July 4th, 1865, "Give to President Johnson your firm and united support, I know he is worthy your confidence." Said Senator Wade in Ohio, "There is not a man in the Nation I would sooner trust than President Johnson." The loyal multitude throughout the land, white and black, turned from the grave of their beloved Lincoln to support his successor in the great work of restoration, upon the basis of freedom and loyalty. Union men of pre-eminent standing and patriotic record who had studied and admired the acts and sayings of Governor Johnson, of Tennessee, were the last to discover the true policy of President Johnson.

Dr. Dostie was the last prominent Unionist of New Orleans to avow his belief that Andrew Johnson was the "Judas of the Republican Party." He continued his prayer "God bless Andrew Johnson," after his departure from Nashville, Tennessee, until that point in national affairs when no true loyal man could longer conceal from his mental vision the fact, that the President of the United States sustained traitors, in their tyranny over the loyal citizens of the South. In proportion as power was snatched from loyal men, by the opposers of the United States Government, it passed into the hands of the rebel element, to be used as an instrument to destroy republican principles. Those who had crouched by the ruins of slavery, silently lying beneath the black pall of treason, throughout the Administration of President Lincoln, formed a coalition with the working rebels who had fought the battles of secession, and suddenly appeared under the political leaders of the Rebellion, to plot afresh, the destruction of the Republic. The Union

Liberty loving men of the South, who had been the standard bearers of their Cause in the conflict between Slavery and Liberty, between republican principles and aristocratic despotism, were the recipients of all indignities. The true character and plans of Andrew Johnson, were known and read to his kindred spirits, the ancient slaveocracy of the South. Men whose political life was conceived in the Black Code and similar documents, were appointed judges of the Courts, Sheriffs of the Parishes, and permitted to fill all the important offices, throughout the rebel States.

The provisional Governors of the Seceded States were, most of them, in harmony with the hidden policy, the working of which soon became visible. No justice could be obtained in the courts by loyal men. If Governors were appealed to for justice the persecuted were advised to look to the President for redress. An appeal to the Chief Executive from a persecuted loyalist was quickly referred to the civil authorities of the reconstructed States. Loyal men were restricted in business, and made to feel in every way that their noble principles were no passport to success, that the government under which they lived was no longer a protection to their persons lives or property. Unionism and loyalty were at a discount; rebellion and treason were more popular in 1865-66 than in 1860-61.

The cause of the war was the conflict between the antagonistic elements of liberty and slavery. It ended when four millions of slaves were liberated. The next question was what are the rights of the emancipated? The true friends of the freedman from one end of the land to the other exclaimed, "let them have the rights of citizens; let them claim the rights of suffrage:" Philanthropists who had spent their lives in advocating freedom from tyranny, were the first to interest themselves in the physical, moral, intellectual, and political rights of the freedmen. Dostie formed one, and that too a conspicuous link in the chain which binds together the friends of equal rights in this age of reform. Said he, "Freedom in the United States entitles white and black men alike to the rights of a citizen, and to the constitutional privileges of all Americans." His views upon negro suffrage made him as obnoxious to the slave-ocracy in Louisiana in 1866 as his views of secession had made him in 1860 to the disloyal. His views upon that subject were in harmony with those of Lincoln, Chase, Stevens, and Lovejoy. The following letter to Governor Hahn he often quoted, as indicating his own views, sometimes adding, "they are not quite as radical as mine."

WASHINGTON, D. C., March 14, 1864.

"*My dear Governor*—I have just been reading with great satisfaction a brief notice of your inaugural and the address you made on the occasion. I am very glad that you propose to make clean work of slavery.

"Will you allow me to suggest one thing more? We can not go to the bottom where the granite is, in order to build without giving the elective franchise to the negro. I am satisfied that if we stop short of that, it will be found that our house is built upon the sand, and when the floods come, and the winds blow, and the rains descend, it will fall, and great will be the fall thereof. The sense of justice which has been awakened in the nation by the rebellion will not rest satisfied to have forgiven rebels who have fought to overthrow the government, and drive away loyal black soldiers who have fought to sustain it. It is not necessary at first that all should vote. You can allow those who can read and write to vote; or you can allow black soldiers to vote. The privilege of voting given to the latter class, to wit: the soldiers, would commend itself, I think, to the whole nation. You may think that this is owing to my overweening anxiety for the blacks, but it is not that alone, nor chiefly. I am satisfied that Providence will not let us settle this question until we settle it on the foundation of equal and exact justice to all, in accordance with the principles of the Declaration of Independence and of the Constitution, which know nothing of black or white, rich or poor, but regard the rights of men, as such, as sacred.

"I was much gratified the other day in a conversation with the President to find that his views on this subject accord with my own. He does not feel that he can require this, as a delegation requested him to do. Still he desires it to be done by the action of the people themselves.

"If Louisiana takes the lead I think all the other States will follow, and then we shall have settled this question on deep and broad foundations, against which the gates of hell cannot prevail. The number of those who are at first admitted to the privilege of the elective franchise does not to me seem essential, for if you let any portion of the colored people vote the rest will follow in time.

"I had a conversation with Governor Johnson, of Tennessee, on this subject. He feels right, personally, but is a little timid as to the public sentiment. I do hope you will see your way clear to take the lead in this matter. You will thus not only do a good thing for your country, but immortalize your name, for I am satisfied the nation will grow to this, if it has not already reached it.

"Excuse me for having intruded my views upon your attention. The brief but pleasant acquaintance I had with you has encouraged me to do it.

Very truly yours,

"OWEN LOVEJOY."

"Governor MICHAEL HAHN, New Orleans."

In September, 1865, Dr. Dostie determined to go to Washington and consult with President Lincoln, believing he had been misinformed as to the true state of political affairs in Louisiana. His radical friends were anxious that their interests should be represented at the Executive Mansion. Like Lovejoy, Major Stearne, and hundreds of others, Mr. Johnson succeeded in deceiving Dostie, in conversation with him, as to his real antagonism to the vital interests of all Southern loyalists. Strengthened in his confidence in the integrity and honesty of the President, whose policy at that time was to conciliate radicals, conservatives, copperheads, rebels and traitors, Dostie writes from Washington: "I am convinced in my interview with the President that his loyal sentiments will never allow him to seriously conflict with the policy of the martyred Lincoln. He has been misled, but will, I am confident, retrace his steps. I think we may safely trust the Administration." After spending several weeks with his aged mother (whom he visited for the last time), his brothers and sisters, he returned to New Orleans, hopeful of the future, and confident of the success of the cause he cherished. Soon after his arrival Dr. Dostie delivered the following address, which was denounced by the Press of New Orleans as an "incendiary speech," the author of it being styled "an insulting advocate of Negro Suffrage."

"FELLOW-CITIZENS—The friends of the Union and Liberty, in reviewing the events that have convulsed our Republic for the past four years, rejoice in the glorious fact that the most gigantic rebellion upon record has been crushed—that the "Confederate States of America" are but an idea of the past. To-day the flag of the United States waves over this vast country, proclaiming the blessings of freedom to every man of whatsoever race or color. Emblazoned upon its ample folds is the motto—No North, no South, no East, no West—the United States of America, one and indivisible. The leading traitors of the nation—the Davises and Breckenridges—with many of lesser stamp, now languish in prisons, awaiting trial and condemnation, or are fugitives from the justice of a people they have clothed in the habiliments of mourning, and who have doomed them to infamy, as the murderers of their fathers, sons and brothers. To-day, fellow-citizens, the nation is sovereign. The Constitution, Laws and Government command treason to be silent that Justice and Liberty may reconstruct the Republic upon a basis that shall forever exclude slavery, and establish universal Justice.

"The friends of emancipation and of equal rights look triumphantly upon the overthrow of that infamous system which was enveloping, with its anaconda folds, our republican structure, and undermining by its subtle poison the noblest of governments, that it might build upon its ruins an oligarchial despotism. We are now a nation of freemen. We claim that the people are the legitimate source of power. They command the enemies of liberty to cease their infernal work.

"The rebellion, which has baptized our country in blood, and caused hundreds of thousands to seal with their lives their devotion to liberty, has resulted in the liberation of four millions of human beings. It was a war of principles—of principles that, when once fairly inaugurated, must result in a full development of the republican elements which lie at the foundation of our Government.

"The progressive spirit of the age sternly demanded that the despotism, which the aristocracy of the South arrogated over the poor man, should cease. That the oppressed should have full privilege to enjoy the inestimable blessings of "life, liberty and the pursuit of happiness." But that the lingering aristocrats of the land seek to withhold these from the masses, we have ample evidence. What mean these late convulsive movements of the enemies of Democratic Republican liberty throughout the South? Why have they combined with the Copperheads of the North to overthrow the great work the friends of republican institutions have accomplished in four years?

"Do we not discover in their attempts the machinations of a relentless, hydra-headed aristocracy repudiating still the immortal truths "that all men are equally free and independent;' that 'Government is instituted for the benefit, protection and security of the people; that no free Government, or the blessings of liberty, can be preserved to any people, but by a firm adherence to justice, moderation and virtue?'

"Why do the Legislatures of the rebellious States so persistently refuse to recognize the fact that slavery has ceased to exist in our country? Alas! are not the men who compose these bodies, and who have met to make laws, the very men who have for the last four years been imbruing their guilty hands in the blood of our heroes? Have not they murdered these noble men that slavery might become the corner stone of their purposed despotism? Can we trust these men to give to freemen their rights? Patriots and statesmen, distinguished for their love of the Union and all who truly love their country, exclaim against the outrage of having such rulers.

"We are told by the Democratic party that this is President Johnson's policy. I do not believe that President Johnson intends to place traitors in power. I have had the honor of several interviews with him, and I was impressed by the conviction that he is a true patriot, an honest man and able statesman. I do not believe it will ever be Andrew Johnson's policy to place political power in the hands of men who have labored to destroy the most beneficent of Governments. His past acts and words have ever been in direct antagonism to this suicidal policy. At Nashville, as Governor of Tennessee, he says: 'I, Andrew Johnson, hereby proclaim liberty, full, broad and unconditional liberty—to every man in Tennessee. Rebellion shall no more pollute our State. Loyal men, whether black or white, shall govern the State.' Again as President of the United States he says: 'In adjusting and putting the Government on its legs again, I think the progress of the work must be put into the hands of its friends. If a State is to be nursed until it gets strength, it must be nursed by its friends, not smothered by its enemies.'

"The great problem of reconstruction before the American people is now being solved by a Republican Congress, with which the President is in accord. There is no worthy basis for the Government of States but that basis which contains the elements of justice and equal rights. The corner stone of all republican governments must be the self-evident truths, that 'all men are created equal; that they are endowed by their Creator with inalienable rights; that among these are life, liberty, and the pursuit of happiness.' Shall the eleven rebellious States, which have declared these immortal declarations to be contrary to their policy of government, be allowed to send their representatives to Congress until they abandon their political heresies, as they have the field? Does not the dignity of the nation demand this? Does not Freedom itself demand that none shall be sent to our National Legislature to represent the vital interests of these States, but those who have been steadfast, devoted upholders of the Union, when the life of the nation was assailed? If this policy is not adopted and enforced we shall have treason again in our Congressional halls, and a new set of Davises, Breckenridges and Slidells will seek to seize the reins of Government and renew their war upon loyal men and upon the Union,

"Heaven grant our Republic may never again be summoned to meet rebellion, begun by Senators, Legislators and Governors—that Liberty and Civilization shall be draped in mourning by traitors; men, who, having taken a solemn oath to maintain the Government, betray it, and thrust their swords of treason into the vitals of the nation! In the name of God, let our Congressional and our Legislative halls be purified from the taint of treason! We cannot trust men to make laws for our State and for the nation, who by their traitorous acts, have disfranchised themselves—have forfeited their right to vote or to hold office under the National or State Governments. Let them remain disfranchised until the evidence of their repentance is perfect. If this policy is not pursued, the peace and unity of this country will be constantly imperilled.

"President Johnson has again and again declared that none but loyal men had a right to rule the country. While Governor of Tennessee he said: 'But in calling a Convention to restore the State, who shall restore and establish it? Shall the man who gave his means and influence to destroy the Government? Is he to participate in the great work of reorganization? Shall he who brought this misery upon the State be permitted to control its destinies?' Again he says: 'Why all this blood and carnage? It was that treason might be put down and traitors punished; therefore I say, that traitors should *take a back seat* in the work of restoration. If there should be but five thousand men loyal to the Constitution, loyal to justice, these true and faithful men shall control the work of reorganization and reformation absolutely.'

"These are words worthy a Democratic Republican President, and we have reason to believe that our truly Republican Congress will sustain these noble sentiments.

Then will treason be made odious, and genuine loyalty and unimpeachable integrity be rewarded. Our Republic will no longer be in danger of being buried beneath the powers of despotism. Treason will no longer threaten the peace, harmony and unity of the nation. Anarchy, convulsion and conflict will be among the things of the past.

"CITIZENS:—In this work of reconstruction, let us earnestly labor with the patriots of our country to establish the principles of universal justice and impartial freedom. That in the reorganization, equity shall prevail. That there shall be no repudiation of just debts, and no recognition of the debts of rebels; no slavery—nothing but justice.

"Should men who made the rebellion be permitted to possess the power they seek, and succeed with the Copperheads of the North in their conspiracies, we may, indeed, fear for the precious boon of Liberty. We want no rebel party in disguise. We must not imperil our glorious heritage by a misjudged magnanimity towards even the remains of an insolent aristocracy. This class are still contumacious rebels, and, as such, are not worthy of confidence. They must suffer the ignominy due their crimes, and receive their just punishment that worketh repentance.

"Long years these traitors have plotted the destruction of our Government—of the Constitution—of Liberty. Let us hope and pray that in this great work of the reconstruction of States this Union may be based upon the National recognition of all men's inalienable rights, and that nothing may be endangered by precipitancy. As Mr. Colfax has said, 'Let the work make haste slowly,' and we can then hope that the foundation of our Government, when reconstructed on the basis of indisputable loyalty and freedom, will be as 'eternal as the stars.'

"Freedom is the watchword of this age of progress. The decree has gone forth that Liberty shall rule supreme in this Republic and throughout the world. The words of our martyred Lincoln were prophetic: 'This nation, under God, shall have a new birth of freedom, and government of the people by the people and for the people, and shall not perish from the earth.'

"In my opinion, before this work of restoration can be fully consummated, this Government must recognize and secure the equal political, as well as religious, civil, and moral rights of men.

"MY FRIENDS, On the question of universal suffrage I feel as did Gadsden, of South Carolina, in reference to the Stamp Act of 1765, when he exclaimed: 'We stand upon the broad, common ground of those natural rights which we feel and know as men.' The two elements now at work in our land are striving, the one to perpetuate Freedom, the other to destroy the power which justice seeks to give man. Whence arises this bitter antagonism to the free, unconditional and equal rights of the oppressed? Are these rights not denounced most fiercely by the infamous instigators of the rebellion—the aristocratic conspirators of this country, who have declared, by words and by war, that power was more potent than right—and oppression than equity? The four millions of human beings made free during the past four years are not recognized as freedmen by their former masters. Their rights are not respected by them.

The terrible events of the past four years have not opened their eyes to sight in this matter. They will not look upon truths which are in accordance with the laws of God and republican principles. Who were the loyal and steadfast friends of the best of Governments in her hour of peril? Who came forward by hundreds of thousands at the call of Abraham Lincoln, and fought with a courage unsurpassed by the bravest soldiers, helping the nation in the darkest hour of danger to turn the tide of battle, and win the precious victory that made safe the Republic? O friends! let us be just, and labor to extend to this portion of our fellow-citizens those rights the God of Nature has bequeathed in common—the right of self-government—of representation—of the ballot—for until these rights are given we cannot become fully a nation of freemen. Refuse the just demands of a brave and loyal people, and internecine war, discord, sectional and national strife will re-appear, in some form, with their blighting effects upon the country.

It is said by the enemies of negro suffrage that this people are uneducated in the science of government, and therefore unfit for the right of suffrage. Have they not already proved to the world their capacity to appreciate all the truths necessary to be understood by the loyal citizens of the United States, in order to maintain the rights of freemen? Do we not find them as anxious for the acquisition of knowledge as the white race? Contemplate some of the developments of freedom to this race. Go into the schools of the freedmen in this State, established by this munificent Government, where upwards of twenty thousand colored people are being educated. See with what avidity they apply themselves to the various branches of knowledge. Examine them in the progress of their various studies. Then, casting aside all prejudice of color, tell us if they have not capacity to understand and appreciate the principles which lie at the foundation of a truly Republican government.

The loyal heart of the nation is fully aroused to the importance of educating the race morally, intellectually, civilly, and politically. The great defender of human liberty, Abraham Lincoln, says in a letter to Governor Hahn, "I congratulate you on having fixed your name in history as the first Free State Governor of Louisiana. Now, as you are about to have a Convention, which, among other things, will possibly define the elective franchise, I barely suggest to you whether some of the colored people may not be let in, as, for instance, the intelligent, and especially those who have fought gallantly in our ranks. They would probably help in some trying time to keep the jewel of liberty in the family of Freedom."

President Johnson said on this question of negro suffrage, "Were I in Tennessee, I would introduce negro suffrage, gradually, first to those who had served in the army, those who could read and write, and perhaps a qualification to others."

The voices of patriots all over the land are proclaiming that freedom and the right of suffrage are inseparable. It has become a historical fact that stands out boldly upon American records that the black men of this country have vindicated this Government, and "cemented its foundation stones with their blood." Shall we then refuse them support to maintain the laws? Can we say, in justice, they shall not become citizens? The voice of liberty in thunder tones which shakes despotisms and make oppressors tremble, says, "Freedom means universal rights, universal justice." That voice has been always speaking, not only in our own country, but through the patriots, statesmen, poets, and philanthropists of other nations. England has proclaimed universal liberty and human rights, through her Wilberforce, her Locke, her Pitt, her Shakspeare, and her Milton. Ireland, through her O'Connell, her Father Mathew, and her Curran, speaks loudly for the precious boon of liberty. Germany —freedom-loving Germany—sends forth her sweetest notes of freedom through her Schiller, Luther, and Humboldt. France breathed the pure, immortal flame of liberty from the fires which burst from the noble heart of Lafayette, whose pulse throbbed with that of our own Washington, as they struggled together for human rights. Italy boasts of her Garibaldi—thousands of voices chant the strains of liberty at the mention of that name associated forever with freedom.

In our own beloved land, the combined voices of millions may be heard speaking for universal freedom, universal justice. Through our martyred Lincoln, our living Johnson, our Banks, our Butler, and hundreds of others we speak. Louisiana has her Durant, her Hahn, and many others who are raising their voices in favor of humanity and universal suffrage.

Can the sneers and scoffs of the enemies of freedom—the hiss of Copperheads, or the combined powers of any despotism silence this voice? Never? Ideas do not travel backwards. This voice of Freedom is now awakening those who have been fighting in the ranks of treason and rebellion. The Stephenses, Bells and Reagans of the "so-called Confederacy"—have recently had the penetration to discover " the truth," that freedom pointed to the right of suffrage. Who knows but we may live to see the rebels who have gone to Brazil, in the hopes of finding slavery, return with the conviction that equal rights, republicanism and democracy are better than slavery and oppression.

God has given human beings reason and energy, and man has no right to chain that reason and energy by oppressive laws, or in any way prevent the exercise of those rights, which in equity belong to all. Kossuth, in reviewing the rights of man, exclaims, " Liberty is Liberty, as God is God."

The adoption of the constitutional amendment has extirpated slavery from our country. God grant that all things pertaining to its unjust laws, or to its spirit may also be extirpated. The rebel Legislature have recently made laws in direct opposition to the Constitutional amendment, which reads: " Neither slavery nor involuntary servitude, except as a punishment for crime, whereof the party has been duly convicted, shall exist within the United States, or any place subject to their jurisdiction."

These Legislatures also, true to their slaveocratic instincts, ignore by their acts the self-evident truth that man has an inherent right to enjoy civil, religious and political liberty.

There is not on earth a Republic but this that legislates the rights of man away. No nation but this disfranchises freedmen because of their color or race. In slaveholding Brazil they do not go so far as do the enemies of negro suffrage in this country. In Brazil, freedmen, regardless of color, are equal before the law, and eligible to any office. In the British West Indies, the blacks were sent to the Republican Chamber of Deputies, as representatives. And yet, in what nation, we ask, have they fought for liberty as they have in our Revolutionary war, in the war of 1812, and in our recent great struggle for freedom?

In regard to political rights, we do not as a nation stand on the same broad basis as did our revolutionary fathers. Washington, Jefferson, Hancock, and Hamilton, went to the polls and deposited their ballots where the negroes did theirs. These revolutionary patriots advocated the cause of equal rights, and maintained the rights of all freedmen to the ballot box. The black man voted under Washington's, Adams,' Madison's, and Jackson's administrations.

In five of the New England States they have been voting ever since the revolutionary war. In Pennsylvania they continued to vote until 1838. In Maryland and Virginia they voted until 1832. In New Jersey until 1839; and in North Carolinia and Tennessee until 1835.

Negroes, after fighting in New Orleans under Jackson, helped to elect the hero to Congress.

"The black people of this country have been ardently and universally loyal, and ever ready to fight against the anti-democratic and anti-republican principles which despots have sought to establish in this Republic. They are Americans by birth, and love freedom with an undying love which they instinctively know is destined for all Americans.

"At New Orleans, Mobile, and other cities, how did they spend the fourth of July, 1865? Was not American freedom honored by them? Was not the memory of Abraham Lincoln glorified by this grateful people? On that day the black men of this nation proved themselves worthy to assist in carrying out the principles inculcated by the Declaration of Independence. They proved on that day the right to demand the same freedom the white man claims.

"The negro wants no protection but just and equitable laws. He only asks, in the spirit of 1776, to be enfranchised from the thraldom of oppression. He knows as well as we do that distinctions growing out of color or race are incompatible with justice. This is an age of progress not only for the white man, but for the black man.

"The black man is becoming intelligent, and looks upon the enemies of liberty just as the intelligent white man looks upon slavery, serfdom, vagrant acts, oppressions and wrongs, as all just men do. He knows that the nation imperatively demands equal rights and justice, and he believes, with us, that this demand will be satisfied. He exclaims with the friends of equal rights, 'Let there be freedom for all, education for all, labor for all!' Justice demands this, and nothing else will be satisfactory.

"We want no more Opelousas ordinance, which prohibits freedmen from coming to town without special permission: which prohibits them liberty on the streets after ten o'clock at night; which declares that freemen shall not reside within the limits of the town, unless they be in the regular service of some white person or former master; which refuses freemen the right to hold public meetings, to preach, or to carry arms; which refuses them the liberty to barter, or to sell goods, without the special permission of their employers, under the penalty of imprisonments, fines or hard labor on the public roads. Neither must these persistent slaveocrats be permitted to put into operation those infamous laws enacted in the rebel Democratic Legislature of 1865, which force freedmen to contract away their labor and submit themselves to slavery under new names.

"We want no negro vagrant laws, no more jail fees, highest bidder, rendition of poor and indigent persons of color! no more reminders of the block, the ball chain, the 'nigger dogs' the fugitive slave laws and the slave gangs of the past.

"Let this people alone to enjoy the same protection we are entitled to claim. Let this people with the aid of justice and liberty, work out their own destiny. If they will not work, let them starve; but give them an equal chance with us in the struggle of life.

"When the slave oligarchy ruled in the plenitude of its power, the rights of the laboring classes were trampled under foot. Free labor was reduced to the level of slave labor. This shall be no more. The fiat has gone forth that labor shall not be subjected to a domineering, unscrupulous aristocracy. A new era has dawned upon this country. Labor in the future will be respectable and dignified, and command the best portion of the fruit it produces.

"The Union party of Louisiana has labored earnestly and faithfully to wipe out the disgraceful laws of this State, that she might become one of the brilliant lights of the nation. Abraham Lincoln was the prime mover in this work of reformation. His sympathies were ever with Republican movements. His voice, which can never be lost to this nation, was heard on the eve of his departure from earth, declaring his sympathy with the Constitution of 1864, which ignored the Black Code of this State, abolished slavery and the laws which governed it from her statute books.

"My Friends, The Republican party of Louisiana—counting white men only—are in a minority in this State. A Rebel Democratic party, composed of domineering aristocrats, who one year ago were fighting against republican liberty, and who to-day are seeking to crush loyal men, both white and black, by a renewed tyranny, continue their Satanic oppressions and wrongs, while they attempt to draw the veil of hypocrisy over their damnable conspiracies.

"The National Republican party, to which all loyal men in the South belong, seeks to establish liberty and justice throughout the land. For the past four years it has been working for freedom and equal rights, against slavery and oppression; against that slaveocratic power which hates with undying hate, free schools, a free press, free speech, and all that pertains to that freedom a just God designs for this mighty Republic.

"We are called upon to battle with these rebellious tyrants. In that work, my friends, we must be united. Our beloved Louisiana is in imminent danger from the deadly foes of freedom. Let us who love the Union and liberty, forget past differences, and combine to fight the oppressors who threaten to crush out the loyal element of this State. Shall we not with our President say: 'Let us be united. I know there are but two parties now—one for the country and the other against it; and I am for my country.' While we embrace this noble sentiment, let us inscribe upon our Republican banner the motto: Union, Justice, Confidence, Freedom, Enfranchisement.

"Freedom must triumph in our State. Louisiana must become the land of human rights—the land where every one can enjoy his own labor, his own soil—where all can claim the right to educate their children, and have all the rights of human beings respected by their neighbor, and maintain the rights of self-government, of the ballot, and all other rights which impartial justice claims for the citizens of a magnanimous Republic. Then we can vaunt our freedom; then will the foreigner no longer reproach America with slavery; then can we say, in truth, our land is the 'asylum of the oppressed and the home of the free.' Men of every nation shall cherish it as the land of human rights—the land where liberty means to enjoy manhood, free and untrammeled, with all the inestimable rights of freedom, in its broadest and fullest meaning. Then may the citizen proudly boast—'I AM AN AMERICAN.'"

CHAPTER XXII.

REBEL LEGISLATURES.

The Governors and Legislatures of the rebellious States, in unison with "my policy" moved on in their work of politically restoring the rebellious elements to power, and of crushing loyalty.

Louisiana seemed to take the lead in this ignominious work. In that State it was considered an honor to have approved the Ordinance of Secession. None who had fought for the Government of the United States were considered worthy of official position under the reconstruction laws of Johnson.

The Legislature of Louisiana was composed almost entirely of men who had fought against the government, and, approved of the rebellion and slavery. The constitution of 1864 was ignored by that assembly. The work of the Convention and Legislature of 1864, which abolished Slavery in Louisiana, and looked to the interests of the freedmen and the laboring classes, were to the Legislature of Louisiana of 1866 what the Emancipation Proclamation had been to the Confederate Government, and was treated with the same contempt, as all other acts which opposed Slavery, and oppression.

In a letter to Senator Howe, of Wisconsin, April 12th, 1866, Governor Hahn writes, "The present Legislature evidently intend to revive the old slavery regulations. A careful analysis of the acts they have passed would convince any man of their true intent, which is to keep up a sort of slavery in spite of the new Constitutional Amendment. I assure you what, Mr. T. W. Conway, lately Assistant Commissioner of the bureau of Freedmen in Louisiana, called the ordinance relative to the police for colored persons, 'Slavery, in substance,' is true of the acts of that Legislature. But you will not be surprised at their unjust provisions when you are informed of their authorship—Duncan F. Kenner is their worthy parent. He was elected a delegate to the Montgomery Convention by the Louisiana Convention which adopted the infamous ordinance of Secession. He helped to frame the Confederate Constitution, and was elected to the Confederate Congress. He remained a member of that rebel body until General Grant extinguished the Codfederacy, when he availed himself of an early opportunity to visit Washington and seek a pardon. And with his pardon he hurried to Louisiana, dismissed the officers of the Freedmens' Bureau from the further preservation of his property, and immediately procures an election to the State Senate, and then becomes the author and advocate of the new Slave laws. With such material in the Southern Legislatures, what good can be expected? If 'Reconstruction' is to be entrusted to such intelligent and influential rebels, "what can we hope to achieve for the good of the country? As to the disloyal character of the Legislature, I will let the published declarations of others speak.

Hon. R. C. Richardson, of New Orleans, writing to Ex-Governor George S. Boutwell, says:

"A prominent member of the Legislature, and an old secession leader, stated to me in conversation a short time before the election, that he was a stronger secessionist than he ever was, and that he hated the United States Government from the bottom of his heart, and if he ever got a chance he would strike a death-blow at it. I state from memory nearly his own language.

"Now, sir, I am prepared to assert that at least nine-tenths of his colleagues entertain the same sentiments, leaving out one solitary Union man elected from one of the country parishes.

"All their proceedings, so far, sustain this conclusion."

Hon. H. C. Warmoth, of New Orleans, in his argument addressed to Senator George H. Williams, of the Reconstruction Committee, after speaking of other rebel influences in Louisiana, adds:

"And finally the Legislature comes with new enactments, in order to more effectually, if possible, destroy the friends of equal suffrage and equal rights. And thus without opposition or question re-enslave the colored people."

But why should I accumulate the *opinions* of citizens, however trustworthy and honorable, when a simple statement of *facts* cannot but bring you to a similar opinion?

The Legislature elected its officers on account of distinguished services to the confederacy, and the criterion of success was persistent devotion and bitterness in the rebel cause.

It refused to have the American flag about its halls until some colored ladies formally tendered it one as a present, which offer, however, was indignantly ignored. It refused action on a resolution offered by Mr. William Brown, of Iberville, as follows:

"*Whereas*, In the opinion of this body, the Government of the United States is the best Government on the face of the earth, and, whereas, the flag of the said Government is worthy of all respect; therefore be it

"*Resolved*, That the Sargeant-at-arms of the Senate be directed to procure a large United States' flag, to have the same properly and tastefully arranged over the President of the Senate's chair."

Shortly after its assembling the Senate expelled Mr. Wm. Brown, the author of the foregoing resolution, and some other Union Senators, who held over in their term from the previous Legislature, on the pretext that they were elected by a small vote of Union men before the rebels had given up the Confederacy.

The present Constitution of Louisiana, framed while most of the members of this Legislature were in the rebellion, contains this provision:

"The Legislature shall provide for the education of *all* children of the State between the ages of six and eighteen years, by maintenance of free public schools, by taxation or otherwise."

The former Constitution, made in the interests of slavery, used the word "white" before the word "children." The members of the Legislature have sworn to carry out the constitutional mandate as it now stands. They assert in their preamble that "sufficient provision is made by the Constitution and laws of the State, &c." They have made no provision for or sign of willingness to open colored schools, and no existing colored school is recognized, fostered or encouraged by their action.

But, you may ask how can these evils be remedied? How can justice be secured to the Union men without dealing harshly with the rebels? My answer is ready. Give EVERY COLORED CITIZEN THE RIGHT OF SUFFRAGE. This will settle all difficulties connected with reconstruction. It is not only just and proper to extend this inestimable right to our colored citizens, but it is a debt we owe them. Let the nation be as scrupulous in discharging its moral obligations growing out of the war, as it is to pay its financial obligations. Let us be true to those who have been true to us. In granting this right we obtain security for the future. By doing this act of justice, by paying this debt, we close the rebellion. There is no other question seriously dividing the people which is not settled, with the discharge of this duty.

Respectfully yours, MICHAEL HAHN.

CHAPTER XXIII.

SCHOOLS, CHURCHES AND FREEDMAN'S BUREAU.

By order of municipal authority, in harmony with the new reconstruction laws, the Public Schools of New Orleans were placed in charge of those who had fled into the "Confederacy" upon the arrival of General Butler in that city in 1862. The Loyal School Board was superseded, with one or two noble exceptions, by a disloyal Board of Education. Wm. O. Rogers was appointed to the position he had held in the schools—when the black flag was considered an honorable emblem of the "Confederate Schools." His subtle influence was used to gradually displace Union teachers. The United States flags, placed over the Public School buildings through the influence of Dostie and his co-laborers, were torn down, the flag staff used for kindling wood and the flags destroyed. The names of Beauregard, Lee, Sidney and A. Johnson were reverenced. The names of Lincoln, Grant, Butler and Banks were treated with contempt by the Superintendent and scholars of the reconstructed Schools.

In one of the rebel sheets of New Orleans we find the policy of the public schools referred to in the following article. "Unless for cause," in that article means volumes of injustice. It pointed to the expulsion from those schools of more than one hundred teachers for their known Union sentiments:

"The policy here, as elsewhere, in relation to our public schools, has been to make no changes of teachers, *unless for cause.* When, however, such men as A. P. Dostie were potential in the management of the public schools in New Orleans, while the war was progressing and less attention was bestowed on education, than on military science, oaths thick as leaves of Vallambrosa were administered to all who proposed to become instructors of the youth of this city, and woe be to him or her who could not swallow the gilded pill, and sol emnly swear to swallow an entire nigger at the same instant."

Glendy Burke was President of the reconstructed School Board. His first proposition in that relation was to "dismiss all the Union teachers from the schools," claiming as his reason for such action, "Their mismanagement and incapacity." Engraved in letters of gold, stands the name of Dr. Goldman in that School Board. This distinguished friend of Union teachers, and liberal education, indignantly repelled the charges of Glendy Burke, and exerted his influence to retain the teachers who had faithfully labored in the cause of the Union.

The churches under the new reconstruction laws were ordered to be given up to their old pastors and congregations.

Palmer, Leacock and Goodridge returned to honor the memory of the "lost cause" and give aid to "my policy" under the garb of Christianity. The following from a leading paper of New Orleans—indicates the spirit with which rebel divines and orators were received by the reconstructed:

DISTINGUISHED ARRIVALS.

"It is our pleasant task to notice the return, after an absence of three years or more, of two of the truest, ablest and most distinguished citizens of New Orleans, the Hon. Pierre Soule and the Rev. Dr. Leacock. The former has always been one of the chief ornaments of the Louisiana Bar, the latter the model of the Southern Divine—pure, simple, charitable and sincere. Many a sunny memory will be recalled by the sight of those noble men on our streets and at our firesides."

"The other day the Carondelet Street Methodist Church, for a long time past presided over by the Rev. J. P. Newman, was restored to the old members of the congregation."

"The Rev. Mr. Newman, who waited on the President the other day to see if he could not get permission to retain possession of a certain church edifice in New Orleans, which he had occupied since the time of General Butler, is said to be quite disgusted at the President's refusal to acquiesce in his request, and to have already written to his friends here that "the war is a dead failure."

The Rev. J. P. Newman was the Luther of the churches in New Orleans during the rebellion. He probably received more censures for his labors in the cause of Christianity—the Union and liberty than did the great reformer.

The Rev. J. W. Horton was another beloved pastor of the Union Church of New Orleans, against whom the vengeance and denunciations of a rebellious community were directed. He was pastor of the church from which his lamented brother the Rev. Wm. Duncan was excluded before the arrival of General Butler in 1862.

After Dr. Dostie's return from Washington, he was prostrated for weeks by sickness. Upon his recovery (as was his usual custom), he started to attend church on Sabbath morning to listen to a sermon from the Rev. J. P. Newman. As he was entering Carondelet Street church, a friend asked the Dr. "If he knew the churches had been given up to their old pastors?" He replied, "If that is true, I do not desire to listen to the enemies of my Government and shall spend the day in jail with my loyal friend Mr. Bennie."

His friend had been sent to jail by Governor Wells for the crime of "embezzlement." That crime consisted in Mr. Bennie's refusal to pay acting Auditor Neville, after Dr. Dostie's unlawful removal from office, his returns as Sheriff of Terrebonne Parish.

The Freedmans' Bureau was another impediment in the way of "My Policy" and the new reconstruction laws of President Johnson. The friends of President Lincoln were those first removed from office in Louisiana by his successor. The folowing letter proves the estimation in which the labors of the Rev. T. W. Conway were held by the martyred President:

EXECUTIVE MANSION,
WASHINGTON, March 1, 1865.

Mr. Thomas W. Conway, General Superintendent Freedmen, Department of the Gulf:

SIR: Your statement to Major-General Hurlburt of the condition of the freedmen of your department, and of your success in the work of their moral and civil elevation, has reached me, and gives me much pleasure.

That we shall be entirely successful in our efforts, I firmly believe.

The blessing of God and the efforts of good and faithful men will bring us an earlier and happier consummation than the most sanguine friends of the freedmen could reasonably expect.

Yours,

A. LINCOLN,

The following article from "the reconstructed Press of New Orleans" indicates the vindictive spirit manifested towards the laborers in the cause of freedom:

"We are told by the telegraph that Major-General Thomas has tendered the superintendence of the schools for freedmen in Tennessee and Kentucky to the Rev. Thomas W. Conway. We do not believe it. General Thomas would hardly appoint an officer that President Johnson had dismissed in disgrace for stirring up the freedmen to acts of sedition.

"While we have the utmost respect for the clergy, we hope to be spared the curse of such preachers as this Reverend who is now in Washington defaming the people of Texas and Louisiana.

"We are all the more incredulous of this item, because Mr. Conway has been an habitual deceiver of journalists for a long while. One-half the frightful stories of inhumanity to the negro originate in his jaundiced mind. His relations exceed those of 'Uncle Tom's Cabin.'"

Ex-Confederate General Humphries, of Mississippi, one of the reconstructed Governors under "My Policy," thus writes of the Freedmens' Bureau:

"To the guardian care of the Freedmens' Bureau has been intrusted the emancipated slaves. The civil law and the white man outside of the Bureau has been deprived of all jurisdiction over them. Look around you and see the result. Idleness and vagrancy has been the rule.

"Four years of cruel war, conducted on principles of vandalism, disgraceful to the civilization of the age, were scarcely more blighting and destructive to the homes of the white man, impoverishing and degrading to the negro, than has resulted in the last six or eight months from the administration of this black incubus.

"How long this hideous curse, permitted of Heaven, is to be allowed to rule and ruin our unhappy people, I regret it is not in my power to give any assurance, further than can be gathered from the public and private declarations of President Johnson."

The following correspondence explains *one* of the acts of reconstruction under "My Policy:"

NEW ORLEANS, April 10, 1866.

His Excellency, President Andrew Johnson:

SIR: It is made my duty, as President of the Senate of this State, to transmit to you by telegraph a copy of a joint resolution relative to the collection of taxes by the freedmen's bureau, for the purposes of education.

The resolution reads as follows:

"*Whereas*, we are informed that the superintendent of the freedmen's bureau for the State of Louisiana is proceeding to enforce the collection of a tax levied by military order in the State of Louisiana, to refund moneys expended, or to provide funds to be expended by the Federal authorities in the education of freedmen in this State:

"*Be it resolved by the Senate, the House of Representatives of the General Assembly concurring*, That General Howard, general superintendent of the freedmen's bureau for the United States, or, in his default the President of the United States, be respectfully requested to suspend the further collection of said taxes, and to procure or make a revocation of the order upon which they rest; and that the president of the Senate and the Speaker of the House of Representatives be requested immediately to communicate this resolution by telegraph to Washington."

I remain, very respectfully, your most obedient servant, ALBERT VOORHIES.

WAR DEPARTMENT, April 12, 1866.

To Albert Voorhies, Esq.:

Your telegram was referred to the Secretary of War, who reports that all orders and proceedings for the collection of taxes by the freedmen's bureau for the purpose of education, have been suspended.

ANDREW JOHNSON.

President Johnson's favorite theory, "The Conflict of Races," met the approbation of his reconstructed friends. "The negro will one day have his misery, and destruction entailed upon his race by the radicals of the day," was the cry of the rebel Press. Such language was no check to men of blood, who hated with undying vengeance radical and just measures.

CHAPTER XXIV.

DOSTIE NOMINATED FOR SURVEYOR OF THE PORT.

The friends of Dr. Dostie were anxious that he should be appointed Surveyor of the Port at New Orleans. Through the influence of Members of Congress and others the name of Dostie was sent by the President to the Senate to be confirmed. This unwelcome news soon reached his rebel enemies in New Orleans, and the President was besieged with the numerous pleadings of his rebel friends to withdraw from the Senate the name of the "Radical fanatic," Dostie. The whole city of New Orleans was thrown into excitement over this supposed victory of radicalism. "What!" said his enemies, "shall this man who has been so conspicuous in the Yankee reign, as a Union man, as a man who has advocated negro rights, be allowed by our President to occupy a position which none but those who defend *our cause* should fill?"

The press denounced his appointment, and his patriotic radical record was soon pictured to the President. The representation to the Chief Executive that Dostie would be an "impediment to his cherished plans of reconstruction," had the desired effect; the name of Dostie was withdrawn from the United States Senate, and a man was appointed as surveyor of the port of New Orleans who would agree with "My policy."

Said Dr. Dostie, when his name was sent to the Senate, "I have not been wrong in placing confidence in the President. He knows me to be a loyal man, and yet he proposes to place me where I may exert an influence against disloyal men." Said one who had lost all confidence in Andrew Johnson, "You will never be allowed to retain any position long under the administration of President Johnson. You are an honest radical; your enemies are the friends of the President." Said Dr. Dostie, after his name was withdrawn, "I am not yet willing to give up my confidence in Andrew Johnson. My enemies have misrepresented me to him. Personally considered I do not so much regret the withdrawal of my name (although I had every assurance that I should have been confirmed by a loyal Senate,) but I knew it would be a victory of the radical party in Louisiana, who are losing all confidence in the President. The appointment by him of a radical Union man would have secured faith in him. I believe he will yet appoint a loyal man to the position, and should he, I shall not murmur." The President's appointee was a man of known rebel proclivities.

The following letter was written by Dr. Dostie to President Johnson at that time:

NEW ORLEANS, Feb. 1, 1866.

"*Andrew Johnson, President of the United States:*

"SIR:—I feel deeply obligated to you for having conferred upon me the appointment of Register of the Land Office for the State of Louisiana, and afterwards you saw proper, without any solicitation on my part, to appoint me Surveyor of the Port of New Orleans, which appointment (after you had sent it to the Senate) was withdrawn by you. Your reasons for withdrawing the appointment are unknown to me, and may be of such a character as to make it desirable (on your part) that I should vacate the position to which you first assigned me. I therefore tender my resignation, to date from the 5th of February, as I had determined upon when I learned of my appointment to the Surveyorship.

"I will cheerfully give way to abler and better men than myself, who seek to serve the country and the cause of the Union. I can assure your Excellency that no one could feel keener than myself any blow that might be aimed against those men who have at all times and under the most trying circumstances stood up for an undivided country, and those great principles you have advocated and defended.

"I remain, respectfully yours,

"ANTHONY P. DOSTIE."

CHAPTER XXV.

DOSTIE'S LOSS OF CONFIDENCE IN JOHNSON.

President Johnson's vetoes of the "Freedman's Bureau Bill," and "The Civil Rights Bill," converted Dr. Dostie from his error in reposing confidence in a traitor to the cause of liberty. Dostie became a radical in his opinions of Andrew Johnson of the class of Wade, Butler and Sumner, and with thousands of others he stood by Senator Wade, when that noble statesman rose in the Senate chamber and said in reply to Senator Lane of Kansas, (who defended the President in his vetoes of the Civil Rights and Freedman's Bureau Bill,) "Who is your President that every man must bow to his opinion, if you please? Why, sir, we all know him—he is no stranger to this body. We have measured him, sir. We know his height, his length, his breadth, and his capacity—all about him, and you set him up as a paragon, and declare here, upon the floor of this Senate, that you are going to wear his collar. Is that the idea—that you are going to be his apologist and defender on whatever he may propose? Three millions of people, sir, exposed to outrages and insults and murder from these worse than human savages, their former masters; murdered, as we are told, every day; their lives taken away; their humanity trampled under foot; and when Congress, under the Constitution of the United States, is endeavoring to tender them some little protection, how are we met here? Every attempt of your Moses has been to trample them down, making them worse, and throwing every obstruction in the way of everything proposed by Congress."

Said Dostie, "Next to President Lincoln I trusted President Johnson. When I was compelled to see in him a traitor to liberty and loyalty my indignation knew no bounds." In the following address delivered before the Republican Association of New Orleans, May 9th, 1866, he thus expresses a measure of that indignation:

"FELLOW-CITIZENS—The conflict between Freedom and Despotism now agitating the nation is rapidly developing those great principles which form the basis of republican government. In the antagonism raging there are two parties in the field—the Republican party, which maintains that liberty, equality and justice are the prerogatives of all men, and should be the foundation of government; the other, the "Democratic" party, which disgraces that name by denouncing human equality and the rights of man.

"In this battle of ideas no middle ground can be taken by friends of freedom, of democracy, of republicanism. The events of the past four years have clearly developed to the American people the fact that the elements in our country at war with republican institutions can no longer with impunity be permitted to endanger the life of the nation.

"Patriots and heroes have written, with pens dipped in the blood of thousands, upon the corner-stone of the Republic: Liberty—Progress—Democracy.

"No human power can thrust this Republic of Liberty

into the depths from which it has been lifted. The plague spot has been removed from the nation, and that *man*, be he 'President, rebel, or conservative,' who dares to conspire against the progress of freedom, equal and exact justice, must eventually incur the just indignation of an outraged people, and be crushed by those 'eternal forces' which have decreed that this shall be a land of free, republican institutions.

"Connected with the events of the past five years are two names that will ever stand out boldly upon the records of the Second American Revolution. These are, Abraham Lincoln and Andrew Johnson. The one, the great leader of the Republican party, the leader of that party which, during the past four years, won so many 'victories for humanity.' Abraham Lincoln was the champion of liberty, the embodiment of the principles and policy of the Republican party. He was ever the friend of patriots, of men loyal to our country, and steadily maintained the principles which honored republicanism and protected loyalty. With mercy he blended justice. Abraham Lincoln was never known to compromise with traitors. None dared approach the man who, by every act of his life, had proved himself invulnerable to the flattery of the enemies of his country, and who never granted favors which would injure the cause of republican liberty. The friends of emancipation, of the Union—men of republican ideas, of true democratic principles—were the men with whom he sympathized and whom he selected to fill places of trust in this Government. Abraham Lincoln never dreamed of a policy that could place traitors in power to crush loyal men who had suffered for the cause of liberty and the Union.

This name, which was made immortal because it stood at the head of that party, whose policy has ever been to extirpate slavery from the land and restore the country according to the laws of right and justice, will ever appear in bright contrast with that of Andrew Johnson.

"A mourning nation turned from the grave of a martyred President to repose confidence in one they believed to be a true patriot, in one whose past acts and noble sayings had marked him as a friend to loyalty, an enemy to treason. The oppressed looked up to Andrew Johnson with confidence, as he told them '*he would be their Moses, and take them through the dark waters which surrounded them.*' Loyal men who had suffered by fighting for their country in her peril, for which they were persecuted by traitors, trusted the 'Moses' of the wronged, and confidently believed that his policy would be to protect the friends of the Government against the tyranny of those who had sought to destroy it. Had Andrew Johnson not said, when Governor of Tennessee, 'Rebellion shall no more pollute our State. Loyal men, whether black or white, shall govern the State?' Had Andrew Johnson not said from his exalted position of President, 'Treason must be made odious, and traitors must be punished and impoverished. Their great plantations must be seized and divided into small farms and sold to honest and industrious men?'

"Traitors were appointed to fill places of trust, but none were willing to believe that the patriotic Andrew Johnson had adopted a policy that would place men in power who had labored for years to destroy the most beneficent form of government. Were not his past acts and words in direct antagonism to this suicidal policy?

Had not he said that 'in the work of restoration, that work should be put into the hands of friends, not smothered by its enemies?' That 'if there were but five thousand men loyal to freedom, loyal to justice, these true and faithful men should control the work of re-organization and reformation absolutely?' Such was the confidence reposed in Andrew Johnson by the loyal Union men of the South that they suffered in silence the persecutions of traitors, believing that when their patriotic President had experimented sufficiently in his restoration policy, he certainly would discover that such a policy sustained traitors and crushed loyal men. They waited hopefully and patiently, believing that when their loyal President should discern the true character of his appointees, they would receive their just reward—that traitors would be punished according to his solemn promises.

"Alas! that Andrew Johnson should have stultified his history, abandoned his party, and fallen from that position where a confiding liberty-loving people had placed him, expecting him to carry out the great principles the lamented Lincoln had pointed out as necessary to save the Republic. Alas! that the Chief Executive should descend from that exalted position so recently occupied by the Great Martyr of Liberty, to denounce the principles of that party, of that Congress who are struggling to maintain the immortal cause for which the leader of Republicanism—the noble Lincoln—had died.

"Liberty bowed her head and wept, methinks, on the night of February 22d, 1866, when the Chief Magistrate of the nation mingled with the traitors of the land to insult a Republican Congress, to strike at the vitals of

Liberty, to treat with contempt the memory of Washington and Lincoln. It was not strange that the nation stood aghast and loyal hearts were filled with shame and humiliation, while traitors shouted and fired guns in honor of their avowed leader.

"President Johnson declares that he is but carrying out the policy of Abraham Lincoln. If he had reconstructed and restored States according to his promises, he would have carried out Mr. Lincoln's policy. Has this been his course? Has he adhered to the principles for which he was elected to restore the States? Has not Andrew Johnson said 'The leaders of the rebellion have decided eternal separation between you and them. These leaders must be conquered and a new set of men brought forward, who are to vitalize and develope the Union feeling in the South?' This was the policy of Abraham Lincoln; this was the promulgated policy of Andrew Johnson, as an avowed Republican. This is not his present policy. His policy is to arm the rebels, to veto Liberty Bills designed to give protection to the loyal against traitors, to denounce patriots as traitors and fraternize with the red-handed monsters of the land.

"Listen to what Governor Brownlow says of Andrew Johnson's policy: 'When I put the President in nomination at Baltimore for the Vice Presidency, I felt that he had so thoroughly committed himself to the Union cause, and had been so badly treated by tha rebels, it was impossible for him ever to get around to them again; but I give him up as lost to the Union party, and as the man who is to head the rebels and Democrats. Every rebel in this country, every McClellan man, and every ex-guerrilla chief are loud and enthusiastic in praise of the President. The men who but a few months since were cursing him for an abolitionist and traitor and wishing him executed, are now for executing all who dare oppose *his policy*, or even doubt its success.' In the eleven rebellious States, can any one point out the 'new set of men?' No. The leaders of the rebellion, through the influence and power of Andrew Johnson, to-day hold the offices and places throughout these States, and openly declare that Andrew Johnson, whom the loyal millions trusted, is the friend and supporter of the leaders of the rebellion, while they know that the loyal Union people are unprotected and subject to the tyranny of the instigators of the rebellion. Andrew Johnson is shamefully guilty of displacing men who have lavishly spilt their blood and expended their treasure to secure an undivided country, and given those places to men distinguished for their treason. The policy of Abraham Lincoln was in bright contrast with this policy. During Lincoln's life, were men known to have been partisans of secession, appointed to govern the States? Were its instigators allowed to hold offices or positions of honor or trust? Did traitors dream of asking such favors from the just and honest Lincoln? They knew that the great object of that noble life was to put down treason and restore the Union. In contrast to Johnson's proceedings, Lincoln acted according to his convictions of right and justice. His acts were in harmony with his words. Andrew Johnson declared that influential and wealthy traitors ought to suffer 'the penalties and terrors of the law,' and now seeks to conciliate them, honors them by placing them in Government employ, and giving them positions of power, where their influence in favor of treason is unlimited. Is this 'arresting, convicting and punishing' men who have been guilty of the greatest of crimes—treason? Is this making *treason odious?*

"Andrew Johnson has recently declared, in praise of his restoration policy, that Louisiana and South Carolina, are now more loyal than they have been for the past twenty five years. The men who have been crushed by the despotic tyranny of President's Johnson's *reconstructed rebels*, because they have fought for the Union and republican principles, place a different construction upon loyalty. The men who have fought treason and slavery for the last twenty-five years, and who have been commissioned by high authority to investigate these important matters, do not talk thus of the loyalty of Louisiana and South Carolina. The true, loyal Union men of these eleven rebellious States know that rebellion is only conquered by the bayonet, that military power alone keeps it in check. Why is the press of these States, if they are so loyal, constantly filling the public mind with the same ideas that were popular during the rebellion.

"Hearken to what Horace Maynard says: 'With the same traitor editors as before and during the war, pardoned it may be, but manifestly unchanged in temper and purpose, there is displayed the same sectional feeling and hatred of the Federal Government, though not the same stomach for fight. Under a thin disguise of of flattery of the President they assail his friends who have stood by him all through the dark years of the conflict, and vilify those whom they call radicals, meaning all Union men who oppose their infamous course and who are now unwilling they should be restored to power over loyal men. Their diurnal venom affords the strongest argument against the admission to their seats of your Congressional representation. The ideas and principles of the rebellion are constantly instilled into the popular mind.' This is known to be true by all loyal men in the South. The unrepentant rebels still resist the laws of the Nation, despise the sacred oaths they have taken, and only took them for the purpose of gaining power through the mysterious *magnanimity* of Andrew Johnson, praise the institution of slavery and despotism, and generally embrace the sentiments of men like T. Yancey, of Mississippi, who says: 'As for recognizing the right of freedmen to their children, I can say that not one Southern man or woman in the whole South recognizes the negro as a freedman, but as other stolen property forced by the bayonets of the *damnable United States Government.*'

"Such are the 'loyal men' in power in these reconstructed States. Such are the men now guarding the vital interests of eleven States of this Republic of Liberty. Does that flag which is the pride of the Nation, in the folds of which may be read 'Liberty, Justice and Equality,' wave triumphantly over these States? Although Andrew Johnson *has* proclaimed the 'insurrection at an end,' *war has not ended*, peace has not come. The Union men of the South yet look upon Federal bayonets as their only hope of salvation, and must so do, until a truly Republican Congress can secure peace to the country by reconstructing the rebellious States upon a loyal basis, until those who are traitors are made 'to take a back seat,' and are shorn of all power to renew their assault upon the life of the Nation. Traitors through the *magnanimity* of Andrew Johnson, have received positions due only to good and patriotic men. Men who had made themselves worthy of favors from the Chief Executive by their adherence to the Government when in peril, demanded, in the name of right and justice, that the sacred interests of this Government be guarded by its sworn and tried friends, and not placed in the power of the leaders of the rebellion, who still plot the destruction of the Republic. Honors bestowed upon traitors will prove that

"Mercy but murders, pardoning those that kill."

Have these pardoned rebels, who to-day, through the influence of the President, govern the eleven rebellious States, shown any evidence of repentance for the crimes they have committed against their country? Do they regard their sacred oaths? Do they not daily declare, while surrounded by Federal bayonets, that they will yet conquer that power which has compelled their submission to the just laws of this Nation, while they acknowledge themselves beaten in the field? that, with the help of *their* President and the Copperheads of the North, they will triumph politically in the Government of this country; that it will be a more decided victory of their principles than they could have obtained by defeating the Republican army upon the battle-field? Is this yielding up the infamous principles for which they commenced and fought a bloody war, that they might become a Confederacy of Traitors, the corner-stone of which was to be slavery? Is this embracing the great truths which give to this Nation 'Liberty—full, broad and unconditional Liberty?' Ought not traitors to be made to feel that by committing the crime of treason against this Government they forfeit their right as citizens, and that justice demands that they be arrested and punished? If they had repented of their infamous crimes, would they not honor and respect their conquerors? Have they done this? No. The fact is notorious that all the influential wealthy leaders of rebellion to-day bid defiance to the Government and laws of the country they have deluged with blood and filled with woe and desolation. The prenciples of these leaders have always moved them to oppose republicanism, human equality and liberty, and to guide the masses under their control to anarchy and rebellion.

"These are the men who to-day, under the policy and administration of Andrew Johnson, occupy the first positions in the States so lately in armed hostility to the United States Government. These men, who led the armies of the rebellion against the Republican hosts, who fought to maintain the Government and establish liberty throughout the land, now lead the armies forth to fight the political battles against their conquerors.

"And whom do they claim as their leader in this conflict between republicanism and despotism, between free institutions and slavery? Who, say the copperhead presses of the North and the rebel presses of the South, shall be their leaders. They evidently believe that their leader is secured to them, that the man who so long suffered on the 'gridiron' because men of republican principles were suffering by the persecutions of traitors, copperheads and rebels, the 'Moses' of the oppressed, the Governor of Tennessee, who declared that loyal men, whether black or white, should rule the State, who said that treason must be made odious, that the wealthy, influential leaders of the rebellion must be arrested, convicted and punished, is now the accepted leader of those who love oppression and hate free, democratic, republican institutions. The leader of red-handed traitors, who have fought to undermine the foundations of this Government, the leader of men whose names stand in the same category of crime with Aaron Burr, of whom Andrew Johnson said, in the days when he denounced traitors: '*Were I President of the United States*, I would do as Thomas Jefferson *did*, in 1806, with Aaron Burr—I would have them arrested, and if convicted, within the meaning and scope of the Constitution, *by the Eternal God, I would execute them.*' Andrew Johnson is President of the United States, and who has he arrested? Who has been executed?—Wirz. The men who founded and instigated conspiracies to overthrow the Government, men who fired upon our flag, took our forts and custom-houses, our arsenals, our mints, our lands, and fought against our liberty, made desolate our homes and murdered our sons and brothers—these are the men who cry, from every portion of the land, upon Andrew Johnson to lead them against that party who has ever stood up boldly for the eternal principles of justice and the rights of humanity, who crushed the infamous rebellion and stayed the revengeful arm of those who struck at the vitals of the Nation, that party which wielded a power that all the Copperheads, rebels and demons in Christendom cannot crush, be their leader Andrew Johnson, Robert E. Lee or Jefferson Davis.

"Notwithstanding the defection of the President, this

great Republic is not to be hurled from the majestic heights to which it has been lifted within the past five years; it is not again to be thrown back into the depths of slavery, oppression and degradation from which it has just emerged. The spirit of the age proclaims the march of Freedom to be onward, and no human power can silence the voice of Liberty, as she proclaims to the nations of the earth her right to rule this Republic. Men may plot to conspire and destroy liberty and republicanism, and build upon their ruins slavery and despotism, but there is a God of Justice who rules the destinies of this Nation, and who, in the events of the last four years, has proved to the American people that from His Eternal Throne He has decreed that this shall be a Republic where the rights of humanity shall be sacred against oppression and tyranny. Human rights have become wonderfully developed by the revolution which has been sweeping over the land. Millions of the enslaved have been, by the Great Emancipator, proclaimed freemen, and are beeoming enlightened on the important events of the age, and appreciate the humane principles of republicanism, to which they owe their liberation from the thraldom of tyranny, notwithstanding President Johnson's recent order to discontinue 'the collection of taxes by the Freedmen's Bureau for purposes of education.'

"We hear a great cry raised about taxation without representation. Andrew Johnson, in his anxiety to admit the leaders of the rebellion in Congress, exclaims that it is unjust to compel States to pay taxes without representation, and declares that it is unjust to bar the Congressional doors against the Representatives now sent from the rebellious States, and says: 'Admit into the councils of the Nation those who are unmistakably loyal.' Does not President Johnson know that nine-tenths of the men sent from the rebellious States are notorious for their treasonable efforts to destroy the Government, and that their constituents daily curse it as 'the damnable United States Government;' that these unprincipled rebels are now laboring with their wealth and unlimited influence to tax four millions of free men, without representation; that they deny them the rights of the ballot, while their loyalty is unquestionable. Andrew Johnson says 'the Revolution was fought that there should be no taxation without representation.' For what, we would ask, has this Second Revolution been fought, if not to establish equal rights in this Nation? Should the Republican Congress be denounced by the Chief Executive because it would maintain the principles for which this great civil war has been fought, because it frowns upon traitors and makes those guilty understand that they have forfeited the right to participate in the legislation of the Nation? President Johnson and Congress do not differ in this matter if President Johnson abides by his words. No true Union man desires to see a loyal man thrust out of Congress, or to see a State unrepresented in the National Legislature, when it can be proven that that State has a trusty republican government and is established upon a loyal basis—a State that will send men to represent her in Congress whose hands have not been imbrued in the blood of patriots. President Johnson declares he stands by the Constitution and Government to resist encroachments. Alas! that he had not been as anxious to guard them from the polluting touch of traitors as he is to denounce their noblest friends. President Johnson is opposed to any further amendments of the Constitution 'at this time.' He desires that this important work be postponed until the restoration of the Southern States, that they may have their influence in determining what these amendments shall be. What kind of amendments are we to expect from traitors whose souls are steeped in the principles of rebellion and slavery, the sworn friends of Jefferson Davis, Robert E. Lee and other leaders of traitors? This being, according to his recent acts, '*the white man's government*," universal suffrage is not in harmony with his ideas of American Government. 'It would bring on a war of the races.' That war commenced when slavery was first established, and will continue until human equality is acknowledged and respected in every State in the Republic of Liberty. That is a self-evident truth, plainly read by every thoughtful lover of right and justice in this country.

"Abraham Lincoln, true to justice and liberty, taught the duty and necessity of equal rights. His words were: 'Universal suffrage before universal amnesty.' Abraham Lincoln understood Southern loyalty, and knew that the rebellious States could not be reconstructed upon a loyal basis until the principal element of loyalty in those States had the right of the ballot and all other rights of American citizens, which all men are entitled to. The withholding these rights, the rights which the founders of this Government acknowledged, has already deluged the land in blood, and points to another civil war unless the just demands of humanity are complied with. Liberty has written upon the flag of the nation, 'Equal

Rights—the Destiny of Republicanism,' and this Nation will never have attained to the glory destined for her until the rights of all men are respected by the Government. How, we would ask, can President Johnson claim to be carrying out the policy of the Martyr of Liberty, when he is doing everything in his power to crush the loyal men in the South, both white and black, by appointing the most powerful leaders of the rebellion to prominent official positions, who still cherish disloyalty in their hearts?

"Lincoln was never known to announce a great principle and act contrary to it. That great and good man said: '*An attempt to guarantee and protect a revived State Government, constructed in whole or in preponderating part from the* VERY *element against whose hostility and violence it is to be protected, is simply absurd.*' Can Andrew Johnson, with these words before him, look at the work that his policy has wrought and believe that it is the lamented Lincoln's policy carried out? Andrew Johnson knows that every political act of that great and just man had a tendency to crush treason and exalt loyalty and liberty; that he never dreamed of traitors governing the four millions of enfranchised human beings. Andrew Johnson calls upon the people to tell him what principle he has violated, from what sentiment he has swerved?—asks them, if any one quotes his predecessor as going in opposition to anything he has done, what principle adopted by him has he departed from? There may have been silence in that crowd when these questions were asked, but the loyal people aver that he has violated his solemn engagement to be the Moses' and lead the oppressed to 'Liberty—full, broad and unconditional liberty;" that he has discriminated against the loyal and in favor of the disloyal; he has been guilty of acts and language calculated to precipitate another horrid rebellion; that he has attempted to usurp the legislative powers of Congress; that he has said he 'did not consider those who opposed his policy as belonging to the Union party;' that he has been guilty, in the following, of shameless interference in the sacred rights of the ballot: 'In reference to the elections in Connecticut or elsewhere *I am for the candidate* who is for the general policy and the specific measures promulgated in my annual message, veto message, speech of 22d February, and the veto message sent in to-day. There can be no mistake in this. I presume it is known, or can be ascertained, what candidates favor or oppose my policy or measures as promulgated to the country.'

" 'ANDREW JOHNSON.'

"These averments and the President's own letter answers the question the President puts. By them it is shown that he has not been true to his own professions, nor have the acts been in keeping with those of his predecessor.

"In connection with the subject of reconstruction, the name of Abraham Lincoln will be lovingly enshrined in the hearts of patriots for his immortal acts, while that of Andrew Johnson will be associated with their woes and their oppressions; he will be remembered as the prime mover in the infamous plans of staying the progress of the noble work commenced by his predecessor.

"A Republican Congress is now acting in harmony with the great work commenced by Abraham Lincoln. That Congress seeks to 'establish justice, insure domestic tranquility, provide for the common defence, and insure the blessings of liberty' to the Nation. The contest between the Chief Executive and that legislative body is not for the restoration of the Union—the Union is indivisible. Congress opposes the admission of rebels to legislate upon the vital questions now before this Nation. It opposes those who are enemies to the Government. The President is laboring to force men who have been the leaders of rebellion into Congress to frame the laws of the country. The civil and political organization of the rebellious States is constitutionally within the control of Congress. It is the duty, under the Constitution, for the Commander-in-Chief of the Army and Navy to suppress insurrection and rebellion, *under the direction of Congress.* Through Congress armies and navies are raised and sustained, and the duty of the President, as Commander-in-Chief, is to execute the laws of that body in carrying out the will of the people. Congress has the right to determine the conditions of peace or war, and it is the unmistakable and the sworn duty of the President to heed and enforce its solemn behests. The Constitution declares that 'it shall be the duty of the President,' as Commander-in-Chief, 'to execute the laws of the Union, suppress insurrections and repel invasions.' But Congress shall 'provide for organizing, arming and disciplining the militia, and *for governing* such part of them as may be employed in the service of the United States,' to provide for the common defence and *general welfare* of the United States, to declare war, grant letters of marque and make reprisal, and make rules for the capture on land and water, to raise and support armies, to make rules for the government of land and naval forces, and to provide for calling out the militia.

"War has not ended. The act of Congress of July 22d, 1861, and the act of four days later, reducing the army to twenty-five thousand men within one year after the existing rebellion and insurrection, cannot be carried out, because of the continuance of rebellion. The men who participated in the rebellion are still armed insurgents. If not armed with the bayonet, they have inaugurated a warfare against freedom and the just laws of this Government, and hold themselves in readiness to strike at the life of the Republic when they shall have obtained the power.

"Under the present policy of reconstruction the rebel States have not chosen their representatives according to law. The proclamation of May 29th, 1865, was utterly disregarded. Men excepted by it voted at the elections, and men thus excepted were elected to the most important offices. Men were elected to aid in the important work of reconstruction who had sworn an oath against the United States Government, who had fought against it, and had given no subsequent acknowledgement by returning to their allegiance, that they were not still its bitter enemies. Are such men fit to represent the vital interests of the States of this Republic within the National or State Governments? Such are not the *set of men* Congress desires should *vitalize and develop the Union feeling in the South.*

"It is a false assertion that a Republican Congress desire to humiliate the South. It is treason and hydra-headed slavery, with their correlatives, aristocracy, despotism, anarchy and rebellion—that Republican loyalty has determined shall perish from this Nation, and with the help of a just God, will crush out from this country, destined to be the land of human rights.

"Justice, ever in harmony with freedom, demands that national crimes be punished and equitable laws established, and that the dignity, rights and privileges of loyal citizens be respected. An outraged people demand that 'as the Government has put down traitors in arms, traitors should be put down in law, in public judgment, and in the morals of the world.' Loyal people believe in no policy that honors, exalts, makes governors, legislators, senators and presidents of men who have sent our brothers and sons to Andersonville and Libby prisons, and made the land to flow with the blood of patriots; men who to-day are singing praises to the traitors—Jefferson Davis, Lee, and Stonewall Jackson, and have erected monuments to rebels, while they curse the memory of our fallen heroes and martyred patriots. We believe the mass of the people in the insurrectionary States, freed from the vile influences of those men who led them into treason and rebellion, would be easily brought back to allegiance and become good citizens; but the leading men, those described in the Proclamation of Amnesty, are 'the conscious, influential traitors,' who wield their power in opposition to republican institutions and draw the masses which they control into the vortex of treason, anarchy and political crimes. Is it strange that the loyalty of the nation demands that the infamous crime of treason 'should suffer its penalty,' that 'it should be made odious,' when we behold the war that it has caused, and the men who yet avow they will accomplish the destruction of free institutions? Are not these unrepentant traitors guilty before the law? Should they not be disfranchised, that they may no longer continue their infernal work of ruin and death? Should not men in sympathy with Jefferson Davis and his co-fiends, men who live to plot, conspire and to undermine a government based upon justice, liberty and republicanism, be excluded from our legislatures? yea, be prohibited from the rights of loyal citizens until they have become such. These traitors, who avow that had they it in their power they would inaugurate a war to-day that would extirpate pure democracy from the land, trample upon the rights of humanity, and crush liberty with the iron heel of despotism. It has been fully demonstrated to thoughtful, candid, reasoning loyal men who have investigated the true state of affairs in the rebellious States, that it would be unsafe to permit the withdrawal of the military forces from those States. That loyal people, white and black, are hopeless of maintaining their rights without military power; that without it they would have no protection for life, liberty or property.

"In view of these facts, should not loyal men demand that the basis of pacification be justice and human rights? Should they not exact justice, and determine never to recognize any government as a republican government, but one based upon the principles which insure 'Liberty—full, broad and unconditional Liberty?' Then, and not till then, can we expect 'peace to come, and come to stay.'

"The Republican party for the last four years has been fighting for the 'general liberty and security of the people.' That party, in Congress and out of Congress, are still battling for what alone will secure the general liberty and security of the nation—justice and equal rights before the law. On the other hand, there is a powerful faction who are opposed to the principles of the Republican party, have been fighting against emancipation, the draft, confiscation, the enrollment and arming of the blacks, the proclamation of martial law, and the arrest and punishment of traitors. The men who opposed the war because they believed it would result in the destruction of their cherished plans against true democratic principles, are those who cheer loudest for the reconstruction policy of Andrew Johnson and applaud his shameless betrayal of the Republican party, and are loud in praise of his denouncement of those who in the National Congress firmly maintain republican principles and resist all attempts to force into their councils traitors who have been connected with the rebellion. What class of men support Andrew Johnson's policy in his vetoes of the Freedmen's Bureau and Civil Rights Bills, and demand the full representation of the rebellious States in Congress, when he denounces as traitors that body whose every act has been to carry out the policy of Abraham Lincoln to 'secure the rights and liberties of the people?' Where do we find the voice of the disciples of Calhoun and the Vallandighams? Why did the rebels and copperheads, North and South, shout long and loud for the Chief Executive of the Republic when he stepped from his exalted position to mingle with a copperhead mob to condemn the leaders of the Republican party for their integrity and loyalty? Are not these admirers of the President's last acts those who said, a little while since, that 'successful coercion would be as great a crime as successful secession;' that 'if any attempt was made to put secession down blood would flow in the streets of New York;' that 'coercion was unconstitutional, illegal?' Are not these the men who opposed the measures for the suppression of the rebellion, opposed the suspension of the *habeas corpus*, opposed emancipation, conscription, loans, legal tender, money and taxation? Such are the men who opposed the policy of Abraham Lincoln, but who to-day embrace the doctrines of the betrayer of the Republican party.

"Andrew Johnson is now the upholder of that party who said of the Martyr of Liberty, 'that the fate of Charles I, should be his doom," that he ought to be put down by the bullet, and found their Booth to carry out their hell-born desire. These admiring friends of Andrew Johnson threatened to hang the military commission that condemned to death the assassins of Abraham Lincoln. These same friends proposed to divide this Union into four quarters, Northern, Western, Pacific and Southern; but now do not object to Union, provided that the country can be ruled by the policy of Andrew Johnson, Robert E. Lee, Jefferson Davis, General Humphries, and other 'loyal' Southerners—provided our Congress can be made up of the leaders of the great secession movement. Are not these men 'Southern patriots,' 'honorable men,' 'Christian warriors,' 'chivalrous gentlemen,' the men who have a right, acquired by their devotion to 'Southern institutions,' and their adherence to the 'white man's government,' to bid defiance to a Republican Congress and a loyal people. Have not these men acquired a right to denounce *that party* which has determined, with the help of Eternal Justice, to establish equal rights and equitable laws in this Republic.

"My friends—we, who are in sympathy with the National Republican party, are called upon to meet the issues that are presented in this contest between human liberty and despotic oppression. The great questions before the nation are of vital importance to us all, involving as they do the moral and political ruin of the country, or the triumph of the principles upon which human rights are based. In the progress of events we can but mark a series of antagonisms which must impress all thoughtful men who are interested in the welfare of our country with the fact that in this terrible conflict, free government and the rights of humanity must be established and respected in this Republic and the Union maintained in its integrity, or the false and dangerous doctrines which the enemies of our National Government have vindicated before, during and since the rebellion, will triumph and overthrow the democratic, republican institutions now the glory of the American Nation. In this case, will not the loyal element, North and South, sustain a truly Republican Congress, which, as a body, is devoted to liberty and loyalty, which is struggling to vindicate the immutable principles of the Declaration of Independence and the Constitution, and 'to continue the Government in loyal hands, and none other;' which has determined that none 'but men loyal to the Constitution, loyal to freedom, loyal to justice,' shall participate in the National Councils, to frame laws for the country or control the work of reorganization? This body of earnest patriots is governed by the fundamental principle that 'the exercise of political power should be confined to the loyal.' One of the noble men of that body, Senator Wilson, forcibly says: 'A loyal people, with the clear instincts of intelligent patriotism, saw amid all the excitements of the present that this was not a struggle for the restoration of the rebel States into the Union; but a struggle for the admission of rebels into the Union; a struggle for the admission of rebels into the legislative branches of the Government of the United States; not a struggle to put rebels under the laws, but to enable rebels to frame the laws of the country. Politicians might deceive themselves, but the people, who had given two and a half millions of men, the blood of 600,000 heroes, and $3,000,000,000, comprehend the issues. The Republican or great Union party of the country, embracing in its ranks more of moral and intellectual worth than was ever organized in any political party on the globe, proclaims as its living faith the creed of the equal rights of man, and the brotherhood of all humanity embodied in the New Testament and in the Declaration of Independence. The best interests of the regenerated Nation, the rights of man, the elevation of an emancipated race alike demand that the leaders of that great Union party that restored a broken Union and gave liberty to four millions of men, shall continue to administer the Government and preserve and frame the laws for the nation.'

"The great Liberty party will sustain this Congress in its efforts to establish in the rebellious States republican governments based upon the fundamental principles laid down in the Declaration of Independence. Until these governments are established the rights of loyal citizens will not be protected—Liberty, peace and permanent Union cannot be secured to the Nation—the natural, civil and political rights of man will not be achieved. The two great elements of republican government are justice and equality. These two elements are wanting in the present governments of the rebellious States. They only contain those elements which, in the words of Abraham Lincoln, 'make the States half slave—half free,' and are, therefore, established upon a basis which cannot permanently endure. They do not secure freedom to all, do not protect the rights of four millions of human beings, who claim and are entitled to the just rights of citizens. They do not, in the language of Andrew Johnson, 'secure exact justice to all men, special privilege to none,' do not provide for the common defence, promote the general welfare, establish justice and secure the blessings of liberty to ourselves and our posterity. These governments, I repeat, are wanting in the great principles upon which must be based republican government. These fundamental doctrines the Fathers sought to establish—Liberty to all, and Equal Rights to all. No State constitution can be republican in form which disfranchises the loyal citizens of the United States. Millions of human beings, within the past four years, have been emancipated from the bondage of slavery, and are now citizens of the United States, loyal patriotic defenders of their country and the firm friends of republican State governments, which will recognize their moral, civil and political rights. These governments will never be established through the influence of traitors, rebels, or any class of men whose lives have been spent in political opposition to republican institutions, and who continue to fight against destiny and the forces which are moving the nations of the world to extend equal rights to all men; the men whom treason has made '*odious*,' the men in command of the rebel goverments, who 'grant protection to the rich traitor, while the poor Union man stands out in the cold, often unable to get a receipt or a voucher for his losses.' These men might legislate forever and they would never establish just laws for all, would never advocate measures by which the rights of all would be secured, would never recognize the great principles of republican government, which comprehend universal liberty, universal justice and universal suffrage, without which this nation will never attain to that grandeur and power which the voice of liberty proclaims the destiny of a united Republic. During the administration of Abraham Lincoln an attempt was made to establish governments in Louisiana, Tennessee and Arkansas, based upon republican principles. These were in harmony with the policy of that Martyr of Liberty, and met the approbation of him who ever desired to promote liberty and popularize progressive principles. It is true an important political element was wanting in these forms of government, which President Lincoln himself more than once hinted at as necessary to enter into truly republican governments. They did not embrace the political rights of all loyal citizens. Alas! Lincoln did not live to carry out that policy which promised universal suffrage; did not live to carry out his pledge that 'the freedom of the enfranchised should be maintained,' and that he should be not only a 'soldier in war, but a citizen in peace.' In the Constitution of Louisiana of 1864, provisions were made for the Legislature of the State to extend the right of suffrage to the enfranchised, to educate them, to draw upon them for defence. Of this Constitution, it was said by the immortal and lamented Lincoln, that he had read it through twice, and 'thought it the best Constitution yet adopted by any State.' Had not the enemies of progress and liberty controlled this State in opposition to the policy of the champion of liberty and loyalty, Louisiana would have stood upon the broad platform of constitutional liberty, when she would have exclaimed through the people, 'I have bent the tyrant's rod, I have broken the yoke of slavery, and to-day she stands redeemed.' But, alas! who, under the policy of Andrew Johnson, the author of these noble words, have been the participants in the work of reorganization? Has it been those 'loyal to freedom, loyal to justice,' men true and faithful to the rights of humanity? What has been the course of action of the Governor of Louisiana, of the State Government, of the Government of New Orleans, the metropolis of the South. History, true to justice, will not fail to point out the true story and give its moral to the future. It will solve this problem of reconstruction and seal the doom of the enemies of human rights. Antagonistic systems of government cannot exist. There is no harmony between liberty and slavery. Their friends will never be in sympathy, can never work together in the vitally important work of reconstruction. Uncompromising and eternal war has been declared between slavery and freedom. Peace will never come until this antagonism ceases, and pure republican, democratic principles triumph over the arrogant slave powers.

"Andrew Johnson says the people will 'give evidence to the nations of the earth and to its own citizens that it has the power to restore internal peace.' Yes, the American people will give this evidence, against all Andrew Johnson's diabolical machinations to inaugurate another horrid rebellion. Let Andrew Johnson beware of treachery in himself, lest he call down the vengeance of betrayed millions.

"My countrymen—the loyal element, regardless of race or color, must master and control the destinies of Louisiana, or the enemies of Liberty, the sworn vindictive enemies of the Great Republic, will again raise the banner of treason and trail in the dust that glorious flag which has inscribed upon its folds, 'Union, Confidence, Justice, Freedom, Enfranchisement—*the salvation and perpetuity of the Nation.*' Lovers of liberty and human rights—I call upon you in the name of our venerated fathers, in the name of the love you bear for the rising generation, to meet with brave hearts and iron resolves the vital issues now before you. In our struggle to achieve and maintain republican institutions, we are sustained by the glorious Congress who are laboring 'TO MAKE TREASON ODIOUS,' and enact governments that will '*insure freedom to the free.*' When this glorious desideratum is achieved, this GREAT Nation will justly claim that Unity and Liberty destined for a land of FREEDOM."

CHAPTER XXVI.

MONROE RE-ELECTED MAYOR OF NEW ORLEANS.

The reconstructed of New Orleans preferred men to govern the city dyed a few shades deeper in the blood of the friends of the United States Government than those already holding the municipal offices. Looking back upon the days of thuggery with evident pleasure, the returned rebels nominated John T. Monroe for Mayor, and Lucien Adams for one of the Recorders of the city.

The following was a reason given by one of the returned Confederates for the nomination of Monroe:

"He is a staunch member of the National Democratic party, an earnest supporter of the reconstruction policy of President Johnson, and an advocate of peace, harmony and good will."

The following is from the pen of an ex-confederate officer who was upon the ticket of municipal officers to be elected in New Orleans on the Monday to which he refers:

"We must stand by Andrew Johnson in his contest with radicalism, already fierce, and destined to become fiercer and more ferocious. We ought to preserve the organization of the National Democratic party in all its completeness and integrity. We cannot afford to lose the present occasion of demonstrating to the President that in his fight with radicalism he has all our sympathies.

"It cannot be objected that in a merely municipal election this is a matter of minor importance, and that our Federal relations have nothing to do with it.

"The chief commercial city of the South will have an opportunity next Monday of deciding by what majority she allies herself with the only party that can save the country from ruin."

The Democratic nominees for the city offices were elected on the 12th of March, 1866. The New Orleans Press and the friends of the Administration were jubilant over the election. Rozier, Rozelius, Fellows, and others who were in sympathy with President Johnson's "reconstructed," considered it a joyful victory over the radical Republican party. Loyal men were overwhelmed with reproaches and threats by the dominant party if they dared resist the encroachments of thuggery by word or act. The state of affairs caused a general indignation in the hearts of the loyal masses, who trembled with fear as they saw the workings of "My Policy," but were powerless to defend justice against the encroachments of the organizations by which they were surrounded. The unanimous voice of the truly loyal in New Orleans was "deliver us from our enemies and the corrupt men in official positions." Even the mild and gentle Canby, who was always disinclined to interfere with civil law, sustained by Executive authority, was startled from his repose upon the announcement of the election of Monroe.

The following orders were issued by the commanding General:

HEADQUARTERS DEPARTMENT OF LOUISIANA,
NEW ORLEANS, La., March 19, 1866.
Special Orders, No. 63.

[Extract.]

2. It appearing that John T. Monroe, who received, respectively, at the late municipal election a majority of the votes for the office of Mayor, may come within the class of exceptions mentioned in the President's proclamation of amnesty, not having received a special pardon, will be suspended from the exercise of any of the functions of his office until his case can be investigated and the pleasure of the President be made known.

By order of Major-General E. R. S. Canby.

WICKHAM HOFFMAN,
Assistant Adjutant-General.

Official.
NATHANIEL BURBANK,
1st Lieut., Acting Asst.-Adjt.-Gen.

HEADQUARTERS, DEPARTMENT OF LOUISIANA.
NEW ORLEANS, La., March 19, 1866.
Special Orders, No. 63.]

[Extract.]

3. J. Add. Rozier, Esq., is appointed Mayor of the city of New Orleans, *pro tempore*, and will act in that capacity until the municipal government of the city is organized, as provided for by the fifteenth section of the city charter, in the case of the sickness or temporary absence of the Mayor.

By order of Maj.-Gen. E. R. S. Canby.

WICKHAM HOFFMAN,
Assistant Adjutant-General.

Official:
NATHANIEL BURBANK,
1st Lieut., Act. Asst. Adj.-Gen.

Can it be supposed by a reflecting mind that, had Arnold applied to Washington for pardon, he would have been reinstated as General of the United States forces? or that, had Monroe sought pardon from Lincoln, he would have been reinstated Mayor of New Orleans?

Andrew Johnson's favorite policy drew to his sovereign feet the chief traitors of the land, who went through with the farce of sueing for pardon, for the known purpose of strengthening despotism. Such suppliants were raised to the highest positions in the State and municipal governments of the rebellious States. Mark the contrast between the treatment of Doctor Dostie, the patriot of New Orleans, and that of Monroe, the traitor of New Orleans, at the hands of the Executive!

To Washington went Monroe, to get permission from the President to control the metropolis of the South, according to his old thuggery principles, in defiance of loyalty, justice, law and order. Upon his return to New Orleans, after an interview with the President, the following notice appeared in the New Orleans papers:

"Mayor John T. Monroe arrived home last evening. While in Washington, Mayor Monroe had several interviews with President Johnson, and obtained from him a special pardon, affixed to which is the President's own signature, which in most cases is only stamped upon pardons issued by the Chief Executive.

"Mayor Monroe, who was received very kindly by Mr. Johnson, upon asking for his pardon remarked to the President that he had supposed he was already pardoned under the proclamation of President Lincoln. Mr. Johnson replied that to all intents and purposes he was included in that proclamation, but that for the sake of satisfying all parties, and to place the Mayor beyond the probability of any future annoyance, he thought it best to grant him a special pardon.

"At half-past eleven o'clock Mayor Monroe repaired

to the City Hall, and once more assumed the duties of Chief Executive of the city."

By the supporters of the President the flattering reception of Monroe at the Executive Mansion was hailed as a propitious omen for their plans.

The Mayor, fully established in office, proceeded to act in harmony with the plan of reconstruction. All policemen known to be tinctured with loyal blood were discharged, to give place to applicants conspicuous in murdering Union men in 1860 and during the rebellión.

Secret organizations were formed, composed of officers of the confederate army, whose avowed object was to protect the rights of their companions, but whose secret purpose was demonstrated to be the destruction of the loyal element of Louisiana. As early as May 27th Hays' Brigade was organized to prepare for future work. Similar organizations, prepared for future emergencies all proclaiming their rule of action to be in unison with the principles of their former master, Jefferson Davis, and their ruler, Andrew Johnson.

The rumors of conspiracy, armed organizations, and secret societies aroused many of the timid and watchful to the danger of the situation; whispers of revenge uttered by the avowed enemies of "Yankees," "innovators," "negro worshippers," and the freedmen fell upon the ears of the alarmed loyalists of New Orleans. To whom should they appeal? Not to the Chief Executive. His decrees had gone forth "to sustain the civil authorities." The civil authorities were the conspirators. To the military alone the defenceless looked for protection.

In the midst of danger the courageous Dostie knew

no fear. He faced his enemies with the same daring spirit with which he had petitioned General Twiggs for a pass in 1861, and passed his enemies, who sought every opportunity to insult him upon the street with stoical firmness.

Said he: "I am reminded daily that my enemies seek my life and attempt to destroy my reputation. I am pointed at as a fanatic, an immoral man; am accused of every crime but that of disloyalty to my Government, and in the eyes of my enemies that is my greatest crime. But I have faith in my God, faith in my Government, and am in possession of a clear conscience. My enemies may be numberless, but my philosophy points me to a happy future."

Surrounded by a despotism which proscribed Union men in their business, deprived them of their political rights; endangered their lives, liberty and property, loyal men naturally sought relief from a tyranny that was depriving them of every blessing due to humanity. The basis of the Constitution of 1864 was liberty, justice and equality. That basis was in harmony with the acts of a radical Congress. To that the loyal people of Louisiana appealed. At the mention of the Convention of 1864, delirium and fury seized the "reconstructed."

According to the following resolutions adopted by the Convention of Nov. 1864, it was proposed to re-assemble that Convention in 1866.

"*Resolved*, That when this Convention adjourns, it shall be at the call of the President, whose duty it shall be to re-convoke it for any cause, or, in case the constitution should not be ratified, for the purpose of taking such measures as may be necessary for the formation of a civil government for the State of Louisiana. He shall also, in that case, call upon the proper officers of the State to cause elections to be held, to fill any vacancies that may exist in the Convention, in parishes where the same may be practicable.

"*Resolved*, That in case of the ratification of the constitution, it shall be in the power of the Legislature of the State at its first session, to reconvoke the Convention in like manner, in case it should be deemed expedient or necessary for the purpose of making amendments or additions to the constitution, that may, in the opinion of the Legislature require a reassembling of the Convention, or in case of the occurrence of any emergency requiring its action."

At this important crisis, Judge Abell of the Convention of 1864, hastens to give the following advice.

"NEW ORLEANS, June 27, 1866.

"*Editors of the Picayune*—If you believe with me that the attempt to reconvene the Convention of 1864 is unlawful and calculated to disturb the peace and good order of the State, you will publish the following, that the people may know how stands the matter. I am bold to say I look upon the whole matter as a conspiracy against the constitution and people of the State.

"I am clearly of the mind that the Convention of 1864 has filled its mission and is a lifeless body, and that it cannot and will not be reassembled by constitutional or legal authority. But if without constitutional or legal authority, it should do so, I will then, as I now do, protest in the name of the people and State of Louisiana, against touching the constitution of 1864 without the consent of the people, expressed at the ballot-box or by the Legislature.

"I am not an apologist of that instrument; it was conceived in usurpation, and brought forth in corruption; but like unto all human institutions, it has some good points, and will answer all the purposes of a State government until the people shall, by deliberation and experience, adopt a constitution to accord with their wishes and interest under the changed state of political and social order.

"Yours, respectfully, E. ABELL."

The concentrated wrath of the leading rebel organ in New Orleans, in view of the daring of loyal citizens, finds vent in the following words:

"The Jacobins of 1864 are at work. They are in league with a Jacobin Congress and seek to overturn our Democratic Government." In 1866, the press of New Orleans, with but two exceptions, (the Tribune, edited by colored men, and the Advocate edited by the Rev. J. P. Newman) was identified with the enemies of liberty and loyalty.

Outside of the men and measures connected with "our cause" and "my policy," nothing relating to political or philanthropic movements escaped the vile attacks of the press. The Freedman's Bureau, the Civil Rights Bill, Republican ideas, the officers of the United States army and navy, Congress, Philanthropists and Reformers, who opposed slavery and rebellion all over the land were subject to their low scandal. Some of their vile epithets were, "The Rump Congress," "The Rump Convention of 1864," "The fool, Abe Lincoln," "The Beast, Butler," "The crazy fanatic Sumner," "The nigger worshipper Dostie," etc.

The 4th of July, 1866, was celebrated in the following manner in New Orleans, by the "Reconstructed Party" of that city. From the New Orleans *Press*, July 5th, we quote the following:

"The ninetieth anniversary of the Declaration of Independence was celebrated in this city on Wednesday.

"There was not a large attendance at the Fair Grounds on the morning of the Fourth.

"About noon, at the central stand, the few hundred people in attendance were called to order, and Mayor Monroe was introduced as the presiding officer.

"In presenting to the audience Mr. I. N. Marks, President of the Firemen's Charitable Association, as the reader of the Declaration of Independence. Mayor Monroe took occasion to say that he differed from one expression of opinion in that document to the effect that "all men were created equal." The nigger could not be considered the equal of the white man; and as the writer of the Declaration, Mr. Jefferson, was a slaveholder, it stood to reason that he never could have meant to include the nigger in that assertion."

CHAPTER XXVII.

CALL FOR A CONVENTION.

On the 7th of July, Judge Howell issued the following proclamation:

Whereas, By the wise, just and patriotic policy developed by the Congress now in session, it is essential that the organic law of the State of Louisiana should be revised and amended so as to form a civil government in this State in harmony with the General Government, establish impartial justice, insure domestic tranquility, secure the blessings of liberty to all citizens alike, and restore the State to a proper and permanent position in the great Union of States, with ample guarantees against any future disturbance of that Union.

And whereas, It is provided by resolutions adopted on the 25th day of July, 1864, by the Convention, for the revision and amendment of the Constitution of Louisiana, that when said Convention adjourns, it shall be at the call of the President, whose duty it shall be to reconvoke the Convention for any cause; and that he shall also, in that case, call upon the proper officers of the State to cause elections to be held to fill any vacancies that may exist in the Convention, in Parishes where the same may be practicable.

And whereas, at a meeting held in New Orleans, on the 26th of June, 1866, the members of said Convention recognized the existence of the contingency provided for in said resolutions, expressed their belief that the wishes and interests of the loyal people of this State demand the reassembling of the said Convention, and requested and duly authorized the undersigned to act as President *pro tem* for the purpose of reconvoking said Convention, and in conjunction with his Excellency the Governor of the State, to issue the requisite proclamations reconvoking said Convention, and ordering the necessary elections as soon as possible.

And whereas further, it is important that the proposed amendments to the Constitution of the United States should be acted upon in this State within the shortest delay practicable.

Now, therefore, I RUFUS K. HOWELL, President *pro tem* of the Convention, as aforesaid, by virtue of the power and authority thus conferred on me, and in pursuance of the aforesaid resolutions of adjournment, do issue this, my Proclamation, reconvoking the said "Convention for the Revision and Amendment of the Constitution of Louisiana," and I do hereby notify and request all the Delegates to said Convention to assemble in the Hall of the House of Representatives, Mechanics' Institute Building, in the City of New Orleans, on the FIFTH MONDAY, (thirtieth day of July, 1866, at the hour of 12 M., and I do further call upon his Excellency the Governor of this State to issue the necessary writs of election to elect Delegates to the said Convention in Parishes not now represented therein.

Done and signed at the City of New Orleans, this seventh day of July A. D. 1866, and of the Independence of the United States the ninety-first.

R. K. HOWELL,
President pro tem.

Attest: JOHN E. NELLIS, Secretary.

On the same day that the above proclamation was issued, the National democratic Committee, of New Orleans, met at St. Charles Hotel, and adopted the following resolutions:

1. *Resolved*, That we highly approve of the reconstruction policy of President Johnson.

2. *Resolved*, That the political principles of the Radicals in Congress are unconstitutional and revolutionary.

3. *Resolved*, That we cordially approve of the proposed call of a National Union Convention at Philadelphia.

July 27th, 1866, Governor Wells issued a proclamation commanding an election to be held by the qualified voters for delegates to the Convention for the revision and amendment of the Constitution of Louisiana.

Governor Well's action in the tragedy of July 30th, is another proof of his vascillating, criminal course. One day a professed Unionist, the next an enemy to his Government and loyal subjects; one day crushing loyal men, another day elevating them; one month exerting his power to abolish the Constitution of 1864, the next changing his plans, and issuing a proclamation reassembling the Convention of 1864. Did Governor Wells foresee danger? Was he the deepest plotter in the great Conspiracy? General Sheridan in his letter to the the Honorable Secretary of War, E. M. Stanton, thus delineates the character of Governor Wells:

"I say now unequivocally that Governor Wells is a political trickster and a dishonest man. I have seen him myself, when I first came to this command, turn out all the Union men who had supported the Government, and put in their stead rebel soldiers, some of whom had not yet doffed their grey uniforms. I have seen him again during the July riot of 1866, skulk away where I could not find him to give him a guard, instead of coming out as a manly representative of the State and joining those who were preserving the peace. I have watched him since, and his conduct has been as sinuous as the mark left in the dust by the movement of a snake.

"I say again that he is dishonest."

The New Orleans *Times* thus comments upon Governor Wells' proclamation—the Secretary of State, etc.:

"It is quite confidently stated that the Secretary of State will refuse to affix his signature and the seal of the State to the proclamation of the Governor ordering elections to be held to fill vacancies in the so-called Convention of 1864. The Secretary will be fully justified in refusing to connect himself with so lawless and revolutionary a proceeding—so flagrantly criminal an act.

"Meantime official notification has been sent to the President at Washington, informing him of the conspiracy of the Governor and others to overthrow the government and institutions of the State by a lawless and revolutionary act. J. Add. Rozier, Esq., is also present at the Federal Government, to represent to the President the proposed wrong and indignity to our State. We have little doubt that the President will take such action as will arrest these reckless conspirators and agitators and protect the people from their evil designs. There is a peculiar appropriateness in the selection of Mr. Rozier for this mission,"

The following notice appeared in one of the city papers on the morning of July 27th:

"FRIENDS OF FREDOM RALLY!—*Universal Suffrage!* A grand mass meeting of citizens who are in favor of universal suffrage, of the reconstruction policy of Congress, and of amending the Constitution of this State to give equal rights to all without distinction of race or color, will be held on Friday night, July 27, 1866, at 8 o'clock, at the Mechanics' Institute. Distinguished speakers will address the meeting. Union men, come in your might and power."

Said the late Adjutant-General of the State of Louisiana, John L. Swift, who descended from his radical platform of 1864 to bow at the footstool of the Chief Executive of the nation in 1865:

"Revolution in Louisiana had a brave and determined leader in Dr. A. P. Dostie. He was a man of unquestionable courage. He was honest and fearless. He possessed many admirable qualities, and he was a revolutionist by nature. In works and acts he was a fanatic." Alas! that some of that honest and fearless "fanaticism" could not have been imparted to his friend John L. Swift, who apparently sympathized in all his fanatical acts in 1864.

"Fanatic!" was the cry when Sumner was struck down by Brooks in the United States Senate. The same cry was heard when Lovejoy was murdered by the enemies of free speech. When Lincoln fell by the hand of an assassin, the dark pall of woe hung over the nation. There was silence in the ranks of the enemies of the Republic, but secret joy that another "fanatic" in the cause of universal liberty had become a victim to the national conspiracy.

For a time that conspiracy was paralyzed before the Nation's woe, but, under "My Policy," was revivified. "Tbe Conflict of Races" was incorporated into the reconstruction measures of Andrew Johnson. Negro suffrage and its advocates in 1866 were to the returned rebels what freedom and Abraham Lincoln were to slaveholders in 1860. Conspiracy and murder are the offsprings of slavery. In 1860 Jefferson Davis defended the spirit of slavery. In 1866 Andrew Johnson defended the same demoniac spirit, and warmed the dying viper into life that it might strike its fangs into the vitals of the Republic.

The following invitation was sent to Dr. Dostie on the morning of the 26th of July:

"NEW ORLEANS, La., July 25, 1866.

To Dr. A. P. Dostie:

SIR: The friends of universal suffrage will hold a meeting in this city at the Mechanics' Institute on Friday evening, the 27th inst., at 7 o'clock P. M., for the purpose of endorsing the policy of the present Congress relative to the Southern States and the call for the reassembling of the Constitutional Convention of Louisiana. You are respectfully invited to be present and address the meeting.

By the Committee.

On the night of the 27th of July a meeting of loyal citizens was held in Mechanics Institute for the purpose of endorsing Congress and to discuss the call for the reassembling of the Convention of 1864. It is to be regretted that Dr. Dostie's speech at Mechanic's Institute was not fully reported as his enemies have taken advantage of that fact, and misrepresent his words upon that occasion. We annex the following report of the meeting:

"NEW ORLEANS, July 28th, 1866.

"By far the most enthusiastic meeting which had assembled in New Orleans for many years, met last night at the Mechanics' Institute, or State House. The meeting was composed of 'citizens who are in favor of universal suffrage, of the reconstruction policy of Congress, and of amending the Constitution of this State to give equal rights to all, without distinction of race or color."

"Long before the time announced for opening the meeting, the large hall of the House of Representatives was crowded to its utmost capacity, and a large and anxious crowd assembled in the street, in front of the State House, where a stand was erected and a separate meeting subsequently organized. The inside meeting was called to order by Judge Heistand, United States Commissioner, who nominated ex-Governor Hahn as chairman. Vice-Presidents composed of prominent Union men from all the districts and parishes in the State, were elected."

The following resolutions were read and adopted:

Resolved, That the 75,000 citizens of Louisiana qualified to vote, but disfranchised on account of color, 20,000 of whom risked their lives in her behalf in the war against the Rebellion may claim from her as a right that participation in the Government which citizenship confers.

Resolved, That we endorse the proposed reassembling of the Constitutional Convention of Louisiana, seeing in that movement a reasonable hope of the establishment in the State, of justice for all her citizens, irrespective of color, and also of the enforcement of that patriotic declaration of President Johnson, "That treason is a crime, and must be made odious, and that traitors must take a back seat in the work of reconstruction."

Resolved, That we commend the course pursued by Judge Howell and Governor Wells, who, regardless of threats, personal violence and unmoved by the ridicule, censure and attempt at intimidation of the rebel press of the city, rise to the hights of the occasion in the performance of acts of duty.

Resolved, That the thanks of the loyal men of Louisiana are due to Congress, for the firm stand taken by that Honorable Body, in the matter of reconstruction.

Resolved, That the military and naval authorities of the Nation are entitled to our gratitude for the security afforded us.

Resolved, That we approve the call issued by the friends of the Republican Party to assemble in Philadelphia on the 1st Monday in September next, and we recommend, that on the 8th of August next, a Convention assemble in this city to select delegates to represent this State in the Philadelphia Convention.

Resolved, That until the doctrine of the political equality of citizens irrespective of color is recognized in this State there will be no permanent peace.

Gov. Hahn, on taking the chair, spoke as follows:

" *Fellow-Citizens:* Although it is not my province to address you on this occasion, I cannot resist the temptation to express to you my appreciation of the honor which I feel in being called to preside over this meeting. The days of the slave oligarchy, of Confederate Provost-Marshals, when colored men could not come together to deliberate over public affairs, has, thank God, ceased to exist. [Applause.] As President Lincoln and the Union army were unable to restore the Union until the colored men came to their aid, so the Union men of this State feel that they cannot maintain the principles of the union of the States without the aid of the patriotic colored men. [Applause.] I remember the day when the teacher of a colored school in this city was ruthlessly arrested and died in prison on a charge of being an abolitionist, and every time I pass that old church where he used to teach, I feel that there are men still living who have the spirit that animated him. [Applause.] The cause which we are here to-night inaugurating in Louisiana is a great and holy cause, and the rebels are trembling in their shoes in consequence. They are realizing the fact that this is a country to be ruled by loyal men, both white and black. There was a time when the term 'Abolitionist' was considered a shame, but I stand before you to-night, raised and educated as I have been in the South, and tell you that I glory in being an Abolitionist and a Radical. [Applause.] When I went to Washington last fall, my Union friends in Louisiana did not come up to the mark of universal suffrage; but when I came back a few months later, the outrage which had been heaped upon them by the rebel Government here had brought them to the mark, and now no man can justly claim to be a Union man unless he favors universal suffrage.

"I would rather every office in the State was in the hands of colored men than in the hands of unrepentant rebels. [Applause.] It is to you that the loyal men of the South must look, and when you separate to-night, make up your minds from this day forward you are as good as any white man in the State." [Great cheering.]

Hon. Rufus Waples next addressed the meeting, reviewing the policy of Congress and the President, as follows: "Congress recognizes the right for the people, in their primitive capacity, in those States destroyed by the rebels, to make their own organic law, and submit it to Congress, and leave it to Congress to decide whether it be consistent with the organic law of the republic.

"The President says all these States have a right to send their Senators and Representatives to Congress as before. If this were true, they might have sent them during the war as well as now. The rebels claim in effect that there has been no war. But let them look around at the desolation they have caused, and they will see their mistake. All loyal men indorse the policy of Congress. It ill becomes the chivalrous men of the South, as they call themselves, to talk of the injustice administered to them by the Government which they tried to destroy. If they do not like the Government, let them go to Brazil or Mexico. They say they were overpowered. Have they just found out that in this country the prime principle is that the majority shall rule. Are they any better than the loyal black man who fought for his country? I say take the whole masses of the colored people in Louisiana, and they are better educated than the rebels are—not in Latin and Greek—but in politics, and that is the necessary education required by a voter. You have learned two important lessons—to hate slavery and to abhor treason. Moral voters are more needed by the Government now than intellectual voters. Congress and the convention of 1864 both favor universal suffrage. We have now no constitution in this State, and you are in your primitive capacity. Then you have already acquired the right of suffrage—you have not got to acquire it. But you are hindered in exercising it, and the object of the convention is to remove these hindrances in conjunction with your friends at the North." The speaker concluded by paying tribute to the efforts made by Sumner, Phillips, and others at the North in the cause of universal suffrage, and assuring his audience that their efforts would not be in vain, and that the great object before them would soon be accomplished.

The outside meeting was called to order by Mr. Judd, who nominated Judge Hawkins as chairman.

Hon. John Henderson was introduced, and spoke at considerable length. He said:

"The convention will meet. He, as a member, wanted no arms. He had the arms of the State and the arms of the military authorities. The convention and the constitution had been supported by two Presidents, and by the army and navy.

Judge Heistand spoke as follows:

"*Fellow-Citizens:* The decree of God has gone forth that there shall be universal freedom and universal suffrage throughout the South. The men who got up this war effected emancipation, and by the course which they are now pursuing they will be forced to yield universal suffrage.

He spoke of the convention, and said, in substance, that if the Executive of the State needed anything to enforce the law, that power was here. The great power of American citizenship was in obeying the laws.

"He asked whether there was any justice in allowing 25,000 to have all the political power and do all the voting for 60,000 men in the State? Congress is abused for not admitting the Representatives from the South by the mass of those who have but recently returned from fighting against the very Government in which they claim a representation. They have the modesty to say: 'We'll do all the voting—you'll do all the working.'

"The Rev. Mr. Horton held up an advertisement of an Accident Insurance Company, with Gen. Johnston at its head, and hence he thought they were all safe here. He alluded to the scene in Boston when Anthony Burns, a fugitive slave was marched down State street, surrounded by a cordon of bayonets, to be carried back into slavery, and regarded the present scene as a contrast. We are here to-night as preliminary to reconvoking the convention of 1864 and 1866.

"Dr. Dostie closed the outside meeting by an eloquent speech, which was applauded to the echo, and the vast crowd, at his request, commenced forming with those from the inside meeting, for the torch-light procession, which was one of the grandest and most enthusiastic displays of the kind which has ever taken place in this city. At least 5,000 loyal disfranchised citizens formed in compact columns, and with bright torches, to the sound of loyal music, marched down Canal street, making the air resound with cheer upon cheer, for universal suffrage, Congress, and the convention which is about to assemble to give them suffrage.

"The steady march and stalwart forms of those composing the procession afforded unmistakable evidence that they had battled for the Union, and were determined, if necessary, to fight again for the right of suffrage, without which their freedom is but an empty sound."

Said William Lloyd Garrison at a public reception given him in England:

"One of the most gratifying incidents of my life was to have been invited by the United States government, together with my dear friend and coadjutor, George Thompson, to accompany General Anderson to Fort Sumter, to see the star spangled banner once more unfurled on its walls.

"We went into Charleston, meeting with a very cordial reception at the hands of the freed men, who extemporised a procession of a mile or a mile and a half long, and composed of old and young, and with a band of music they marched us through all the principal streets of that city, singing 'John Brown's body lies mouldering in the grave, but his soul is marching on.' [cheers]—and giving cheers for Abraham Lincoln and a good many other persons. I began the Anti-Slavery cause in the North in the midst of brick-bats and rotten-eggs: I finished the struggle on the soil of Carolina, in Charleston, almost literally buried beneath the wreaths and flowers which were heaped upon me."

The same liberty-loving spirit which led Garrison to rejoice in the freedom of humanity in Charleston, actuated Dostie and his friends, on the night of the 27th of July—when he marched at the head of thousands of free colored men, and assembled around the Statue of Henry Clay on Canal street, New Orleans—to sing praises to the memory of John Brown, and to exult over their future prospect of political rights.

Previous to the meeting of July 30th, Mayor Monroe wrote to the Commanding General the following letter:

"MAYORALTY OF NEW ORLEANS,
CITY HALL, July 25, 1866.

"Brevet Major-Gen. Baird, Commanding, etc.

"GENERAL:—A body of men, claiming to be members of the Convention of 1864, and whose avowed object is to subvert the Municipal and State Governments, will, I learn, assemble in this city on Monday next.

"The laws and ordinances of the city, which my oath of office makes obligatory upon me to see faithfully executed, declare all assemblies calculated to disturb the public peace and tranquility unlawful, and, as such, to be dispersed by the Mayor, and the participants held responsible for violating the same.

"It is my intention to disperse this unlawful assemblage if found within the corporate limits of the city by arresting the members thereof and holding them accountable to existing municipal law, provided they meet without the sanction of the military authorities.

"I will esteem it a favor, General, if, at your earliest convenience, you will inform me whether the projected meeting has your approbation, so that I may act accordingly.

"I am, General, very respectfully,
"JOHN T. MONROE, Mayor."

To that letter General Beard replied as follows:

"HEADQUARTERS DEPARTMENT OF LOUISIANA,
NEW ORLEANS, LA., July 26, 1866.

"Hon. JOHN T. MONROE, Mayor of the City of New Orleans.

"SIR: I have received your communication of the 25th instant, informing me that a body of men, claiming to be members of the Convention of 1864, are to assemble on Monday next.

* * * * * * *

"You believe it to be your duty, and it is your intention, to disperse this assembly, if found within the corporate limits of the city, by arresting the members thereof, and holding them accountable to the existing municipal laws, provided they meet without the sanction of the military authorities.

"As to your conception of the duty imposed by your oath of office, I regret to differ from you entirely. I cannot understand how the Mayor of the city can undertake to decide so important and delicate a question as the legal authority upon which a Convention, claiming to represent the people of an entire State, bases its action.

"This doubtless will, in due time, be properly decided upon by the legal branches of the United States Government.

* * * * * *

"If these persons assemble as you say is intended, it will be, I presume, in virtue of the universally conceded right of all loyal citizens of the United States to meet peaceably and discuss freely questions concerning their civil governments—a right which is not restricted by the fact that the movement proposed might terminate in a change of the existing institutions.

* * * * * *

"Lawless violence must be suppressed, and in this connection the recent order of the Lieutenant General, designed for the protection of citizens of the United States, deserves careful consideration. It imposes high obligations for military interference, to protect those who, having violated no ordinance of the State, are engaged in peaceful avocations.

"I am, sir, very respectfully, your obedient servant,

"A. BAIRD, Brevet Major General,

Commanding Department of Louisiana.

July 28th the following letter was sent to the Secretary of War:

HEADQUARTERS DEPARTMENT OF LOUISIANA,
NEW ORLEANS, La., July 28, 1866.

To the Hon. E. M. Stanton, Secretary of War, Washington, D. C.:

A Convention has been called, with the sanction of Governor Wells, to meet here on Monday. The Lieutenant Governor and city authorities think it unlawful, and propose to break it up by arresting the delegates. I have given no orders on the subject, but have warned the parties that I should not countenance or permit such action without instructions to that effect from the President.

Please instruct me by telegraph.

A. BAIRD,
Brevet Major-General Com.

Judge Abell had denounced the meeting of the Convention of 1864 as unlawful, and in his charge to the jury, had pronounced its members criminals before the law.

On the morning of July 30th the following appeared in the city papers of New Orleans;

WASHINGTON, July 28, 1866.

Albert Voorhies, Lieut.-Governor Louisiana:

SIR: The military will be expected to sustain, and not obstruct or interfere with the proceedings of the Courts. A dispatch on the subject of the Convention was sent to Governor Wells this morning.

ANDREW JOHNSON.

Mark the contrast!

The last public act of Abraham Lincoln sustained the loyal people (black and white) of Louisiana. The one act more infamous than any other in the administration of Andrew Johnson was that act in which he sought to crush the friends of his predecessor in Louisiana.

CHAPTER XXVIII.

MASSACRE OF JULY 30TH, 1866.

At 12 o'clock of the night of July 29th the police were withdrawn from their beats and assembled at their respective station-houses; and, besides the weapons usually used by policemen, each was given a large-sized navy revolver. Thus armed, they were held at the station-houses to await orders. In addition to these measures others had been taken by Harry T. Hays, Sheriff of the Parish of Orleans, ex-General of the rebel army, pardoned by the President to enable him to assume that office. He reorganized a portion of his old brigade as deputy sheriffs, and they were ordered to be in readiness on that occasion. They were doubly armed with revolvers, and prepared to act with all the efficiency of military discipline.

On the morning of July 30th, as the members of the Convention and their friends started to go to Mechanics' Institute, they discovered an unusual excitement, which deterred many from going. Crowds of citizens upon the streets appeared disturbed and restless. They were seen to whisper from time to time, to look at each other and, with looks of scorn and contempt, seemed to bid defiance to the members of the Convention and their friends. Says Judge Howell, President of the Convention: " A few minutes past 12 o'clock the meeting was called to order. Prayer was offered by the Rev. J. W. Horton. The roll was called amid perfect silence; only twenty-five answered to their names. A motion to adjourn for an hour was adopted for the purpose of procuring the attendance of many of the members of the Convention known to be in the city. It was expected that several days might be occupied in obtaining a quorum. I did not expect the military to protect the Convention. I could not realize the probability of disturbance. Those comprising the Convention had a right to meet as they did, and could not be properly disturbed in that right, unless they abused it by a violation of law and public order. Surely, twenty-five men meeting in the capitol building could do very little towards overturning the government of the State of Louisiana. It is wonderful how much terror they created among the recent destroyers of the State and National governments. The members of the Convention had learned that a Grand Jury in Secession on that day might under the charge of Judge (Abell) indict them as an unlawful assembly, and that Sheriff (Hays), might arrest them, and it was understood among them that, although there was no law against such assemblies, they wauld quietly submit to any attempted arrest, however unwarranted by law, give bail, and proceed in their efforts to obtain a quorum."

With the United States flag floating over Mechanics' Institute, surrounded by the United States army and navy, that Convention was left to the mercies of an armed mob. Lincoln rested in his tomb. Butler was powerless to save. Sheridon was not in the midst of the danger. Beard had not studied the plottings of the great Conspiracy. Justice slumbered, and Treason triumphed over the liberties of Louisiana.

The State officials of Louisiana, the municipal officers of New Orleans, with the armed policemen and fire companies under control, (all reconstructed under the policy of Andrew Johnson), knew that the victims of treason were defenceless in Mechanics' Institute, when thousands rushed upon the Convention assembled in its walls to crush the friends of liberty and equal rights.

When the attack was made by the mob, many of the members of the Convention and their friends had gone into the city, as a recess had been given. Judge Howell, Governor Hahn, Dr. Dostie, Alfred Shaw, Esq., Dr. Hire and the Rev. J. W. Horton, were quietly conversing with their friends when the shouts of the crowd outside the building, pursued by the mob, were heard in the streets. Negroes, followed by the excited mob, sought refuge inside Mechanics' Institute. A rush was made for the door of the Convention room. Alfred Shaw, ex-Sheriff of Orleans, was requested to inform the police, who were in pursuit of the crowd, "that inside the Hall no resistance would be made to any loyal officers claiming the right to make arrests." Mr. Shaw was met by that police with shouts of "Kill him!" "Kill him!" "Shoot the Scoundrel!" Wounded and exhausted, he was hurried to jail and thrown into a cell.

The terrible massacre outside the building progressed; hundreds of the defenceless were wounded, others brutally murdered. The Sergeant of Arms had barricaded the doors of the Convention Chamber, but soon policemen and citizens made a rush at them and broke them in. A volley of shots were poured in upon the defenceless inmates by their enemies.

The Rev. J. W. Horton attempted to hold up a United States flag in token of non-resistance. When it was recognized, policemen exclaimed, "Not one of you shall escape here alive!" and the noble Horton was shot, saying: "We offer no resistance; we surrender!" Then followed scenes of blood and carnage which can never be revealed. The assembly room was filled with the wounded and dying, whose cries and groans mingled with the oaths and demoniac laughter of their murderers. Shouts of Jefferson Davis and Andrew Johnson fell upon the ears of the dying victims of "My Policy." Numbers who came to Mechanics' Institute with those who loved liberty and delighted in the policy of Abraham Lincoln, died on that terrible day by the bloody hordes of the supporters of Andrew Johnson, who had declared that "The civil authorities must be sustained."

They were sustained, and loyal hearts ceased to beat. Thousands of the reconstructed, under the policy of their leader, rent the polluted air of New Orleans on that day with shouts of victory over loyalty. Said an eye-witness of that terrible scene:

"The Convention had been broken up an hour ago—if that were the object of Mr. John T. Monroe and his rebel soldier policemen. The negro procession had been scattered, its leaders killed, and dozens of innocent negroes struck by the same hapless fate, if *that* were their object. But still the authorities and citizens continued the riot.

"An innocent negro carrying a roll of cotton samples under his arm, quietly passed the St. Charles Hotel. Four hackmen pounced upon him, began beating the frightened non-resistant, and collected a crowd. A policeman rushed up, and without a word of inquiry, discharged every barrel of his revolver at the prostrate negro, who kept crying: '*Arrest me, I've done nothing; arrest me, but for God's sake don't kill me in cold blood.*' To the amazement of the crowd every shot missed him. "But," exclaimed a reputable citizen—let the expression be set down forever to his honor with those who know him—"if I'd a pistol, I'd have killed the miscreant policeman."

"Carts were constantly passing, laden with the bodies of murdered negroes. In one I counted six; many had two and three. *All were greeted with laughter; occasionally one evoked a cheer.* Now and then a carriage passed with some wounded white man, and not unfrequently the crowds would make a rush upon him to see if he were one of the obnoxious Radicals.

"One fell thus near the noted millinery-shop of Madame Sophie, a few doors below Blelock's bookstore. A gentleman—so far as clothes go and general demeanor—stepped out from the sidewalk and devoted a minute or two to vigorously kicking the dead body. A bystander made some expressions of horror and disgust, when a policeman turned sharp on him with 'Are you one of them, *say?*' He protested that he was not. 'He lies,' exclaimed another; '*he's a yankee soldier!*' The luckless person protested that he was not; the policeman fiercely questioned him, and at last allowed him to escape on the express ground that he '*guessed he wasn't a Fede-*

ral soldier after all.' This occurred in *sight and hearing of at least one late General of our army, who stood on an adjacent upper verandah.*"

Said another eye-witness of that revolting scene:

"I was standing on the corner of a street near Mechanics' Institute, when great cheers came up from the Institute, and a dense mob crowded along Common Street toward the St. Charles Hotel. As they approached, we could make out four policemen with cocked revolvers, and in their midst, with hat knocked off, with coat nearly torn from his shoulders, with blood clotted over his head and about his neck, with citizens rushing at him, striking at him, shouting, 'kill him!' partly limping and partly jerked along by the infuriated policemen, came Michael Hahn, ex-Member of the United States House of Representatives, ex-Governor of Louisiana, and United States Senator elect from the Legislature of Louisiana—the man to whom Abraham Lincoln confidently wrote that 'negro suffrage might yet, in some hour of peril, help to keep the jewel of Liberty in the family of Freedom!' In ten minutes he was lying bleeding and feverish in a cell of the city jail!

"My companion and myself 'moved on.' In less than a square, a regiment in blue—thank God for the color at last!—came up Canal Street on the double quick, and obliquing from side to side, left no rioters behind the artillery.

"A Union ex-Major General walked down, an hour later, to demand of Mayor Monroe, in the name of common decency and humanity, the release from the stifling jail where these wounded men still lay, of Governor Hahn, Sheriff Shaw, Dr. Dostie, and the rest. He was met by the smiling Mayor with the inquiry '*if the thing hadn't been pretty well done?*' While he was getting his question fitly answered, in walked Cavalry Kautz.

"'Is this Mr. Monroe?'

"'Yes, Sir.'

"'I am directed, Sir, to relieve you of any duties as Mayor of the city, and assume command as military governor. Yourself and other officials will await my orders.'"

Night drew her sable curtain over a scene of woe. The first act of the terrible tragedy of July 30th had been performed. A stroke of "My Policy" had been struck. The reconstructed had made use of a powerful argument in favor of the "Conflict of Races." The jails, police stations and hospitals of New Orleans bore evidence of that "conflict." The dead, the dying, those who mourned over their murdered fathers, brothers, husbands and friends, were all evidence of that "conflict." The agony of despair revealed by those who sought in vain to find the mangled remains of their loved ones, who had left their homes in the morning with hopeful hearts to be murdered by the enemies of liberty, knew that their sorrow was caused by the "Conflict of Races." They required no arguments to be convinced of the simple logic of "My Policy" and the triumph of the demon spirit of Slavery over Liberty.

Mayor Monroe and his colaborers, with their thuggery principles, had carried out their programme, upheld by the Chief Executive, who had declared that the "Civil authority must be sustained." Mechanics' Institute, in the capital of Louisiana, was a slaughter house, where the city police and the reconstructed had waded in the blood of their victims. Said one who had looked into Mechanics' Institute after the massacre: "The floor of the Convention room was covered with the blood, limbs, hair and brains of human beings, at which policemen and citizens laughed with fiendish pleasure. The hall and stairway dripped with human gore. The sidewalk was covered with blood and tattered garments."

At police stations and in the streets, citizens and policemen looked upon their dying victims; heard their cries for water, and pleadings for mercy without rendering them any assistance. "Let the wretches die," they exclaimed with a fiendish laugh, and the innocent victims of despotism perished with their pleading eyes fixed in vain upon their relentless murderers.

At the jails, and at the gates of hospitals many lay in the agonies of death. When policemen and citizens were asked if nothing could be done to relieve in some measure their sufferings, the reply was, "We know our own business. The wretches ought to suffer." "For what?" was asked. A terrible oath was the only reply.

The Rev. J. W. Horton, who had opened the Convention with prayer, was shot, stabbed, and beaten by policemen until deprived of reason. He was then dragged to jail and thrown into a cell by order of the city officials, who in order to keep the peace of the city and "sustain the civil authorities, ordered the arrest of the rioters." Therefore, the dying Horton, among whose last conscious acts, was an appeal to the God of Nations to protect a Convention which had met to uphold the cause of justice, was thrown by his assassinators as a rioter into jail. "*That was an act of justice.*" "The rioters must be arrested," said the Press of New Orleans the morning after the massacre. "The peace of the city must be preserved. The city authorities must be sustained."

In another cell lay the Rev. Mr. Jackson, who had been beaten with clubs, stabbed, and left to die by his enemies. His groans were heard by a friend of suffering humanity, in time to save him from bleeding to death from his terrible wounds.

In another cell, John Henderson, a member of the Convention of 1864 and 1866, who had so nobly opposed Judge Abell in his attacks upon Constitutional liberty, lay mortally wounded, arrested as one of the rioters."

In a distant part of the city lay the lifeless body of a German Federal officer. Captain Loup in the morning said to his wife, "There is no Government I cherish as this Republic."

That noble German was sacrificed for his love of the American Republic. "So much for your uniform," was the cry of his rebel murderers, as they dealt their death blows. The lifeless body of Captain Loup was carried home in a cart followed by a mob. It was thrown upon the floor before his loving wife. She lay unconscious of her woe, beside the lifeless form of her beloved husband, with her children clinging to their widowed mother. The mob tore from her person—her watch and rings—tokens of affection given her by her husband. Captain Loup did not live to be arrested by the "reconstructed."

Revenge, no doubt, was sweet to Judge Abell, Mayor Monroe, and other officials, acting under new "reconstruction measures." These traitors reposed that night in the calm conviction, "that the civil authorities had been sustained," and the "conflict of races" commenced with so little loss to "our cause."

CHAPTER XXIX.

DR. DOSTIE'S DEATH.

On the morning of the 30th of July, 1866, Dr. Dostie went to the Mechanics' Institute, conscious that his enemies desired his destruction. With no faith in Andrew Johnson, the unrepentant rebels, the City authorities, or the authorized bands of policemen; upon the military alone he relied.

Said he, "my enemies may assassinate me as they have often threatened, but the Convention has nothing to fear in presence of the United States army." Dr. Dostie was closely watched by the conspirators. He had been so surrounded by the snares of his enemies, that whatever movement he made, whichever direction he took seemed a step towards death. "Dostie is marked!" "Dostie will never make another speech!" "Dostie shall never come out of the Mechanics' Institute alive!" with many similar expressions were proof that his destruction was the aim of the conspirators. He was an impediment to the plans of rebels in New Orleans. "We now have Dostie and his Convention friends where we want them," said Lucien Adams and his band of policemen, as they saw their systematic organizations ready for action. An alarm was given by bells—such as had been ordered by Monroe when General Butler approached the city in 1862—and five hundred armed policemen, and companies of firemen armed and equipped for murderous action, combined with a mob of citizens, rushed from different parts of the city to Mechanics' Institute, to commence their massacre upon its defenceless victims. Upon hearing confusion in the street, a gentleman said to Dr. Dostie, "A policeman has fired upon a negro, he is begging for mercy." He replied, "we cannot prevent it, we are defenceless."

When the mob rushed to the Convention room, Dr. Dostie forgetful of self, exclaimed to the excited crowd within, "Be quiet and seat yourselves upon the floor, we shall soon be protected by the military. The United States flag waves over us."

When the mob commenced firing upon the members of the Convention and its friends, he said, "What do you want? Have you an order of arrest? We surrender." "They will kill us. We had better try and save ourselves," said a friend. Dr. Dostie replied, "I am wounded; we will beg for protection."

He went to the door where he met the infuriated mob and asked them to spare his life. He was knocked down by a brick-bat and shot—dragged down stairs by the hair of his head and thrown upon the pavement. Citizens and policemen gathered around the seemingly lifeless body of their victim and thrust it with their swords. Urged on by the mob, news-boys pierced his head with penknives. The chivalry shot and stabbed him, and shouted for Jefferson Davis and Andrew Johnson. Said an eye witness to this scene, General Alfred L. Lee, an officer of Cavalry under Banks and Sheridan:

"There was a noble man who represented the Radical sentiment of the city—Dr. Dostie. He was not a member of the Convention, but he was in the hall; he was struck with a brick and knocked down. Policemen were standing near, but instead of arresting the assaulter they stepped up to Dr. Dostie and deliberately fired into the body of the defenseless man. A citizen standing by, drew his sword from his cane and thrust it into his body. Still the doctor was not dead, and was dragged by the police through the crowd and placed in a common dirt cart. I saw this myself. One policeman sat on his body and one sat near his head. The poor man attempted to raise his head, and I saw the policeman lift his revolver and strike him on the face."

Said another eye witness, an Ex-Major General in the United States army:

"I saw four policemen bear out the seemingly lifeless body of Dr. Dostie, (an earnest, sincere patriot, a pre-eminent Free Mason, and a gentleman against whose character no true charge was ever brought) his head hung down till it almost dragged upon the pavement, blood was streaming from his wounds, and marking the path by which he was borne. Around his inanimate form the mob rushed and blasphemed. At last a cart was reached and the body thrown in; before it was reached several blows had been rained upon the bleeding body. The news flew among the rioters that Dostie was killed, the tidings were received with cheers and expressions of positive delight. 'Yes,' said the reconstructed all over the city: 'Dostie has fought our cause for years, and now we have our revenge.'"

Another rioter had been arrested and must be taken

to the police station. Nearly two miles from the Mechanics' Institute, opposite Jackson's Square, in which the monument stands, erected to the memory of Jackson, upon which in 1862, General Butler caused to be engraven the words, "The Union must and shall be preserved," the mangled bleeding body of the patriot Dostie was taken, and in sight of that monument erected to the memory of one he had cherished, he was thrown upon the stone pavement in front of the police station by the enemies of his Government—to perish. For hours he lay on that pavement suffering the agonies of death. Six rebel physicians passed him only to mock at the agonies of the dying martyr. A friend of suffering humanity desired to raise his head at the request of Dr. Dostie, but was not permitted to do so by the policeman who guarded his "prisoner." Governor Hahn upon hearing where Dr. Dostie had been conveyed, requested his sister to go to his friend and take him to some place of safety. She hastened to the police station in her carriage, and found the Dr. in a dying condition. Said he, "I am dying, tell my friends to bury me by my beloved wife, my only love." The Dr. was interrupted by the wretch who was guarding him, "Dr. Dostie is under arrest and cannot be removed without an order from the city authorities," said the chivalric policeman. The order was obtained, and the Dr. was removed to the Hotel Dieu, where he was tenderly and thoughtfully cared for by friends. "Never would Dostie have lived to have been carried to Hotel Dieu had we known that he was in the hands of his friends," said his enemies. Destiny had not decreed that the last moments of the noble Dostie should be spent in listening to cheers for Jefferson Davis and Andrew Johnson. On the night of July 30th, the dying patriot was surrounded by friends who prayed earnestly that he might be spared to labor for his beloved cause. His noble heart, patriotic life and unselfish course, had endeared him to his numerous friends, who vainly hoped that his assassinators might be cheated of their victim, and the reformer be spared for future usefulness.

Said the unselfish Dostie on that night, "I am grateful for the kindness of my friends, but there is danger in your remaining with me. Place yourselves under military protection. I cannot recover; my enemies have murdered me; I forgive them all. I should be glad to see the end of the great conflict between freedom and slavery!" Upon the suggestion of a friend that his mind might act with greater power in another world than in this, and that he might be conscious of the passing events of this world, he smilingly replied, "What a consoling thought, and in a better world I shall meet the spirit of my beloved wife, who for years has been waiting for me to meet her in Heaven. To night, I trust in her Saviour!"

A wounded policeman was taken to Hotel Dieu, who occupied a room near that of Dr. Dostie's. The Dr. upon hearing his expressions of pain, inquired who was suffering? "A policeman, perhaps, one of your murderers," was the reply. "Go," said he, "and see if the agonies of that man can in any way be relieved. If I forgive my murderers, should not my friends do the same." Six days Dr. Dostie lived after he had been mortally wounded, to prove to the world that he who had been proclaimed a "fanatic," could die a Christian, a patriot, and a philosopher. Weak from the loss of blood, suffering at times the most intense agony from his numerous wounds, he yet insisted upon seeing his friends, who came in crowds to receive a parting word from one who had ever greeted them with kindness. Said he, "I am dying, and I do not wish my friends to feel that I do not appreciate their kindness in coming to see me." Never speaking of his own sufferings, his constant anxiety was for his wounded friends. Daily, as the sister of Governor Hahn administered to his dying wants, did he question her about her brother, Mr. Shaw, and others of the wounded, saying, "Do not deceive me, I want to know if they are in danger."

An allusion to the massacre, and the sufferings of his white and colored friends, was exceedingly painful to him. Said he, "Justice will avenge the sufferings of the colored race." Some colored friends called to enquire after the Dr. "Let them come to me," said he. "I want them to know that I sympathize with them in their afflictions." "I shall die for their cause, and they will remember me kindly." During a week of intense suffering, not an impatient word was uttered, not a murmur escaped his lips. Said the dying Christian, "I await my death with perfect resignation. I know that I may die any hour as my friend and physician Dr. Avery has informed me, that my death may be very sudden from the nature of my wounds. The change of worlds will not be unpleasant to me. My trust is in the Rock of Ages."

On the morning of Dr. Dostie's death, he requested a friend to write several letters, that he desired to dictate. Said he, "write to General Butler, that in my opinion, had he been in New Orleans on the 30th of July, that massacre would not have occurred.

Write to General Banks, that my dying request to him was not to forget the cause of the colored man and liberty in Louisiana. Write to my mother, brothers and sisters, that I remember them in my dying hour with affection."

On Sabbath morning he seemed to have recovered strength. Many of his friends had hopes of his recovery, and thinking quiet was what he required, he was left to the care of one or two friends and the Sisters of Hotel Dieu. While conversing pleasantly with a friend, he suddenly exclaimed: "I am dying. I die for the cause of Liberty. Let the good work go on." With his fine eyes irradiated, he lifted an arm heavenward and with a placid smile, suddenly expired.

Such was the death of the liberty-loving Dostie. Said he, "I loved liberty when a child." "I die for the cause of Liberty. Let the good work go on," were his last words. At the tidings of his death, sadness fell upon the hearts of his friends, but strange to relate, the venom of his enemies was re-enkindled at the announcement of the death of their victim—that venom was thrown into the columns of every rebel newspaper in New Orleans, to be quoted by the press in sympathy with the rebellion througout the country.

The most scurrilous articles were set afloat when Dr. Dostie lay upon his dying bed, utterly powerless to defend the truth. Some of those articles were read in his presence. Said he, "Do my enemies persist in following me to the grave with their scandal? When will the enemies of liberty learn to be just and write the truth?" To the grave they followed their victim with falsehood and calumny. His friends proposed that his funeral should take place at Mechanics' Institute, and the military be invited to protect the funeral procession.

"If there is any demonstration over the body of Dostie it shall be torn into a thousand pieces, and his friends shall meet his fate," were the words of the infuriated murderers of July 30th.

Consternation and fear filled the hearts of his mourning friends, who would gladly have followed the remains of their friend to his last resting place. Many said, "Let us remain at home that the body of our friend may repose in peace."

The following is from the pen of Henry C. Dibble, Esq., who followed the remains of the lamented Dostie to the grave, published in the *Advocate*, edited by the Rev. J. P. Newman:

"On the evening of the 6th day of August, a few of the friends of Dr. Dostie followed his remains to the tomb. The occasion was one of unusual solemnity, and when glancing around upon the faces of those dozen or more friends of the murdered man, you could not but be impressed with the depth of feeling expressed—a commingling of poignant sorrow and just indignation.

"The burial ceremonies were performed by the Rev. Mr. McDonald of the M. E. Church. His remarks were few yet touching; calm, but very forcible. No one present felt like speaking. When the heart is oppressed by grief the lips refuse to give utterance thereto. The sorrow we felt was not of the nature which we experience when lamenting the removal of a friend by the natural visitation of Death—when we can attach no blame upon man. But while our tears fell upon the bier of our friend, we could not but dwell upon the atrocious crime, which had snatched him from our side; and then a choking indignation demanded JUSTICE.

"He was a popular man in every sense of the term. Earnest in his labors, fervent in his attachments, true to his word, and generous towards all, he gathered about him a host of friends, and at the same time, as all men of positive character must, gained not a few enemies.

"As a public speaker, the Dr. was forcible and intensely earnest, his native talent and earnestness in denouncing wrong; his honesty of purpose and consistency of action enabled him to carry conviction when others would have failed. In politics he seemed to agree with a distinguished humorist of the day. "If you are right, you cannot be too radical." However, he was not the agitator which his enemies would represent him to have been. Bold as a lion and loving truth for truth's sake, he denounced error and the advocates of wrong in terms of bitterness. Much had been said about his speeches a few nights before his murder; his words stung his enemies because they were pointed with the steel of truth. But he did not speak in the terms which the papers of this city represent. They willfully misstate his language, and for this are *jointly responsible with those who committed the crime for his murder.*

"Socially, Dr. Dostie was genial and obliging. In appearance, he was a handsome man; of medium height, straight as an arrow, and well formed, with a dark piercing eye which seemed to flash at times with enthusiasm.

"He was stricken down in the prime of life, not because his murderers bore him personal malice, but because he held and advocated political opinions conflicting with their own. He died a martyr in the cause of human rights."

The following is the announcement of the death of Dr. Dostie in the *Tribune*, a paper edited by colored men in New Orleans:

"Dr. A. P. Dostie died of wounds received at the Mechanic's Institute, Monday, July 30th, 1866, by the rebel spirits who ruled in that dark hour of the reign of terror. He died for a principle, and that principle is the *right of suffrage* to the colored men, and the right of Union men to govern the State. He died on Sunday at half past five o'clock P. M. Calmly and nobly did he bear his fearful wounds; and nobly said, 'if those principles could be sustained he would die content.' They shall succeed!"

The following is taken from the New Orleans *Times*, edited by Wm. C. King, who has immortalized his name by his unceasing labors in the cause of Andrew Johnson's reconstructed:

"Dr. Dostie, wounded at the riot of Monday last, expired yesterday near half past five o'clock.

"Death came upon him sudden as a thunder-stroke; came to him when not a single friend but the attending Sister of Charity was at his bed-side. Before 7 o'clock the Hotel Dieu swarmed with them."

Common humanity, suggests the propriety of treating death with a respect due to civilization. But that spirit which has ever reveled in the blood of the victims of despotic slavery, fearful of the exposure of conspiracy and crime, assailed one in his grave, whose spirit had passed beyond the limits of the cruel vengeance of his enemies. The name sacred to Liberty was held up, while yet the blood of Dostie stained the streets of New Orleans, by the vindictive press of that city as one linked with "fanaticism, revenge and riot." Before the grave could receive the mangled remains of the murdered victims, the conspirators had prepared their scurrilous articles for the press, hoping thereby to shield their crimes from an enraged nation, who saw the spirit of Free Institutions outraged in the massacre of July 30th, and in the reconstruction measures of Andrew Johnson, the revival of the Spirit of Slavery.

We quote the following article from the New Orleans *Times* on the riot of July 30th:

"The incendiary teachings of a pestilent gang of demagogues have produced their natural fruits—tumult and bloodshed. Fearful indeed is the responsibility which rests on the heads of those who have been concerned in the great crime of attempting to overturn all civil authority among us, and of superseding it by a wicked usurpation.

"A band of poor, deluded negroes, urged on by unprincipled white men, have, unfortunately for themselves, been the principal sufferers. Armed with pistols, clubs and razors, they collected in great numbers in the neighborhood of Mechanics' Institute, for the avowed purpose of defending the revolutionary Jacobins who had raised the banner of negro suffrage, and the result of their folly is sorrowfully apparent.

"The riot was commenced in every instance by negroes, spurred on by white men, and it is highly creditable to the police of the city that they succeeded in quelling it without any military aid. Many of them were wounded, but it is not likely that the results will prove fatal in more than two cases.

"And so the Convention of 1864, which commenced in usurpation, has ended in riot and bloodshed. As Mr. Roselius declared yesterday: "Every participant in the treasonable scheme should be arrested and sent to jail.' This, it must be remembered, is not the opinion of a political adventurer, but of a grave jurist, an original Union man, a sober, quiet citizen of the highest respectability."

On the 2d day of August, Judge E. Abell, true to his mission in the reconstruction measures of the Chief Executive, charges the jury as follows:

"Gentlemen, if you are satisfied that a riot has taken place in the city of New Orleans, then I charge you that it is the duty of all peace officers of the State to assist in suppressing the riot, using no more force and violence than is necessary; and it is the duty of every citizen to aid the officers of the law, using the like caution, and if it becomes necessary to slay one or more of the rioters in order to put it down, it is not murder but excusable homicide. If more force and violence was used than was reasonably necessary upon the circumstances of the case, then the party using the excess will be guilty of murder, manslaughter or assault and battery, according to the circumstances of the case, and the nature, fierceness and magnitude of the riot to be suppressed."

The following is an announcement in the New Orleans *Times* of the progress of the foul conspiracy:

"Sheriff Hays last evening began the re-arrest of the

members of the ex-Convention and participants in the riot, whose release from custody by General Baird has already been noticed. Judge R. K. Howell, 'President pro tem,' and O. H. Poynot, were released by Judge Abell upon bonds of $1500 each. G. H. Flagg was still in the Parish Prison at 9 o'clock last night, unable to procure the necessary amount of bonds; also several others in the same predicament. We suppose those who are now at large will be taken to day, and be held to answer for their revolutionary proceedings."

The editor of the New Orleans *Times* attempts in the following to quote the words of the dying Dostie as evidence of an insurrectionary spirit:

"The conspirators, whose recent attempt to overthrow the State Government and usurp the reins of power was defeated in so disastrous and lamentable a manner, have incautiously uttered expressions on several occasions which confirm a fact of which those who investigated their movements were previously convinced, viz: that a portion of the preconcerted plot was to cause the shedding of blood—a collision between whites and blacks. Dr. Dostie has given additional proof of this fact in a recent declaration at the Hotel Dieu.

"On Tuesday Colonel De Witt Clinton, of General Baird's staff, and Recorder Ahern visited Dr. Dostie to take his dying declaration. The *Picayune* recounts the following incident of the visit:

"'He inquired in regard to John Henderson, Jr., and was told that he was dead. He paused for a moment, and remarked: 'Well, it is a strange coincidence. We were born upon the same day, and embarked in the same glorious cause. I had reason to be apprehensive, to fear a bloody attack, but not he. Strange!'"

We turn from the enemies of loyalty and liberty and welcome the vindicators of truth, patriotism and justice. In the following letter of Mr. Dibble he denies the false assertions of the New Orleans *Times*:

"NEW ORLEANS, August 4, 1866.

"*Editor Times:*

"SIR: Your accustomed falsification of truth, in the evening edition, cannot pass over unnoticed. You say, speaking of the members of the Convention and other loyal citizens who were shot down by the police: 'We know not a single one of them who is not forced to admit, when cornered by direct question, that he was conducted safely from the building," etc. Now, sir, Dr. Dostie states, in his *dying declaration*, that he was shot down, cut, beaten, and left lying in the street by the police. The Rev. Mr. Horton was shot and beaten by the same persons. Mr. Fish, whose statement will be found in the *Advocate*, which I send you, was shot by policemen, to whom he surrendered himself. And further, sir, I have heard as many as twenty persons say that they saw policemen shoot negroes who were unarmed and making no resistance.

"You should beware, sir, how you falsify facts, for the investigations now going on will prove to the world what we in New Orleans know, that you have no respect for truth, and lack the ability to hide your falsehoods.

"Let me commend to your perusal the *Advocate*.

Yours, etc.,

HENRY C. DIBBLE."

At the Dental Convention in Boston on the 3d of September, Governor Bullock was present and made a speech in which he said:

"I have, for the last two or three days, in reading the account of the most deplorable occurrence in a remote city of this Union, had my attention directed to the fact so striking, so sad, and so educational to us, that an eminent member of your profession, Dr. Dostie, of New Orleans, fell by the hands of a populace angry with him because he was exercising the rights of an American citizen. I trust and believe that the same spirit of devotion and loyalty to freedom and the Government of the country which animated his heart, animates the hearts of all the members of his profession." [Applause.]

Said Rufus Wopples in an address before the Executive Committee of the Republicans of Louisiana on the 8th of August, 1866:

"The cause of colored suffrage is not new in Louisiana. After the redemption of New Orleans from rebel rule, the cause awoke from its slumber. I will not recount the history of its progress. To-day we behold it cut down, but not destroyed. It has been stricken down by the hand of organized assassination, some of its noblest advocates have given their lives for the cause. Let it be remembered, 'The blood of the martyrs is the seed of the Church.'

"Truth crushed to earth will rise again,
The eternal years of God are hers,
While error wounded writhes in pain,
And dies among her worshippers."

"'I am willing to die,' said the brave and magnanimous Dostie to me on the day of his death, 'if my death shall promote the cause of Liberty.' He felt that it would yet live; and he, with that spirit of unselfish devotion for which he was remarkable, seemed perfectly reconciled to his fate. I answered, 'I hope you are, in other respects, willing to die.' He said, 'That is all right—I have made my peace—that is all right.'

"I said to him, 'Dr. Dostie, I remarked yesterday to some friends that you are the man, who, in case of yellow fever, small-pox or cholera epidemic, would work night and day, and risk your life for a friend—and I believe you would do it for an enemy.' He promptly plied, 'I would do it for the rebels.' I trust that

"The sunset of life gave him mystical lore
And coming events cast their shadows before;"

that he saw the God of Justice vindicating his prerogatives, and the cause which he loved, succeeding in the future.

"I saw Rev. Dr. Horton die. I was with him an hour before his death, and witnessed his last agony. He died a martyr for that Christian religion which teaches the great doctrine of human brotherhood. The eloquence of his prayer to the King of Nations had scarcely ceased to echo from the walls of the people's Representative Chamber; his touching allusion to the assassination of the beloved and lamented Lincoln had scarcely ceased its thrill in loyal hearts, when this brave and true soldier of the cross was summoned to join the noble army of martyrs. If not a sparrow falleth to the ground unnoticed, the fall of this noble man will not be in vain. His blessed Master fell a victim to the mob because he preached unwelcome truth, but the cause of human brotherhood still lives, and we advocate it to-day."

In a letter of General Banks he thus writes of Dr. Dostie:

"I knew him well. No country ever gave birth to a more unselfish man, a truer patriot, or a more devoted friend of liberty. He and his associates were dangerous men to the enemies of this country. The unseen hand that smote him was that which applied the torch to the city of New York, and by which Lincoln fell. His death will be avenged, and in this, as in all trials of good men, the blood of the martyrs will be the sustenance of the church."

General Butler in an address delivered in New York, thus vindicates his friend and the cause of justice:

"I now remember a man who came to me in New Orleans and took me by the hand and with tears in his eyes said, 'I thank God that you have come; I bless God that your flag waves over me again—the symbol of justice and protection of my country,' and yet I have seen that man murdered in cold blood. That murdered man was Dostie, the best and purest Union man that ever trod the soil of Louisiana, for he periled his life, when he had no hope, in defense of the flag. I speak with feeling, for he was one of my best and staunchest advisers and aided me by all means in his power. As long as I had a command, my flag sheltered him and every other man within my territory. And that that man should be murdered with that flag flying over him —not to him an emblem of power and protection—and we be told that these men are our brothers. [Applause.] The rattlesnake may be a brother of the copperhead, but not mine—not mine! And what was his offense! He went to a convention to discuss their rights as we are assembled here to-night, a right guaranteed by the Constitution of the United States, and under the protection of the flag.

"The whole North was aroused by the New Orleans massacre, following up, as it did, the Memphis riot. President Johnson telegraphs to General Sheridan, putting what lawyers call leading questions to draw out a favorable answer. He don't send on to General Sheridan, saying, 'come tell us all about this riot.' The President's dispatch asked for as kindly a report as possible of the affair.

"When the President asks General Sheridan if the civil power is sufficient to take care of these men he answers: 'I should say emphatically they are not.' This is after the President had issued his proclamation of the 18th of August that peace reigned and civil authority is sufficient protection for all citizens. I am sorry to see that in face of the facts that Horton the clergyman, Dostie the pure patriot, Loup and others are dead, and wounded men are coming North with the testimony of all these unavenged, with Northern people unprotected so that they are obliged to leave New Orleans, that the President has issued his proclamation that peace has obtained throughout all the land, and the civil courts are ample to protect life and liberty. And in the face of General Sheridan's emphatic disavowal of the ability of the civil authorities to protect the citizens, the President on the 18th of August turns over every Union man in the South to the mercies of the thugs, assassins and murderers of Lincoln and Dostie."

At the Southern Loyalists' Convention which met at Independence Hall, Philadelphia, in September, 1866, the following resolutions offered by Colonel Moss of Missouri, were read and adopted:

"*Whereas*, The lamented A. P. Dostie, of New Orleans, one of the true patriots who signed the call of this Convention, has been foully murdered since said call was issued; we recognize the spirit of this faithful Unionist as a delegate in this Convention, whose voice shall ever be remembered, and whose wrongs shall never be forgotten until the principles he maintained shall perish from the earth. Be it further

"*Resolved*, That this Convention wear the usual badge of mourning in memory of the brave friends of liberty who perished at New Orleans on the 30th day of July last, and that a copy of these resolutions, as a tender of sympathy, be forwarded to the families of those who perished."

CHAPTER XXX.

CONGRESSIONAL INVESTIGATIONS.

On the 6th of December, 1866, Congress resolved:

"That a committee be appointed to go to New Orleans and investigate into all matters pertaining to the riot of July 30th, 1866." That investigation resulted in the exclusion of the three prominent upholders of President Johnson's reconstruction measures in Louisiana. The following letter from General Sheridan explains that action:

"HEADQUARTERS FIFTH MILITARY DISTRICT,
New Orleans, June 6th, 1867.

"To General U. S. Grant, Commanding Armies of the United States:

"*General*—On the 29th of March last I removed from office Judge Abell, of the Criminal Court of New Orleans; Andrew S. Herron, Attorney General of the State of Louisiana; and John T. Monroe, Mayor of the city of New Orleans. These removals were made under the power granted me in what is usually termed the Military Bill, passed March 27th, 1867, by the Congress of the United States.

"I did not deem it necessary to give any reason for the removal of these men, especially after the investigation made by the military board of the massacre of July 30th, 1866, and the report of the Congressional Committee on the same massacre, but as some inquiry has been made for the cause of these removals, I should respectfully state as follows:

"The Criminal Court over which Judge Abell presided is the only Criminal Court of the city of New Orleans: for a period of at least nine months previous to July 30th, he had been educating a large portion of the community to the perpetration of this outrage, by almost promising them no prosecution in his court against the offenders, in case such an event occurred. The records of this court will show that he fulfilled his purpose, as not one of the guilty ones has been prosecuted. In reference to Andrew S. Herron, I considered it his duty to indict these men before the Criminal Court.

"This he failed to do, but went so far as to attempt to impose on the good sense of the whole nation, by indicting the victims of the riot instead of the rioters, in other words, making the innocent guilty, and the guilty innocent.

"He was therefore an abetter of and coadjutor with Judge Abell in bringing on the massacre of July 30th. Mayor Monroe controlled the element engaged in this riot, and when backed by an Attorney-General who would not prosecute the guilty, and a Judge who advised the Grand Jury to find the innocent guilty, and let the murderers go free, felt secure in engaging his police force in the riot and massacre. With these three men exercising a large influence on the worst elements of this city, giving to these elements an immunity for riot and bloodshed, the General-in-Chief will see how insecure I felt in letting them occupy their positions in the troubles which might occur in registration and voting in the reorganization.

"I am, General, very respectfully,
"Your obedient servant,
"P. H. SHERIDAN.
"Major-General, United States Army."

In the place of Andrew S. Herron, B. L. Lynch was appointed Attorney-General of the State of Louisiana, a man identified with the Union cause in that State. In the place of John T. Monroe, Edward Heath was appointed as Mayor of New Orleans, whose sympathies every New Orleans loyalist knew to be in harmony with a radical Congress, and opposed to a policy that had permitted the policemen of New Orleans to murder hundreds of defenceless citizens.

In the place of Judge E. Abell, General Sheridan appointed under the new reconstruction laws of a radical Congress, Major Howe, of the Federal Army, a man of anti-slavery and loyal principles, who could appreciate love of justice and order.

Hon. B. Flanders was appointed under the Congressional reconstruction acts in place of J. Madison Wells.

The following correspondence will explain Governor Wells exit from that high position which he had maintained with such undignified contortions under the eye of the Chief Executive. Upon the removal of Governor Wells, for being an impediment in the way of the reconstruction laws of Congress—he writes to his successor as follows:

"STATE OF LOUISIANA,
EXECUTIVE DEPARTMENT,
NEW ORLEANS, June 7, 1867.

"Hon. B. F. Flanders:

"I refuse to recognize the authority of General Sheridan to remove me from office, and I therefore decline to vacate the same. If put out by force, I cannot resist; but I protest against the act of violence as an aggravation of his unwarrantable proceeding in removing me from office. Respectfully,

J. MADISON WELLS,
Governor of Louisiana.

The following letter from General Sheridan proved an effective missive:

"HEADQUARTERS FIFTH MILITARY DISTRICT,
New Orleans, La., June 7, 1867.

"Mr. J. Madison Wells, Ex-Governor of Louisiana, New Orleans, La.:

"SIR—Governor Flanders has just informed me that he made an official demand on you for the records of the office which you have heretofore held as governor of Louisiana, and that you have declined to turn them over to him, disputing the right to remove by office from me, which right you have acknowledged and urged on me up to the time of your own removal. I therefore send Brevet Brigadier General James W. Forsyth, of my staff, to notify you that he is sent by me to eject you from the governor's room forcibly, unless you consider this notification as equivalent to objection.

"P. H. SHERIDAN,
Major General, U. S. Army,
Commanding Fifth Military District."

Upon the removal of General Sheridan, for these noble acts, by Andrew Johnson, President of the United States, General Mower, the Commanding General of the Gulf Department, appointed in the place of Harry Hays, Ex-Colonel of the Confederate Army, Dr. George W. Avery, as sheriff of New Orleans. Dr. Avery was a Surgeon in the United States Army, under General Butler, and during the massacre of July 30th, went to the police station, jails and hospitals, to attend the wounded and dying—was the friend and physician of the dying Dostie and Horton.

On the 4th of July, 1867, Mechanics' Institute was crowded with white and colored citizens, who had met to celebrate the day consecrated to American Independence. On that day the Radical Congress of the Republic was gratefully remembered by the vast assembly within Mechanics' Institute. On that interesting occasion; after the reading of the Declaration of Independence, by H. C. Dibble, Esq., the Rev. J. B. Smith, an intelligent colored man from Boston, Mass., spoke as follows:

"FELLOW CITIZENS:—It becomes my pleasant duty to read to you, as next in order, another very commendable document—a fit appendage of the one to which you have just listened with so much interest and pleasure; an instrument second in importance to no other ever promulgated by any Government. It imparts to the Fourth of July a character for honesty, eartnestness, and sincerity that it never enjoyed before, and makes it something more than a mere gala day for pompous declaimers and arrogant rhetoricians. To the five millions of colored people in this country the declaration of independence has a significance that it never possessed before.

"We will ever hold in grateful remembrance the noble President who issued it; we honor the Congress who had the justice to ratify it, and the people who have the will and the determination to observe and maintain it. I refer to the emancipation proclamation of President Lincoln."

After the reading of the emancipation proclamation, an address was delivered by J. R. G. Pilkin, from which we quote the following:

"One year ago to-day I stood as now within these walls and assisted in a commemoration welcome to every American citizen. The same declaration that you have heard this morning, was then as reverently read, and with glad pulses we at last retired to our homes. But the month that dawned with such wholesome cheer closed with a sunset of fearful crimson; our July is henceforth the solemn memory of both a benediction and a scar. Friends who sat upon this platform and upon these seats before me, communed then for the last time with us in this annual assemblage. They are to-day in their graves, dear to us by the fidelity of their lives, and still dearer by the brutality of their sacrifice. Yet the shot and stab of the assassin insured no lasting triumph except for those that fell—the valor of the one and the infamy of the other are historic.

"But these martyrs were not all who last year crossed yonder threshold for the last time. There were likewise hundreds of men from whose wrists the gyves had been smitten off—men, who sat here with hearts to aspire for and hands to defend our sacred liberties, and yet with brains to wonder that their skin was a bar to an equal enjoyment of them. To-day I see many of their faces again, but they have entered this hall new and different men—no longer freedmen but freemen, equal with us in all things—a stern, loyal impulse in their souls, and a citizen's ballot within their hands.

"Few local events ever so aroused the American people as the wanton massacre of July 30, 1866, and wrought so material a result. It became the cardinal text in the campaign last autumn of a score of the States of this Union—the angry admonition of each loyal constituency to its representative—the accepted symptom of a murderous rebel tempter, which that representative should resent through his measure of reconstruction, and I am by no means extravagant when I say that our national Congress caught the dying whisper of our Dostie, 'Let the good work go on,' and dipping its pen in the mingled blood of black men and white shed upon this spot, inscribed his solemn caution upon its legislative page, and beneath it the bold and glorious decree of enfranchisement!

"We have gathered here as honest democrats, to grasp like true brethren the hands of all that are not recreant to a freeman's faith, and to thank God that we all may now render our first public acknowledgment that four millions of new freemen share with us henceforth in the title to our national Declaration of Independence."

On the 30th of July, 1867, a funeral ceremony in memory of the victims of July 30th, 1866, was observed at Mechanics' Institute. The oration on that occasion was delivered by Rufus Waples, Esq., from which we quote:

"This is the first anniversary funeral of the patriots massacred here on the 30th of July, 1866, the day memorable as the culminating point of the lawless policy of him who had sworn to enforce the laws.

"Within this hall, one year ago this day, sat an assembly of citizens, peaceably convened and peaceably inclined, gathered together for a lawful, patriotic and praiseworthy purpose. Suddenly they were surrounded and attacked by armed enemies of law, order and liberty; suddenly they were made the victims of preconcerted violence, and these walls resounded with the report of firearms, the heavy stroke of the bludgeons, the fall of the dead, the agonizing shrieks and groans of the wounded and dying. The floor ran blood. The prayers and expostulations of the innocent sufferers were drowned amid the oaths and execrations of the assailants. In vain was raised the flag of truce; the minister of peace who bore it was ruthlessly shot down with the white emblem in his hand. In vain was exhibited the banner of the country; it only excited its enemies to deeper hate. The stunned, bleeding and apparently lifeless bodies of respectable and virtuous citizens kicked and spat upon by traitors—the bodie of the wounded thrown roughly into carts with the dying and dead, and hauled off to hospitals and graves; the survivors of the carnage ruthlessly conveyed amid the jeers and mocking, the hisses and curses of crowds, to a filthy dungeon with the intent that they should be massacred at night according to the programme of the plotters. You remember it all; you will forget it never.

"Here fell the brave young Victor Lacroix, cut from head to foot, butchered and mutilated in the most shocking and barbarous manner. He had served with honor and distinction upon the field fighting for liberty and law, but his bright career of glory was thus suddenly arrested, and

"'Now lies he there,
Marred, as you see, by traitors.'

"Here fell Jean Baptiste, Henry Berquier, as faithful a citizen, as loyal a heart, as the country could boast, victimized by enemies of the Government just because he was faithful and loyal. He, too, had proved upon the field his devotion to the flag—that flag which, in the hands of a recreant Executive, had failed to protect him.

"Captain Loup, who had also faithfully served in the national army and had passed through the fiery ordeal unscathed, fell a victim to a dastardly stab in the back. He was a good officer, possessing the confidence of his superiors, and ever faithful to the cause of freedom.

"Telesphore Auguste and Dalcy Duval, who had served three years in the 1st National Guards, and who had been honorably discharged, were here, in this hall, shot down like dogs, and then carted away and buried before their relatives and friends had had the poor satisfaction of looking upon their mangled remains.

"Peace to the ashes of the brave soldiers! The living will keep green the memory of Auguste and Duval, Berquier, Loup, and Victor Lacroix. Let their names be embalmed in the pulsating blood of your living hearts; let their deeds be written in letters of gold upon the scroll of fame! Rest, noble champions of liberty! Yes

"On fame's eternal camping ground
Your martial tents are spread,
And glory guards with solemn round
The bivouac of the dead."

"More than a hundred victims of the massacre lingered in the Marine Hospital, wounded in almost every conceivable way, and the hearse was there a daily visitor. There the Rev. Dr. Horton died, going down with the sun in the stillness of a beautiful Sabbath evening. He was a gentleman of education and irreproachable character, a preacher of the gospel of peace to his fellow-men. Like his blessed Master he fell the victim of a mob. He had, by invitation, invoked the blessing of Heaven upon the efforts of those who had convened here to promote the good of society. He had bravely stepped forward when the armed policemen rushed into the door of this hall, and with his country's flag and a white handkerchief attached as the emblem of peace, he sought to prevent the effusion of blood. His latest act showed him to be a hero in his mission—the holy mission of love and human brotherhood. He was shot down with the national banner and the flag of truce in his hands, with words of peace upon his lips! He died heroically in the van, a brave soldier of the cross.

" Around his dying bed sat his disconsolate wife and a few weeping friends. Looking upon his last agony no eye could restrain its tears. He had suffered a week from several wounds, most of the time being unconscious. Once, in a lucid interval, he said to his wife, 'I was not wrong, I cannot think I was wrong in consenting to open the convention with prayer.'

"His last hour was almost without a struggle; he gradually sank to rest as a child closes its eyes in slumber.

"So fades the summer's cloud away;
So sinks the gale when storms are o'er;
So gently shuts the eye of day;
So dies a wave along the shore."

" In another apartment of the Marine Hospital, John Henderson lay, chafing with mortal wounds. He had been long known in New Orleans as a lawyer well versed in the knowledge of his profession. His enemies were the enemies of his country, and they had not only cut him down because he loved it, but they then derided him, even in the public prints, for having once suffered from such mental malady as had affected some of the ablest jurists, sciotists, and philosophers whom the world has known.

"After suffering excruciating pain for several weeks, John Henderson died, and his name was inscribed by the angel of liberty on the scroll of the martyrs.

"Dr. A. P. Dostie died at the Hotel Dieu on the same Sabbath evening, and about the same hour that saw Rev. Mr. Horton sink to rest. Prominent as a Unionist all through the war; active in every effort to call back the tide of lawlessness that was invading the land, he was long an object of malignant hate to the foes of liberty. His Spartan energy and perseverance, his Roman firmness and bravery, made him a shining mark for these assassins. They knew him by his manly voice and fiery eye; they felt him by the electric shock which earnest men always convey to those about them. When, with bold step he walked out of this hall at the front door, and looked his assailants in the eye, had they been of the true chivalry, they would have admired his courage. When, all unarmed, he asked them to spare his life, had they been of the true chivalry, they would have stayed their hands. But the cry was, 'Kill him! kill him!' with oaths and imprecations which cannot be here repeated. They added indignities to death. They trod upon what they supposed to be his lifeless body, and continued to add other wounds and bruises to those which were already mortal. Let us turn from the painful scene.

"On the day he died, when the lower half of his body was paralyzed. and when his last hour stole on apace, his reason was yet clear, and his mental energy remarkable. Nobler sentiments never escaped dying lips than those uttered by Dr. Dostie. 'I want no one to avenge my death,' he said to the kind Sister of Charity who ministered to his wants.

"With patriotism worthy of the dying Sidney, he said a short time before he breathed his last, 'I am willing to die, if my death will promote the cause of liberty.'

"Some of you here were among the few who attended the burial of Dostie, at a time when even the solemn rites of sepulchre were in danger of outrage; when the public prints were endeavoring to excite further persecution; when a public funeral of any one of the martyrs would have been in danger of demoniac assault. The time and place of Dostie's interment was not generally known, and among his hosts of friends, not many were present at the burial. A few words were spoken; a fervent prayer was offered, and his mortal part was laid away in the narrow house, to rest till the last morn shall beam upon the world.

"Others died and were buried. I cannot enumerate all. Some of them have friends to visit their graves, dressing them with flowers in the spring, and watching them with paternal solicitude through all the year. Some are at rest whose sepulchres are known only to him who looks down and watches their dust till he shall bid it rise in the newness of immortal life. Scarcely less than a hundred killed, and four hundred wounded, was the result of the massacre. So far as possible the names of all the victims should be collected for inscription upon the proposed monument to the patriot martyrs."

"But are they dead? What, they whose souls had
power
To scatter life around them as a shower?
Who did their deathless selves dispense so well
That freedom grew immortal where they fell?
Ah, no. As soon would mingle wave with flame,
Or hate with love as death with hero's name."

In faith, the American people look to Justice to vindicate, to establish, to make certain forever the republican principles upon which is erected a national structure, above which floats the American flag, upon which is engraven a charter of rights to mankind, in letters of living light, so that prejudice shall not misinterpret them; wilfullness shall not misunderstand them, nor perversity whether of King or President shall dare to interfere to prevent their fullest fruition. "To this, republicans stand pledged by the teachings of our patriot sires now echoing through our country; by the hallowed blood of our sons slain upon the battle field or starved in prisons; by the sacred memories of the bleeding corpse of the assassinated Lincoln; by the dying prayer of the murdered sainted Horton, the victim sacrificed on the altar of equal rights; by the sole legacy of the pure patriot Dostie, massacred to establish wrong and sin, bequeathing to his mourning country in his last dying words—'Let the good work go on!'"

Yes, unnumbered, glorious heroes of the battle! yes, thousands of suffering patriots murdered in prisons, now beatified, seeing your lives were not spent in vain! yes, martyred President! yes, sainted teacher! yes, noble-minded patriot! the good work by you begun, for which you laid down your lives, shall go on until every footprint of wrong or oppression by man to his fellow man shall be blotted out forever!

"They slumber, and the stranger's tread
May spurn our country's noble dead;
Yet, on the land they loved so well,
Still shall their burning spirit dwell.
Their deeds shall hallow minstrels' themes,
Their image rise on warriors' dreams,
Their names be inspiration's breath,
Kindling high hopes and scorn of death,
Till bursts immortal from the tomb
The flame that shall avenge their doom."

APPENDIX.

"We have passed the Red Sea of slaughter; our garments are yet wet with the crimson spray. We have crossed the fearful wilderness of war, and have left our four hundred thousand heroes to sleep beside the dead enemies of the Republic. Before us is the land of promise, the land of peace, filled with possibilities of greatness and glory too vast for the grasp of the imagination. Let us as Representatives of the people, whose servants we are, bear in advance the sacred Ark of Republican Liberty, with its tables of the Law inscribed with the 'irreversible guarantees' of Liberty. Let us here build a monument on which shall be written not only the curses of the law against treason, disloyalty, and oppression, but also an everlasting covenant of peace and blessing with loyalty, liberty, and obedience, and all the people will say, Amen."—*Hon. J. A. Garfield of Ohio, in the House of Representatives*, 1866

CONGRESSIONAL REPORT.

APPENDIX.

February 11th, 1867, Mr. Eliot from the select Committee on the New Orleans Riots, made the following

REPORT:

"Mr. Eliot and Mr. Shellabarger, being a majority of the select committee appointed to investigate matters connected with the New Orleans massacre of July 30th, 1866, and to report such legislative action as the condition of affairs in the State of Louisiana required, submit the report of the Committee as follows:

"On the 6th day of December, 1866, the House of Representatives passed the following resolution:

"*Resolved*, That a Committee of three members be appointed by the Speaker, whose duty it shall be to proceed to New Orleans, in the State of Louisiana, to make an investigation into all matters connected with the recent bloody riots in that city, which took place the last of July and 1st of August, 1866, and particularly to inquire into the origin, progress, and termination of the riotous proceedings, the names of the parties engaged in it, the acts of atrocity perpetrated, the number of killed and wounded, the amount and character of the property destroyed, and whether and to what extent those acts were participated in by members of the organization claiming to be the government of Louisiana, and report the facts to the House; and * * * to report such appropriate legislative action as may be required in view of the condition of affairs in the State of Louisiana.

"On the 10th of December the Committee was appointed. They entered upon their duties on the following day, and proceeded to examine witnesses, citizens of Louisiana then residing for the time at Washington, and continued their labors here until the 15th of December. On the 22d of December the examination of witnesses was resumed at New Orleans, and was closed in that city on the 3d of January, 1867; it was resumed at Washington on the 15th of January, and finally closed on the 2d of February. The whole number of witnesses examined is 197; of which 159 were before the Committee at New Orleans. Of these forty-seven were examined at the request of the citizens of that city.

"There has been no occasion during our national history when a riot has occurred so destitute of justifiable cause, resulting in a massacre so inhuman and fiend-like, as that which took place at New Orleans on the 30th of July last.

"The character and position of the gentlemen—members of the Convention which had originally assembled in 1864—who were the subjects of the attack in common with the unoffending negroes, whose political condition, claims, and rights it was their ultimate purpose to consider and determine, give to the events of July significance and national importance.

"The massacre was begun and finished in mid-day; and such proofs of preparation were disclosed that we are constrained to say that an intention, existing somewhere, to disperse and to slaughter the members of the Convention, and those persons, white and black, who were present and were friendly to its purposes, was mercilessly carried into full effect. What parties had formed that intention, and what other persons knowingly or unwittingly co-operated with or aided them, the Committee has endeavored to ascertain.

"The direct cause of the riots which resulted in the massacre of several members of the Convention and in the slaughter of many citizens of Louisiana was the re-assembling of that Convention pursuant to a call made by honorable R. K. Howell, acting as president *pro tempore.* The Convention of 1864 had been held on the first Monday of April in that year, in pursuance of a proclamation issued by Major General N. P. Banks, while in command of the department of the Gulf. That portion of the proclamation which related to the Convention is as follows:

"In order that the organic law of the State may be made to conform to the will of the people, and harmonize with the spirit of the age, as well as to maintain and preserve the ancient landmarks of civil and religious liberty, an election of delegates to a Convention for the revision of the constitution will be held on the first Monday of April, 1864. The basis of representation, the number of delegates, and the details of election will be annonnced in future orders."

It is in evidence before the Committee, and we find the fact to be, that the only action contemplated at the meeting of July 30th was the ascertainment officially of existing vacancies; and if a quorum of members should appear, it was proposed to postpone all further action until such vacancies should be filled and the writs of election for the choice of members from unrepresented districts should be complied with, and the whole State represented. These elections were ordered to be held on the third day of September. The whole State being represented, it was then intended to consider certain articles in amendment of the Constitution, and have them submitted to the whole people for their action. If approved by the people, the Constitution, thus amended, was to be submitted to Congress.

It was understood that two subjects of vital interest would call for discussion and decision, both of them affecting the elective franchise—one in limitation of the right, applying to certain classes of rebels who had waged war against the Government, and one enlarging the right, so as to enfranchise citizens who had been during the rebellion at all times loyal to the Union, but who had been disqualified as voters by reason of their African descent. It was the apprehension that amendments of the State Constitution in these respects would be recommended by the Convention, and finally ratified by the people, which created popular excitement. Obviously no such amendments could be proposed for discussion in Convention until a quorum of its members should assemble, and the proof before the Committe is ample that no intention existed to take any action even then until after the election had been held, and delegates chosen from unrepresented districts. This time could not arrive until after the third of September; but it was deemed safer by the parties who were opposed to the agitation or discussion of either of these questions to interrupt at once the proposed Convention. * * *

THE RIOT.

The riot and massacre of citizens, members of the Convention and others, white and colored, occured at and near the hall of the Mechanics' Institute, on Dryades Street, commencing on Canal Street, at or near the corner of Burgundy Street, between eleven and twelve o'clock on the morning of July 30th.

The Committee examined seventy-four persons as to the facts of violence and bloodshed upon that day. It is in evidence that men who were in the hall, terrified by the merciless attacks of the armed police, sought safety by jumping from the windows, a distance of twenty feet, to the ground, and as they jumped were shot by police or citizens. Some, disfigured by wounds, fought their way down stairs to the street, to be shot or beaten to death on the pavement. Colored persons, at distant points in the city, peaceably pursuing their lawful business, were attacked by the police, shot, and cruelly beaten. Men of character and position, some of whom were members and some spectators of the Convention, escaped from the hall covered with wounds and blood, and were preserved almost by miracle from death. Scores of colored citizens bear frightful scars more numerous than many soldiers of a dozen well-fought fields can show—proofs of fearful danger and strange escape; men were shot while waving handkerchiefs in token of surrender and submission; white men and black, with arms uplifted praying for life, were answered by shot and blow from knife and club; the bodies of some were "pounded to a jelly;" a colored man was dragged from under a street-crossing, and killed at a blow; men concealed in outhouses and among piles of lumber were eagerly sought for and slaughtered or maimed without remorse; the dead bodies upon the street were violated by shot, kick, and stab; the face of a man "just breathing his last" was gashed by a knife or razor in the hands of a woman; "an old, gray-haired man," peaceably walking the street at a distance from the Institute, was shot through the head; negroes were taken out of their houses and shot; a policeman riding in a buggy deliberately fired his revolver from the carriage into a crowd of colored men; a colored man two miles away from the Convention hall was taken from his shop by the police, at about four o'clock on the afternoon of the riot, and shot and wounded in side, hip and back; one man was wounded by fourteen blows, shots, aud stabs; the body of another received seven pistol balls. After the slaughter had measureably ceased, carts, wagons and drays, driven through the streets, gathered the dead, the dying and the wounded in "promiscuous loads," a policeman, in some cases, riding in the wagon, seated upon the living men beneath him. The wounded men, taken at first to the station-house or "lock-up," were all afterwards carried to the hospital. While at the station-houses, until friends found them with medical aid, they were left to suffer. When at the hospital, they were attended to with care and skill. But this was done at no cost to the city or to the State. Without asking permission, so far as the Committee learned, those wounded men were carried to the hospital under the care of the Freedmen's Bureau, and shelter, surgical treatment, and food were furnished at the cost of the United States.

There was evidence before the Committee that for several hours, the police and mob, in mutual and bloody emulation, continued the butchery in the hall and on the street, until nearly two hundred people were killed and wounded. The number was probably much larger than this; but of that number the names and residences are known. Some were injured whose friends conveyed them at once quietly away. There is evidence tending to show that some who were killed were privately carried away and buried. One witness testified: "I saw a dray taking five or six of those who were wounded away. I heard a drayman say, "Where will I take them to?' And a policeman said, 'Throw them in the river.'" Several witnesses testify that the killed and wounded exceed two hundred. One witness says that he saw from forty to fifty killed. Another states that he saw from twenty to thirty carriage loads of killed and wounded. How many were killed will never be known. But we cannot doubt there were many more than are set down in the official list in evidence.

THE RIOT NOT AN ACCIDENT, BUT PRE-ARRANGED.

This riotous attack upon the Convention, with its terrible results of massacre and murder, was not an accident. It was the determined purpose of the Mayor of the city of New Orleans to break up this Convention by armed force.

We state one fact in this connection, significant both as bearing upon the question of preparation and as indicating the true and prevailing feeling of the people of New Orleans. Six months have passed since the Convention assembled, when the massacre was perpetrated, and more than two hundred men were slain and wounded. This was done by city officials and New Orleans citizens. But not one of those men has been punished, arrested or complained of. These officers of the law living in the city, and known to that community, acting under the eye of superiors, clothed with the uniform of office,. and some of them known, as the proof shows, to the chief officer of police, have not only escaped punishment, but have been continued in their office.

The gentlemen who composed the Convention have not, however, been permitted to escape. Prosecutions in the criminal court under an old law, passed in 1805, were at once commenced, and are now pending against them for a breach of the peace. These facts tend strongly to prove that the criminal actors in the tragedy of the day were the agents of more criminal employes, and demonstrate the general sympathy of the people in behalf of the men who did the wrong against those who suffered it. * * * *

But the evidence establishing the fact of determination to suppress the Convention, and preparation for attack upon the members and those friends, whoever they might be, that should attend its meetings, is derived from many witnesses.

Before the day arrived there was general denunciation of the Convention in different circles and in casual meetings on the streets; wishes were expressed and expectations declared that it should be dispersed; anonymous letters of warning and threatening violence were sent to several of the members and their friends; a funeral notice, announcing in advance the death of the Convention, was posted in the streets on Sunday; declarations were made that the "niggers and half niggers should be wiped out;" members of one of the fire companies absent from the city on Sunday declared that they must return and be on hand the next day. They said, "Hay's brigade will all be there, and will clean out those damned Yankees." One man remarked, "I have spotted Dostie myself." (6375.) It was freely said, "We are going to hang Hahn and Dostie;" that "No man should come out of the Convention alive;" that "We will show you what will happen to-day;" that "You will see fun to-day;" that "It is no sin to kill a nigger."

"Fire engines were brought out, one of which had pistols in the box. Fire companies gathered near the Institute at the same time from different parts of the city. In the early morning a man was ascertaining the names of those who were willing to aid in suppressing the meeting. A school was dismissed because there was to be a riot; badges of different kinds were worn by 'citizens' in the street; men were seen buying pistols and cartridges; citizens encouraged the riot in different ways; there were crowds of citizens at different parts of the street; they cheered and shouted for Jeff. Davis, and for Mr. Johnson. When the wounded men were brought nto the 'lock-up,' members of the city council cheered the policemen 'in their bloody work,' and finally, no one of the rioters, either policemen or citizens, has been complained of or punished.

"On Sunday night the police were withdrawn from their stations, that they might rest until Monday morning, when they were ordered to report at their different headquarters. Early on Monday the whole police force, numbering between four and five hundred, were massed at different stations; they were ordered to come armed, and arms were furnished to those who were without hem; the greater part of the police was kept at the station-houses until the time arrived when their work should begin. Soon after noon an unusual 'alarm' was given—such as had been used when federal armies were investing the city—and then the combined police, headed by officers and firemen, with their companions, rushed with one will from different parts of the city toward the Institute, and the work of butchery commenced. In these acts of violence, police and fireman and citizen acted in concert. Different 'badges' were worn on the streets; many policemen had their hat bands reversed so that their 'numbers' could not be distinguished. No effort was made by the mayor or chief of police to control or check these men, but the slaughter was permitted until the end was gained. Facts of this description were put in proof with other circumstances, demonstrating, as we judge, that the slaughter of these men was determined on by the chief executive officer of the city, and was prepared for by him on the night before the meeting was held." * * *

THE MEETINGS ON FRIDAY EVENING—THE RIOTS NOT CAUSED BY THEM.

"It is charged as a prominent and direct cause of these riots that incendiary and turbulent meetings were held on Friday evening, July 27.

"On Saturday morning, July 28, Lieutenant Governor Voorhies and Attorney General Herron sent the following telegram to the President:

"New Orleans, July 28, 1866.

"President Johnson, *Washington, D. C.*:

"Radical mass meeting composed mainly of large number of negroes last night, ending in a riot; the committee of arrangements of said meeting assembling to-night. Violent and incendiary speeches made; negroes called to arm themselves. You bitterly denounced. Speakers Field, Dostie, Hawkins, Henderson, Heistand, and others. Governor Wells arrived last night, but sides with the Convention movement. The whole matter before the grand jury; but impossible to execute civil process without certainty of riot. Contemplated to have the members of the Convention arrested under process from the criminal court of this district. Is the military to interfere to prevent process of court?

"Albert Voorhies,
Lieutenant Governor of Louisiana.
"Andrew S. Herron,
Attorney General of Louisiana."

"The committee inquired carefully into the alleged facts upon which this telegram was founded. There were three meetings upon this evening. One was held within the hall of the Institute, one outside the hall at the same time, and one at the City Hall, in the street, after the close of the former meetings.

"The meetings at the Institute were held upon public notice to consider the questions which would ultimately come before the Convention. They were called by parties friendly to the objects of the Convention, and the speakers were well known as identified with the Union or radical party in Louisiana.

"The following is substantially the testimony as to the character of these meetings:

"John Heistand: 'On the Friday night previous to the Convention there were public meetings in the city of New Orleans. Nothing was said or done at either place which, in my estimation, would authorize a magistrate to bind the party over to keep the peace. I know of no disturbance during that night.' Answer 8."

Rufus Waples: "In the Hall on Friday night everything was well-behaved; no disturbence whatever, and no unusual excitement." Answers 285 and 292.

S. S. Fish: "I never heard of any armed aid (to the Convention,) but had heard it spoken of that caution should be used, not to have armed men there; and I know too that Dr. Dostie, who nearly always carried a revolver with him, that he took it from his person, and left it with a barber in this city, by whom he was accustomed to be shaved." Answer 442. "I heard the speaking inside, and nearly all outside the hall on the 27th of July. I heard no request for any one to come armed as has been asserted. I was present when the meeting was dissolved, and afterwards went with the procession in front of the City Hall, and was there when Dr. Dostie made the speech that is said to be inflammatory. The meeting was orderly so far as any thing I saw. Nothing was said by Dr. Dostie as to the employment of force.

Charles S. Souvinet: "All the time I was up stairs (Friday night) the meeting was orderly. I heard several speeches. As well as I can remember the purport of those speeches, were that the Convention would be supported when it should meet. It was composed, the speakers said, of loyal men, and they would extend the right of suffrage to the loyal men, the colored people." Answer 534.

Judge Howell testifies: "On Saturday evening preceding the meeting of the Convention, several gentlemen came into my house and told me that the general effect of the meeting of Friday evening was favorable to quiet." Answer 575.

"Charles W. Gibbons called on Dr. Dostie and warned him on Monday morning (July 30) that 'I had heard one policeman say to another, in a little grocery on the corner of Custom-house street, on Sunday night, that 'By G—d, we are going to hang Dostie and Hahn.' Dr. Dostie made the remark to me, 'I am going unarmed; I know they want to take my life, but I think it a good cause to die in; if they want to take my life they can do so.' Said I, 'you can do as you please. I thought it my duty to call and tell you, as, in your remarks at the meeting on Friday night, you told the people to come out and attend the Convention.' He said on that night, 'Go home—go quietly—go orderly—behave yourselves, and if there is anybody, white or black, that disturbs you, protect yourselves.'" Answer 1789.

"Mr. Richard L. Shelley, an intelligent witness, makes this conclusive statement:

"I went out to the meeting held in front of the Mechanics' Institute, and after Rev. Mr. Horton had delivered his speech, standing on the platform, within a few feet of Dr. Dostie, I listened attentively to the speech he made. There was nothing whatever in the remarks of Dr. Dostie which could be said to excite or invite in any way acts of hostility upon the part of the colored people against any of the white citizens of New Orleans. After the meeting had adjourned at the Mechanics' Institute a procession was formed with torch-lights and a band of music, and proceeded down Canal street to St. Charles, and then into Camp street and up to the City Hall. On the route to the City Hall some of the men comprising the procession were attacked by some white persons and maltreated. On arriving at the City Hall a short speech was delivered by Dr. Dostie. Among other things, he told them he felt very much pleased with the quiet and orderly manner in which they had conducted themselves, and regretted to learn that the procession had been attacked by a body of evil-disposed men. He recommended them to return quietly to their homes, and that if they were assailed and their lives put in jeopardy, he recommended that they should defend themselves to the extent of their ability.

"6793. Except at that time, was there anything in Dr. Dostie's speech calculated to excite animosity or hostile action?

"No, sir, there was not.

"6794. At the meeting outside of the Mechanics' Institute, did Dr. Dostie say to the men to whom he was speaking that they all ought to fight for their votes; that they ought to come armed to the Convention, and that no cowards were wanted; that the stones of the streets were crying out for the blood of rebels, or any expressions equivalent to these, or anything like them?

"I can swear that he made no such remarks.

"In a public speech delivered at St. Louis, on the 8th of September, by President Johnson, the following charge was made:

"The time has come when it seems to me that all ought to be prepared for peace—the rebellion being suppressed, and the shedding of blood being stopped, the sacrifice of life being suspended and stayed, it seems that the time has arrived when we should have peace; when the bleeding arteries should be tied up. [A voice: 'New Orleans; go on.']

"Perhaps if you had a word or two on the subject of New Orleans, you might understand more about it than you do. [Laughter and cheers.] And if you will go back [cries for Seward]—if you will go back and ascertain the cause of the riot at New Orleans, perhaps you would not be so prompt in calling out New Orleans. If you will take up the riot at New Orleans and trace it back to its source, or to its immediate cause, you will find out who was responsible for the blood that was shed there.

"If you will take up the riot at New Orleans and trace it back to the radical Congress [great cheering and cries of 'bully,'] you will find that the riot at New Orleans was substantially planned—if you will take up the proceedings in their caucuses you will understand that they there knew [cheers] that a Convention was to be called which was extinct, by its powers having expired; that it was said, and the intention was, that a new government was to be organized; and in the organization of that government the intention was to enfranchise one portion of the population, called the colored population, who had just been emancipated, and at the same time disfranchise white men. [Great cheering.] When you begin to talk about New Orleans [confusion] you ought to understand what you are talking about.

"When you read the speeches that were made, or take up the facts, (on Friday and Saturday before that Convention sat,) you will there find that speeches were made incendiary in their character, exciting that portion of the population, the black population, to arm themselves and prepare for the shedding of blood. [A voice, 'That's so,' and cheers.] You will also find that that Convention did assemble in violation of law, and the intention of that Convention was to supersede the recognized authorities in the State government of Louisiana, which had been recognized by the government of the United States, and every man engaged in that rebellion—in that Convention, with the intention of superseding and upturning the civil government which had been recognized by the government of the United States—I say that he was a traitor to the Constitution of the United States, [cheers,] and hence you will find that another rebellion was commenced, having its origin in the radical Congress. These men were to go there, a government was to be organized, and the one in existence in Louisiana was to be superseded, set aside, and overthrown. You talk to me about New Orleans! And then the question was to come up, when they had established their government—a question of political power—which of the two governments was to be recognized; a new government, inaugurated under this defunct Convention, set up in violation of law, and without the consent of the people. And then, when they had established their government, and extended universal or impartial franchise, as they called it, to this colored population, then this radical Congress was to determine that a government established on negro votes was to be the government of Louisiana. [Voices, 'Never,' and cheers, and 'Hurrah for Andy.']

"So much for the New Orleans riot; and there was the cause and the origin of the blood that was shed, and every drop of blood that was shed upon their skirts, and they are responsible for it. [Cheers.] I could trace this thing a little closer, but I will not do it here to-night. But when you talk about New Orleans, and talk about the causes and consequences that resulted from proceedings of that kind, perhaps, as I have been introduced here, and you have provoked questions of this kind, though it don't provoke me, I will tell you a few wholesome things that has been done by this radical Congress. [Cheers."]

Such charge from any other source would not have been considered. But the high position and public character of President Johnson have made it right to examine the grounds on which it rests.

Before the 30th of July, Judge Howell, president *pro tem.* of the Convention, had been at Washington. While here he had conversation with several members of Congress in regard to the proposed meeting of the Convention. During his visit here there was a caucus held of the republican members of Congress. The testimony of Judge Howell disclosed all the encouragement he received from Congress, and full proof has been given that at the caucus referred to no action concerning the Convention was taken or proposed.

When President Johnson felt it to be his duty to make the charge above stated, the official report of Brevet Major General Baird to the Secretary of War had been laid before him, and the testimony taken before the military commission over which Brevet Major General Mower presided had been closed, and the report of the commission had been made. Congress was not in session at the time of the massacre. Its members were at their respective homes, and the committee fail to discover any grounds upon which so grave a charge should be made. It was an unwarranted and unjust expression of hostile feeling, without pretext or foundation in fact."

ACTION OF THE PRESIDENT.

But it becomes important, in this connection, to bring into one view certain other facts.

At and before the time when Lieutenant Governor Voorhies and Attorney General Herron sent the telegraphic despatches of July 27 and July 28 to the President, one or more persons were at Washington who had been commissioned by parties in Louisiana to communicate with the President to obtain from him aid in suppressing the obnoxious Convention. J. Adolphus Rozier testifies: 'I left here on the Wednesday or Thursday previous to the riots. I arrived at Washington, I think, on Friday. I went to Washington at the request of members of the legislature here, also at the request of certain citizens, to see the President of the United States relative to the Convention of 1864.' (Answer 3306.) He further states that he saw the President and conferred with his friends in New Orleans by telegraph; (answer 3342;) that his object in going was to see how the Convention should be prevented; (answer 3343;) that his idea was to represent to him (the President) 'exactly the state of things here—what this Convention of 1864 was; that its effects had been injurious to the interests of the State and the general government; that the men who wished to reassemble this Convention were a revolutionary body: and I endeavored to impress upon the President my views that the civil authorities constituted the only legal body to take charge of this affair, and, after proper indictment, to arrest the members of this illegal Convention, and that, after their arrest, in accordance with the usual forms of civil law, our Supreme Court would decide whether that Convention was a legal body or not.'

The President was apprised when these telegrams were received, of the exact state of things at New Orleans. He knew that Hon. R. K. Howell, president pro tem. of the Convention, had issued a proclamation for the reassembling of the Convention. He knew that Governor Wells, the acknowledged chief executive of the State of Louisiana, had issued writs of election to fill the vacancies in the Convention, and that certificates of election were to be forwarded to the office of the Secretary of State. He knew that these writs of election could not be complied with until after the 30th of July, when the first meeting was to take place, and that some time must elapse before the Convention could be full and the whole State represented. He knew that Governor Wells was at New Orleans, and that he concurred and was co-operating with Judge Howell in assembling the Convention. He knew that it was contemplated to arrest the members of the Convention upon criminal process; and being asked, 'Is the military to interfere to prevent the process of court?' the President replied by telegraphic note, not addressed to the governor of the State, but to the lieutenant governor, as follows:

"EXECUTIVE MANSION,
Washington, D. C., July 28, 1866.

"To Albert Voorhies, Lieutenant Governor of Louisiana, New Orleans, Louisiana:

"The military will be expected to sustain and not to obstruct or interfere with the proceedings of the Court. A dispatch on the subject of the Convention, was sent to Governor Wells this morning.

"ANDREW JOHNSON."

The effect of this dispatch was to assure Lieutenant Governor Voorhies and those acting with him, that they would have the support of the President in their proposed action.

The President knew the condition of affairs in Louisiana, in July last, he knew that "rebels" and "thugs," and disloyal men had controlled the election of Mayor Monroe, and that such men composed, chiefly, his police force; he knew that Mayor Monroe, then an unpardoned rebel, had been after his election suspended from discharging the duties of his office by military order; he knew that he himself had subsequently pardoned him; he must have known the rebel antecedents of Albert Voorhies and A. S. Herron; he knew that riot and bloodshed were apprehended; he knew what military orders were in force; and yet without the knowledge of the Secretary of War, or of the general of our armies upon whose immediate responsibility those military orders had been issued, he gave directions by telegraph which, enforced, as it was intended they should be, would have compelled our soldiers to aid the rebels against the men in New Orleans who had remained loyal during the war, and sought to aid and to support, by official sanction, the persons who designed to suppress by arrest on criminal process and under color of law the meeting of the Convention; and that although this Convention was called with the sanction of the governor and by one of the judges of the Supreme Court of Louisiana claiming to act as president of the Convention.

The effect of the action of the President was to encourage the heart, to strengthen the hand, and to hold up the arms of those men who intended to prevent the Convention from assembling.

In their disclosed intention to arrest, by police or sheriff, the members of the Convention, they were assured of his support and aid. And it was believed with good reason, that whatever steps the Mayor should take, in his office and under color of law, to suppress the meeting of the Convention, would have the sanction of the President.

If the telegram of General Baird to the Secretary of War, of July 28th, had been communicated to the President, we know from the telegraphic message which he sent on that day to Governor Voorhies, that such directions would have been given as would in fact have required General Baird to sustain by military force what was called the civil authorities—that is to say, the Mayor and his police.

If, then, the armed police had engaged in the work of slaughter which destroyed the Convention, the soldiers of the army of the United States would have been charged with the responsibility of the act.

GENERAL BAIRD'S DESPATCH.

The fact that the telegram from General Baird had not been communicated to the President has been the subject of comment, and we give in this connection the statement made by the Secretary of War in relation to that matter. Mr. Stanton says:

That on the forenoon of Sunday, the 29th of July last, I received at my residence in this city a telegram from General Baird, commanding at New Orleans, a copy of which is hereto attached. This telegram was the first information communicated to me that a Convention was to be held at New Orleans, or that there was any difference or controversy on the subject of a Convention or assemblage to be held there. From the telegram of General Baird it appeared that the Convention was to meet with the sanction of the Governor of Louisiana, that its legality was questioned by persons who proposed to break it up by arresting the members, and that General Baird had warned the city authorities that he would not permit this to be done without instructions from the President, and he applied to me for instructions. There was no intimation in the telegram that force or violence was threatened by those opposed to the Convention, or that it was apprehended by General Baird. Upon consideration, it appeared to me that his warning to the city authorities was all that the case then required, for I saw no reason to instruct him to withdraw protection from a Convention sanctioned by the Governor, and in the event of any attempt at arrest, General Baird's interference would bring up the case with all the facts for such instructions as might be proper, and in the meantime, under his general authority, he would take measures to maintain the peace within his command. On Tuesday, the 31st of July, the morning papers contained telegraphic despatches in respect to the occurrences at New Orleans, and on the same day I was informed of the communication that had passed between the President and Governor Wells, Lieutenant Governor Voorhies, and Attorney General Herron."

Mr. Stanton had heard nothing of the Convention; had no knowledge of Mr. Rozier's presence in Washington or interviews with the President; had not been informed of the President's telegraphic correspondence, and saw no reason why General Baird should have new instructions, or why conference with the President was required.

THE RIGHT OF THE CONVENTION TO ASSEMBLE.

Had the citizens who were members of the Convention of 1864 a legal right peaceably to assemble on the 30th July, 1866? Judge Abell, of the first district court of New Orleans, denies their right, and in his charge to the Grand Jury on July 3d, 1866, he says: "I charge you that the Constitution makes no provision for the continuance of the Convention of 1864; that any effort on the part of that defunct body to assemble for the purpose of altering or amending the Constitution is subversive of good order and dangerous to the peace of the State, and that any overt act tending to subvert the

Constitution by any officers of the State, renders them liable to the Criminal Code of the State. It is my duty and your duty to oppose factional usurpation and stand by the reconstruction policy adopted by the President of the United States, which proposed at once to unite the country and make it great and prosperous."

CONDITION OF AFFAIRS IN LOUISIANA.

What is the condition of affairs in Louisiana, and what legislative action should be had? It has been made the duty of the Committee to report to the House upon both these questions.

"The present Constitution of Louisiana was held to be ratified by the suffrages of the people on the 5th day of September, 1864, and has hitherto been accepted, willingly or otherwise, as the organic law of the State. It was the result of military action deemed at the time essential to the proper civil government of the State. The justice or expediency or legality of that action have not been subjects of inquiry by the Committee. Possibly, if the general surrender of rebel armies and the entire annihilation of rebel organizations, civil and military, had not occurred as it did, or having occurred, if civil rule could have been retained in loyal hands, and vanquished traitors at least not pardoned and paid for treason, the strength of loyalty would have been increased, and the body of the people, disloyal theretofore by reason of public pressure, or moral duress, or military force, would have returned to their allegiance and sustained with heart the Government they had fought against, but which had at all times treated them with parental kindness. And when the surrender was fresh, and the defeated leaders had yielded up the sword and political traitors were fleeing from the land or seeking quiet away from public life, such did appear to be the well-founded hope of loyal men and the promise of the near future. But it began to be soon apparent that treason, defeated and disarmed, was to have one chance more to retrieve its fortunes. Under the provisions of an act of Congress entitled to be and designed as an act to suppress rebellion, but conferring, in one of its sections, power upon the President, before conviction had, or charge or complaint made, to grant amnesty and pardon, the people of Louisiana found that pardons were granted and properties restored to rebels who had held high office, military and civil, and that a policy was being pursued which discountenanced punishment and looked to speedy restoration to political favor and offices of trust of the men who had been active in field and in council in support of the rebellion.

There were at this time large bodies of men returning to their homes in Louisiana, who were, when the Constitution of 1864 was ratified, in the armies of the rebel government. There were at home large numbers of men who had in different ways supported the rebellion. Among both of these classes were many men who would have been found and would have remained loyal if it had not appeared to them that the Chief Executive Magistrate was disposed to pardon and to honor by office and political favor their military and civil leaders. And the effect of this policy became apparent in the language and deportment of the people. At first willing to yield and to return to true allegiance, they became assuming, bold and defiant. Under the Constitution of 1864 these men claimed to be restored to political rights and to vote at the polls; and so it came to pass that substantially all governmental authority, most of the offices in the State, and all legislative and municipal power have been conferred upon 'returned rebels' and are now controlled by them. This is eminently true in the city of New Orleans, where known and distinguished rebels, and only such as they, occupy the chief places of trust and power. The Mayor, confessedly a bold and bad man, who was also mayor during the rebellion and marked for violent and bitter hatred of the government of the Union and of men who loved the government, both white and black, of southern or of northern birth, is now Mayor of the city by the choice of the people of New Orleans. The High Sheriff, General Hays, was an active officer in the rebellion. He was in service at the time of the surrender in April, 1865, and has filled his present office since the early part of 1866. All the appointees of the Mayor, the whole constabulary and police force, with almost no exception, are composed of men who have rendered efficient service against the United States Government. There have been more than ninety witnesses examined, who speak of the condition of affairs in Louisiana, and of the sentiment toward and treatment of Union men, known to be such in the community where they live. Of these forty-seven were called at the request of the committee of citizens, who desired to vindicate the character of their city and to establish the loyalty of the State. On the part of these witnesses there was a general expression of satisfaction with the policy of the President. It was stated by most of them that the fact of being a Union man was no hindrance to success in business. Mr. Jacob Barker said that 'men of every party and description patronize my bank. I do not think there is any difference.' The opinion was given by most of these witnesses that it would be safe and judicious to withdraw the military forces and the Freedmen's Bureau and to admit Representatives to seats in Congress.

We have examined with care and weighed the proofs on either side. We have come to clear conclusions, which we believe to be accurate and just.

THE LEGISLATIVE REMEDY REQUIRED.

In view of the facts proved we are constrained to say that the time has fully arrived when Congress should intervene and should so legislate as to secure to the people of Louisiana a republican form of government. The condition of things existing there cannot continue consistently with the safety, security, or peace of loyal men.

Since the surrender of the rebel armies rebellion has assumed another form, and now controls the government through the same agencies that led those armies in time of war.

During the rebellion there were large numbers of men who remained steadfast to the government. In the midst of treason they were found loyal. While armed traitors were in the field contending with loyal armies and struggling to destroy the nation, these men, at personal peril, and despite of obloquy which construed loyalty to the Union to be treason to the State, continued firm in their allegiance.

These men are now made to feel the vengeance of unrepentant although it may be, pardoned rebels, and in person, property, and life are exposed to continual attack. Nothing but the pressure of military power at this moment measurably protects them from injury. It does not protect them from insult, from social ostracism, or the supercilious arrogance of men accustomed to own the labor they employed.

If the government ought to protect its constant friends against men who were its constant enemies, the obligation is disclosed to adopt and enforce such legislative action as the facts existing in Louisiana require.

When men are driven from their homes and their lives threatened and their property destroyed; when, in business, they are proscribed; when recent rebels hold all places of trust, and, having power, use it to oppress and punish loyal men because they are and have been loyal; when the whole body of colored men, who have never flinched from duty as radical loyalists when the days were gloomiest and the dangers greatest in the time of war, are persecuted by system, hunted like wild beasts, and slaughtered without mercy and with entire impunity from punishment; there is no room left for doubt that some legislative remedy should be applied.

These are matters of fact and not of opinion; and, in our judgment, but one course is open, and that should pursued without hesitation or delay.

According to the judgment of all who have felt the pressure of rebel rule, and have stood firmly and fearlessly for the Union when treason was nearest to success; whose judgment, given upon oath, is based upon facts within personal experience; who give opinions resting on knowledge, and speak of what they have seen and know; the present civil government of Louisiana, existing without sanction of national law, should be superseded by act of Congress, and a provisional government, established and maintained by military power until the time has come when Louisiana is controlled by loyal men, and may be restored to her former 'practical relations to the Union' without endangering its security and peace.

The war was conducted on the part of the Government to prevent her from permanently disuniting the States of the Union. Now, the end of war is peace, and the peace to be established must be secured in view of the requirements of the Constitution itself.

Until a loyal State of Louisiana exists in full political accord with the United States, and the demand of the Constitution is complied with that a government republican in form shall be guaranteed to the State, the objects of the war will not have been attained.

To accomplish that end the condition of affairs in Louisiana requires the temporary establishment of a provisional government.

By the loyal people of Louisiana such constitution must be ordained and such civil government formed as will assure to the Republic a loyal and free State, worthy of a place within the Union.

In the mean time the safety of all Union men within the State demands that such government be formed for their protection, for the well-being of the Nation, and the permanent peace of the Republic.

THOMAS D. ELIOT.
SAM'L SHELLABARGER."

The exposure of the powerful and the protection of the weak; these are not only invaluable liberties, but commanding duties.

At last the country sees that Andrew Johnson, who came to supreme power by a bloody accident, has become the successor of Jefferson Davis in the spirit by which he is governed, and in the mischief he is inflicting on his country.

Pardon me if I read a brief lesson:

"The dogmas of the past are inadequate to the stormy present. The occasion is piled high with difficulty and we must rise with the occasion. As our case is new, so we must think anew, and act anew. We must disen thrall ourselves, and then we shall save our country."

These are the words of Abraham Lincoln. Let us heed the lesson.—*Charles Sumner, Senate Chamber, January 18th,* 1867.

www.ingramcontent.com/pod-product-compliance
Lightning Source LLC
LaVergne TN
LVHW010135110826
845151LV00002B/359

* 9 7 8 1 4 2 5 5 3 9 4 4 3 *